TO WEAR A CITY'S CROWN

THE BEGINNINGS OF URBAN
GROWTH IN TEXAS, 1836–1865

TO WEAR A
CITY'S CROWN

THE BEGINNINGS OF
URBAN GROWTH IN
TEXAS, 1836-1865

KENNETH W. WHEELER

HARVARD UNIVERSITY PRESS

CAMBRIDGE, MASSACHUSETTS

1968

TO MY WIFE GRETA, MY FATHER,
AND THE MEMORY OF MY MOTHER

PREFACE

In recent years scholars have begun to build an important body of knowledge in the field of American urban history. Comparative studies have been made of colonial cities, revolutionary cities, cities of the western frontier, and late nineteenth-century industrial cities, but no study has been made of the last urban frontier of the Old South. The raw Texas towns of that frontier, rising during a period of urban boom in the United States, had many characteristics in common with other new American cities and with cities in other eras and areas, but the Texas cities also developed peculiarities of their own.

Various facets of this growth raise questions. Why did certain cities prevail over their rivals? Why did cities develop diverse characteristics when they seemed to share essentially the same cultural heritage and geographical advantages? What economic determinants underlay the forms of expansion? How did the interaction of various groups affect areas of development? When did these figurations begin to form a permanent shape so that the future growth of these communities could be predicted? These and other questions incited this examination.

Initial research included all major Texas cities as well as others which at some time in their histories showed promise of becoming significant. It covered the time span between the early eighteenth century and the mid-twentieth century. The focus soon centered, however, on the nineteenth century, and as the study progressed, many communities, particularly in the north and west of Texas, were eliminated when their development was obviously not highly relevant to the basic question of early urban pattern-ing. After extensive research, designs clearly emerged indicating that the forms for permanent urbanization in early Texas began with independence and were clearly established by the end of the Civil War, and that the cities involved were Galveston, Houston, Austin, and San Antonio. This book, then, presents a descriptive, comparative, and analytical study of the emergence and evolution of the economic, municipal, cultural, and social conditions in these four cities between 1836 and 1865.

KENNETH W. WHEELER

BOSTON UNIVERSITY
BOSTON, MASSACHUSETTS
MARCH 1968

ACKNOWLEDGMENTS

The author wishes to express his appreciation to the countless librarians, archivists, and clerks who have helped him in the libraries, archives, government offices, and other depositories where the research for this manuscript was conducted. Their patient efforts have been invaluable to this study. Thanks are due to the author's wife, friends, and colleagues who helped fill great gaps in his knowledge of important areas related to the subject, who patiently endured his endless queries, who gently corrected many of his errors, and who guided him to further treasures. Special gratitude is due to the University of Rochester and to Professor Richard C. Wade, of the University of Chicago, under whose guidance this project was first conceived in a doctoral dissertation. The Harris and Eliza Kempner Fund and the American Philosophical Society furnished financial support for the final research for this book.

CONTENTS

LIST OF ILLUSTRATIONS

(Following p. 114)

Samuel A. Maverick, an early San Antonio leader. Courtesy of the Daughters of the Republic of Texas Library at the Alamo.

John K. Allen, a founder of Houston. Courtesy of the Daughters of the Republic of Texas Library at the Alamo.

View of Austin. From the book *Texas in 1840,* courtesy of the Austin Public Library.

Alamo Fire Association No. 2 of San Antonio. Courtesy of the Express Publishing Company.

Ox-carts on a San Antonio street. Courtesy of the Daughters of the Republic of Texas Library at the Alamo.

Newspaper mastheads from San Antonio and Austin. Courtesy of the University of Texas Library.

J. M. Brown house, Galveston. Courtesy of the University of Texas Library.

Powattan House Hotel, Galveston. Courtesy of the University of Texas Library.

The Governor's Mansion, Austin. Courtesy of the University of Texas Library.

Mission San Antonio de Valero (the Alamo). Courtesy of the University of Texas Library.

A fandango in San Antonio. From *Leslie's Weekly,* 1858, courtesy of the Express Publishing Company.

Houston theater playbill, about 1839. Courtesy of the Harvard University Theater Collection.

Invitation to the Inaugural Ball, Austin, 1849. Courtesy of the University of Texas Library.

The Confederate recapture of Galveston. From Harper's Weekly, January 31, 1863, courtesy of the Rosenberg Library, Galveston.

TO WEAR A CITY'S CROWN

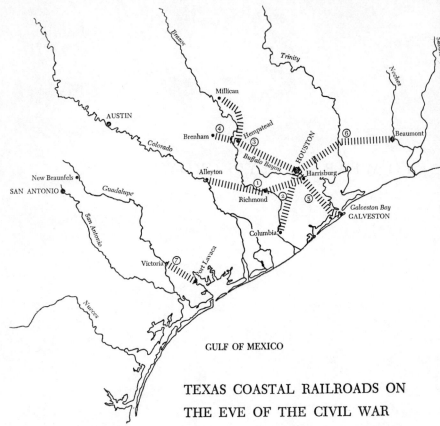

TEXAS COASTAL RAILROADS ON
THE EVE OF THE CIVIL WAR

1. Buffalo Bayou, Brazos and Colorado RR (1856). From Harrisburg, through Stafford's Point to the Brazos River across from Richmond; then across the river to Bernard (or San Bernard) to Eagle Lake to Alleyton.

2. Houston Tap and Brazoria RR. From Houston to Peirce Junction to Columbia.

3. Houston and Texas Central RR. Houston to Eureka then northwestward to Cypress, Hockley, Walker, Hempstead, Narasota, Millican.

4. Washington County RR connected Hempstead with Brenham.

5. Galveston, Houston, and Henderson RR. Galveston to Harrisburg to Houston.

6. Texas and New Orleans RR. Houston to Sheeks to Liberty to Devers to Beaumont.

7. San Antonio and Mexican Gulf Railway. Port Lavaca west 5 miles to Powderhorn, then stopped at Victoria (did *not* go to San Antonio).

I

THE YOUNG TOWNS OF
A NEW REPUBLIC

The first Texas cities were offspring of the Republic of Texas. Social and political conflicts between the Texas colonists and the Mexican government precipitated the Texas Revolution, and the victory of Sam Houston in 1836 over Mexico's erratic and brilliant leader, Antonio Lopez de Santa Anna, won freedom for Texas and began the period of nearly a decade during which Texas was an independent nation. Houston, Galveston, and Austin were founded within three years of the decisive Battle of San Jacinto, and San Antonio began its transformation from village to city during this time. Until the opening of this exciting period, the vast territory between the Rocky Mountains, the Gulf of Mexico, the Red and Sabine Rivers, and the Rio Grande lay beyond any civilization and had little population.

Within ten years of the passing of Mexican governmental control the population of the region more than tripled. Independence and immigration required new centers of commerce, industry, government, culture, and social life. Widespread speculation in town sites followed, and hundreds of communities materialized. Observers were astounded to find swarming settlements where but months before only wilderness had existed. "Towns and villages have been raised as by magic," wrote an English visitor. "Perhaps there is not in the records of history any instance of a Nation rising so *rapidly* as the Republic of Texas has done."[1] Among these new urban creations three were to dominate the early history of the state: Houston, Galveston, and Austin.

Within six months of the last shot at San Jacinto, and only twenty-four miles from its site, carpenters constructed the first dwellings and business houses of Houston, the city which was to become the South's most important trade and transportation center. A. C. Allen and J. K. Allen, shrewd speculators from New York State, were quite aware of the significance of Sam Houston's victory to the future of Texas. Calculating that newcomers would flock to the frontier, they carefully sought out the point in the rich cotton and timber lands between the Brazos and Trinity rivers where water transportation would be possible. They selected the confluence of the Buffalo and White Oak bayous, and here they staked out streets, naming the projected town for the young republic's most illustrious hero and first president.

Despite an unhealthy climate and an aesthetically unexciting locale, Houston boomed to the extent that it was soon considered "the grand focus of the Republic." It was a raw and explosive town where economic competition was ruthless, yet community cooperation was notable. It held the traditional frontier suspicion of intellectual life, yet it urged a wide base of general education. It sneered at "effete Eastern cities," yet it envied and sought the trappings of more cultivated living. Before the end of the Republic, the merchant class had firmly entrenched itself not only in financial leadership, but also in political dominance. Houston's function was trade, its survival depended upon trade, and Houstonians realized this early. Compromise in other areas might be necessary; Queen Commerce was never slighted.

Early European explorers knew that Galveston Island had the best harbor on the Gulf of Mexico between New Orleans and Vera Cruz. Sea captains used the island as a temporary storm haven, and, later, Jean Lafitte held it as headquarters for pirating operations, establishing a small semipermanent settlement. The island's location and harbor induced the Mexican government to locate the provincial customs house at the east end, and the young republic followed this precedent.

It was not, however, until Colonel Michel B. Menard founded his Galveston City Company with Samuel May Williams, Thomas F. McKinney, Gail Borden, and others, that a lasting community was planted. John J. Audubon visited the island in the spring of 1837 and found almost nothing but deer, snakes, mosquitoes, alligators, and a few wretched Mexicans and Indians.[2] He little realized that within a month word would fly about the Republic and throughout the States of the exciting plans for the new city.

By June, heady speculation in Galveston lots was noted in the United States, where a general urban real estate boom was widespread. Galveston prospered despite epidemics and hurricanes. Its commerce flourished, construction could not keep abreast of the influx of population, and the island teemed with activity. A British visitor exaggerated when he related that in 1837 Galveston had only three houses and that in 1840 he found six hundred dwellings and a population of "upwards of 4,000 Souls," but he did not miss the spirit of optimism and growth of what many hoped, and some believed, would one day be the South's rival of New York.[3]

The city of Austin was specifically planned to serve as the

3

capital for the young nation. Using the American city of Washington as an example, Texas's second president (1838–1841), Mirabeau Buonaparte Lamar, energetically promoted the construction of the new community. General Lamar, cavalry hero of San Jacinto and political enemy of flamboyant Sam Houston, was frequently impractical. He often initiated outlandish projects which threatened the very existence of the infant country, and many of his contemporaries felt the proposed new capital was another absurd dream.

The site was far beyond the line of settlement; it was subject to attacks by the Mexicans and to continual harrassment by Indians. Moreover, it was inconvenient to the centers of population and activity. Despite all this, Lamar felt that the capital should be permanently located nearer to the geographical center of the nation where the anticipated great land routes would meet on an inland water route to the Gulf. Thus he planned an economic as well as a governmental center.

When Lamar first visited the upper Colorado river valley on a hunting expedition in 1837 or 1838, he was delighted by the beauty of the surrounding wooded hills, the winding lethargic river, and the gentle light. He is said to have commented to his companions, "This should be the seat of future Empire."[4] As president, the Texas Congress authorized him in 1839 to supervise selection of a site, and the commissioners approved his visionary choice of a spot in the bend of the Colorado, calling it Austin in honor of Stephen Fuller Austin, father of this country.

Despite the determined opposition of former President Sam Houston and the majority of East Texans, work on the capital began, and within six months the rude governmental buildings were ready for occupancy. Forty wagon-loads of the archives, books, supplies, and furniture of the young republic made the trek from Houston to the new capital. Throughout its early years the "seat of Empire" struggled for life. Indian depredations, threats of invasion from Mexico, scarce and expensive provisions, and difficult and undependable communication with the populated areas made survival difficult. Even the government, the city's original raison d'être, was at one time withdrawn. When the Mexicans recaptured San Antonio twice in 1842, the exasperated (and possibly frightened) administrators left Austin, and Congress met until 1845 in Washington-on-the-Brazos or in Houston. The citizenry of Austin, although small in number, was brave and stubborn; they refused to permit the removal of the archives, an act which probably saved the embryonic city.[5] Despite reversals and hardships the meager community of pioneers fought for its hopes. The effort was not in vain, for this struggling village ultimately became the governmental and educational heart of Texas.

In contrast to these newly founded Anglo-American cities of Houston, Galveston, and Austin, San Antonio was over a century old and its population was almost totally of Mexican origin. During the precarious first years of independence the threat of Mexican invasion left the town uneasy. The facts that several of its citizens had played prominent roles in the Texas Revolution, and that within its limits lay the Alamo, shrine of Texas liberty, did not quiet the suspicions of the rest of the nation, which believed San Antonians less than enthusiastic about the severance from Mother Mexico. Moreover, San Antonio's distance from the other Anglo-American communities tended to encourage the continuance of Comanche and Apache raids. In addition, its primary trade and communication lines, which ran to Mexico, were often interrupted during the Republican Era.

Isolated, ignored, and maltreated, San Antonio nonetheless began the painful alteration which was to transform it from a tiny Mexican military outpost into a cosmopolitan entrepôt. Economic and governmental leadership of the community shifted sharply. In the municipal elections of 1837, all but one of the forty-one candidates for office were of Spanish surname while a decade later only five out of a total of twenty-one indicated Mexican background.[6] Economic leadership included such entrepreneurs as Samuel Maverick and John Twohig. Yet the new population was not always so desirable. Transient speculators, attracted by the opening of the Land Office in 1838, mixed with the more stable and energetic. The Texas Revolution, then, profoundly changed the character of San Antonio, breaking its century-old continuity.

While Texas has been under six flags, no such significant modification of its character accompanied any other transfer of government as that which took place when Texas established its independence from Mexico. Three centuries before the Texas Revolution, Spanish explorers eagerly sought cities—the mythical, fabulous gold-wealthy cities of Cibola and Quivera. Francisco Vásquez de Coronado's expedition and a portion of Hernando de Soto's searched, but these opulent places were not found. Instead, the explorers of the early sixteenth century found a variety of Indian tribes cultivating land and dwellings in small villages. Unpromising descriptions by the Spaniards dampened interest in Texas. Although the myth of rich centers would someday become a reality, the early reports helped delay the realization of actual cities for three hundred years.[7]

Ironically, when Spain did renew her interest in her northernmost province, the time coincided with the period when the Comanches began to migrate from the Yellow and Platte river regions of the northwest to the Texas plains. Prior to 1700, the Indian had constituted no major threat in Texas, but after this date his raids on the white man began with a viciousness which remained unabated until the latter half of the nineteenth century. These tribes had come in search of the horses which the Apaches had only recently begun to domesticate.[8] Wild mustangs, descended from those brought to the New World nearly two centuries earlier by Europeans, provided their main source of supply. The Spanish themselves had unwittingly introduced the device which was to thwart their new colonizing efforts more than any other factor, for, once mounted, the Indians were transformed into fierce, nomadic warriors.

Frightened by the successful expansion of the French-Indian trade into their territory in the early eighteenth century, the Spaniards busily constructed missions and presidios across the lower part of the province. By 1722 ten missions, protected by four presidios, stretched from Coahuila to Louisiana. The Marquis Martín de Alarcón, Governor of Coahuila and Texas, founded San Antonio in 1718, when he established the Mission San Antonio de Valero and the Presidio and Villa de Béjar. The Mission San José y San Miguel de Aguayo was founded two years later. A separate provincial government for Texas began in 1721, with the founding of the Presidio de Nuestra Señora del Pílar and a mission and small temporary civil community near the Neches River in East Texas. This capital was near the Louisiana-French outpost of Natchitoches, and the two settlements defined the limits of colonial expansion of their mother countries.

Economy measures, lack of interest, and Indian problems forced withdrawal of a majority of Spanish military troops from Texas by 1730. The following year three of the East Texas missions relocated at San Antonio. The missions remaining in the east declined, and those in the west suffered from Indian attacks. Except for San Antonio, Spain abandoned the province for fifteen years, but special consideration to it during this period gave the sole outpost the first permanent civil settlement in Texas.

San Antonio was the most important mission center in northern New Spain. The missions of San Antonio de Valero and San José y San Miguel de Aguayo, developed by 1720, and in 1731, San

Francisco de la Espada, Nuestra Señora de la Purísima Concepción, and San Juan Capistrano relocated at San Antonio. The presidio and the villa where the soldiers and their families lived completed the community. The Spanish king, disappointed by unsuccessful efforts to transfer settlers from the Mexican interior, moved fifteen families there from the Canary Islands. Transported by the government to Mexico City, the new settlers walked to San Antonio to pioneer in the civil activities of Texas. As a reward, the king ennobled them with the title of *hidalgos* and supported them for a time from his own treasury.

The first years were difficult. Before the arrival of the Canary Islanders, San Antonio's non-mission population numbered about forty-five military personnel and their families.[9] By 1740, the population had increased slightly, and the community boasted about forty small houses; some were now constructed of stone rather than adobe. But the people had built no church and no government buildings. The civil settlers grew enough for their own survival, but as yet they had produced no surplus to raise their living standard.[10]

In time, however, the settlers adjusted to the new conditions, and the community grew and prospered. In 1767, a French visitor estimated that the town had about two hundred houses of which two thirds were stone. By 1779, parishioners had built a church, regular monthly mail service ran to and from Mexico City, and, a short while later, a school was actively operating. The principal employment had become the raising of horses, mules, cows, and sheep, and those who prevented their herds from running wild reportedly owned as many as five to six thousand head.[11]

Except in the villa at San Antonio, military authority had governed Texas during the Spanish period. The villagers exercised their legislative privilege diligently. In 1761, the city fathers passed reform ordinances prohibiting loitering, carrying arms, drinking and gambling, fandangos, and the public grazing of animals. Ordinances required the erection of fences, and farmers were warned against disposing of their savings to the extent of leaving their families in want.[12] No record of enforcement exists, and it is suspected that this executive function was neglected, as the same problems legislated against in 1761 were still present in the community at the turn of the twentieth century.

The role of the mission in the history of San Antonio is significant not only in the founding of the town, but also in its subsequent development. The Spanish first conceived the mission system in the Valley of Mexico as a method of converting and civilizing the settled and often urbanized Aztec groups. Its transplantation to the northern nomadic plains Indians proved less successful, but in full prime, this organization served an important function. San Antonio was the center of activity, and its five missions, stretched at intervals of one to three miles along the river, ministered to nearly a thousand Indians who dwelt, worked, and worshiped within their confines. The prime years of San Antonio missionary activity were between 1730 and 1775. Their zenith was short-lived, partially because of Comanche raids, but the San Antonio missions were used for over a century and left a permanent mark on the character of the city.[13]

A third attempt at colonizing the rest of Texas began in 1745, again because of apprehension over increased French trade. Authorities organized several new missions and presidios. One, San Sabá, was placed far to the north to aid the wily and fickle Apaches in their contest with the Comanches. Hoping to control the savages better, the military launched a series of Indian wars, which ended disastrously for the Spanish. In 1759 under a French flag and with French arms, a force of Taovayas and Comanches repulsed the Spaniards roundly near the Red River in the worst defeat inflicted by the Indians in Texas history. As a result, many of the missions withdrew. Thus, Spanish efforts at settling the province again failed dismally.

The acquisition of Louisiana at the Peace of Paris, in 1763, was no blessing for the Spanish government. Already distended with her traditional colonies, she now was responsible for more lands which were surrounded by hostile neighbors. A revision of policy determined complete withdrawal of all missions, military posts, and settlements except those at San Antonio de Béjar and La Bahía. The settlers of East Texas were removed to San Antonio in 1773. Small numbers of these remained; the significant result of this forced migration was a determined return of the majority to found the town of Nacogdoches in 1779.

The mission system then began a severe decline, efforts at colonization ceased, and settlements dwindled, until at the beginning of the nineteenth century only three villages remained in Texas; San Antonio de Béjar with some two thousand inhabitants, La Bahía del Espíritu Santo with fourteen hundred, and the new community of Nacogdoches with five hundred. Of the three, San Antonio was the most advanced. The government of the province had been transferred to San Antonio in 1773, and the presence of the governor and his retinue lent some civilization to the village. The American explorer, Zebulon Pike, relates in his memoirs that he found the society of San Antonio pleasing. The officials were well educated and courteous, and they offered him a satisfying social life during his stay.[14] But this oasis was the only one in the province.

The purchase of Louisiana in 1803 placed Americans one step nearer to Texas, and not a small number of these northern foreigners illegally crossed the border beginning at this date. From 1803 until 1820, Spain, beset with internal, colonial, and foreign problems, tried futilely to save her disintegrating empire. But even in death throes in the New World, the Spanish were determined to keep constantly threatening outsiders from intruding. In 1818, for example, two Napoleonic generals, Charles Lallemand and Antoine Rigaud, set out with a group of French exiles and assorted other recruits and established, with the aid of the pirate Jean Lafitte, a settlement of about four hundred persons on the lower Trinity River. The settlement lasted less than two years. Frightened by reports that the Spanish were advancing to destroy their village, Champ d'Asile, the settlers fled to Galveston Island and dispersed from that point.[15]

The Mexican Revolution caused further turmoil in Texas. Spanish troops drove away the inhabitants of Nacogdoches in 1819 and 1820, and the town was totally broken up. Its inhabitants sought refuge near the Louisiana town of Natchitoches. San Antonio and La Bahía also suffered considerably during the strife. By 1816 San Antonio was almost depopulated because of the unrest during the independence movement, and in 1819 a flood destroyed much of the town.

Thus, when Mexican independence was achieved, the result of Spanish efforts at colonizing Texas was to be seen in three wretched little villages. The Mexicans would not prove more adept at colonizing the province with their own people, but during their control events surged to a significant climax: the independence of Texas and the beginnings of its urban growth.

The history of Texas and Mexico had been singularly altered in 1820 with the acceptance by Ferdinand VII of the liberal Spanish Constitution of 1812. This gave the final impetus to Mexico's independence movement. But before independence was achieved, a decree was issue by the Cortes in Madrid, on September 28, 1820, reversing the historic exclusion of foreign settlers in Spanish dominions. The new law encouraged foreign colonists, who needed only to accept the Constitution of 1812 and the laws and the customs of the country. They were expected to take an oath of allegiance to the King, embrace Catholicism, and show evidence of good character and ability to support themselves in a trade or profession.[16]

Shortly after the passage of this act Moses Austin arrived in San Antonio. Austin, a former subject of the King of Spain, was then an unsuccessful lead miner from Missouri. He had come hoping to secure permission to establish a colony of Anglo-Americans in Texas. Anglo-Americans had been coming into the province since the beginning of the nineteenth century, but, with rare exceptions, they were residing illegally in the Spanish territory. Armed with the permission received from the provincial governor, Austin began his journey back, but he died before the trip was over. His son, Stephen F. Austin, a competent young man of twenty-seven who had held responsible governmental positions and who was a proven administrator, continued to organize and direct the project.

Stephen F. Austin and about eighty families arrived in 1821, to find a state of turmoil existing in the infant Republic of Mexico, now the supra-government of the Province of Texas. Austin hastened to Mexico City, where he obtained recognition of his father's contract from the emperor, Agustín I, shortly before the latter's abdication. Recognizing the necessity for a guarantee from the new authority of the rights of the colonists, Austin petitioned the Mexican national Congress and received its verifying decree in April of 1823.[17]

The young empresario retraced his steps to Texas and ushered in the new era. The backed-up tide of westward migration in the United States, which had long been dammed at the Sabine, began seeping through. Austin's land commissioner, Felipe Enrique Neri, Baron de Bastrop, received his authority in 1823 and began issuing liberal land grants. By terms of the National Colonizational Law, each family received one *labor* (177 acres) of land if they were farmers and a *sitio* or league (about 4,428 acres) if they were stock raisers. The colonists were exempted from taxation for ten years. A few of the newcomers were large planters like Leonard Groce, whose move from Alabama involved fifty wagons tended by ninety slaves. So considerable an enterprise as Groce's demanded more land, and he was allowed ten leagues, or over 44,000 acres. Other large planters received similar grants. The large planter was rare, however. By 1830, Austin had settled nearly eight hundred families, and his authority extended over 4,500 people.

Austin was not the only empresario, but he was by far the most important and certainly the most conscientious. He alone tried to comply with the requirements that a school be founded to teach Spanish, and he made efforts to construct a church and see that a priest was available to minister to the people. Hayden Edwards began colonization in East Texas in the area of Nacogdoches, but his efforts to form an independent nation, Fredonia, aborted in a revolutionary attempt, and his activities ended in 1827. An Irish-Mexican colony began with headquarters at Refugio, and another primarily Irish group, the McMullen-McGloin colony, established itself below San Antonio and founded San Patricio.

The character of the early colonists was unusually good. Composed essentially of small farmers with some means and a high rate of literacy, the colony presented a picture of industry and thrift. Crime was rare, since Austin and the other empresarios required the sellers to furnish proof of good character, and Austin was particularly vigilant in evicting undesirables from his colony. The majority of these frontier people were from the interior South, but many were from northern states. Word of the prosperity of these early colonists circulated in the United States, and this, plus cheap lands, attracted even greater numbers of immigrants.

Although they had encouraged initial Anglo-American colonization, the Mexicans became apprehensive at the numbers pouring into Texas from the north, while their efforts at relocating their own citizens from Central Mexico proved futile. As a result, the Mexican Congress passed the Law of April 6, 1830, which prohibited further immigration from the United States. Austin was able to admit a few hundred more Americans by the plea that his contract was unfulfilled. However, except for this small number, there was no legal immigration of Americans into Texas between 1830 and 1834.

The Mexican government had hoped to balance the northern colonists by encouraging Swiss and German peasants to come to Texas, and by transplanting groups of their own population. Their efforts failed, however, and in 1834 the law was revoked and Americans poured across the border in unprecedented numbers. It is believed that between January and March in 1835 as many as two thousand persons arrived at the mouth of the Brazos alone. The Mexican government had greatly annoyed the early settlers by its legislative and administrative ineptitude, and the Law of April 6, 1830 antagonized them further. With the older settlers dissatisfied, the Mexicans unwisely admitted a new flood of foreigners whose heritage and sympathies were with the United States. Mexican policies were to cost dearly—indeed, in the end, half the land of their nation.

The older towns had declined under the late Spanish period, and, except for Nacogdoches, the Mexican era did not improve them. The government was so weakened by instability and economic difficulties that it could give little help in Indian defense. San Antonio suffered particularly during these years. Much of the rich farm land near the city was abandoned because of the frequent maraudings. Attacks on the town itself were not rare, but more frequently the Indians would simply invade the community, as in the summer of 1825, when several hundred Indians spent six days committing depredations and insulting and threatening inhabitants. The townsmen did some trading with peaceful Indians, however. A visitor in 1823 recorded that while he was in the town, about a thousand Indians came on a treaty expedition, bringing dried buffalo meat, deer skins, and buffalo robes, which they hoped to exchange for sugar, beads, and other articles.[18]

The town's population was estimated then at less than five thousand and was entirely Mexican except for three or four American and French merchants. Some of the missions were still operating on a small scale in the early Mexican period, but most of the savage converts had dispersed long before. Observers always commented on the delightful climate, but few found the town attractive. Many of the buildings were of stone, but they were neither beautiful nor comfortable. The other structures were built of mud and logs, giving the community a squalid appearance.[19]

San Antonio suffered again in 1824, when the provinces of Coahuila and Texas were governmentally merged and the capital removed to Saltillo. The residence of the governors had enlivened San Antonio, but with the absence of operating missions and of the government the town continued to deteriorate. Benjamin Lundy, who would later achieve immortality as an abolitionist, was one of the few Americans living in San Antonio between 1833 and 1835. He estimated the population at about two thousand before an epidemic of cholera in the fall of 1834 drove the population away and gave the town the "appearance of a 'deserted village.'" Juan Almonte visited San Antonio officially in 1834 and in his report estimated that the population had dropped from five thousand in 1806 to twenty-four hundred in 1834.[20]

Nacogdoches, on the eastern border, was totally deserted when Austin passed that way in 1820, but it began to revive through its Indian trade and the stimulation of immigrants traveling the San Antonio Road. Its population in 1836 was probably about a thousand. Goliad was in a state of ruin, its citizens impoverished and living in a primitive condition. They managed to eke a living from a few horses and cattle and by raising some corn.[21]

The Anglo-American colonies developed several small trade and administrative centers during the early years. Focal community for Austin's colony was the village of San Felipe de Austin, some eighty miles up river from the mouth of the Brazos. The community was active, but as late as 1827 all houses were constructed of logs. Mina (Bastrop) was founded in 1832, at the point where the San Antonio Road crossed the Colorado River.

All the villages were located on rivers. Velasco, Brazoria, Columbia, San Felipe de Austin, and Washington were on the Brazos. At the mouth of the Colorado was Matagorda, while Mina was located two hundred miles up river; Victoria and Gonzales were on the Guadalupe. Texana was near the confluence of the Navidad and the Lavaca, and Harrisburg was on Buffalo Bayou. None of these eleven was to achieve significance as an urban center. Of the fourteen communities in Texas on the eve of the Texas Revolution, only one was to acquire such status. Many disappeared, others remained small towns, but San Antonio alone would claim greatness.

Several factors hampered development of towns during the Mexican period. Money and banking facilities were virtually nonexistent. Barter, the means of trade, was not conducive to creating large commercial centers, and the absence of roads thwarted business by preventing adequate communication and transportation. The province grew from four thousand in 1820 to twenty-five thousand in 1836, but this increase was almost exclusively rural, as the empresario system favored the agriculturalist. The early frontiersman was largely self-sufficient, and money which he might have used for commodities he placed back in the land. The villages which were begun during the early Anglo-American era failed to grow because they were not well situated. Placed earlier as administrative, transportation, and trade centers, they were ineffective later when the governmental boundaries were altered and the railroad, highway, and improved navigation changed transportation routes.

A number of factors lay behind the Texas Revolution, including resentment by the colonists against tariffs and immigration restrictions and, especially, the Mexican government's refusal to separate Texas from Coahuila. The situation was further aggravated by the suspicion of the Mexican government that the United States coveted Texas. The ultimate catalyst, however, was Santa Anna's attempt to establish virtual dictatorship over Mexico and, in particular, a threatened military occupation of Texas. The war opened with a minor fray, known as the Battle of Gonzales, and ended with the dramatic and decisive Battle of San Jacinto.

Separation from Mexico radically changed the future of Texas. Independence meant that Texas would be assured a population of northern European, not Spanish-Indian, background. It also meant stability of government. From the time of her own independence Mexico had been in anarchistic upheaval. Little trained in methods of self-government, the Mexicans had found themselves in the embarrassing position of governing men who were accustomed to effective self-government. The relationship was short-lived. In brief, then, independence meant that Texas would become an Anglo-American community, under an Anglo-American form of government, housing Anglo-American institutions. These factors attracted many who before had been reluctant to chance the strange and the uncertain.

Other factors encouraged the great increase of population to come under the Republic. The new government had little money, but it did have land, and land attracted population.

Liberal grants were offered to those who would come to aid in the battle for independence, and soon after its formation, the young nation offered her public lands to potential immigrants at low prices and under excellent terms. Conditions in the United States aided growth. The Panic of 1837 and subsequent economic difficulties in the early 1840's ruined many people. Often, men who sought a fresh beginning could only gain in migrating to the newly opened frontier. Southerners, always land hungry, were particularly enticed by the climate and soil, which were conducive to the production of cotton.

A singular phenomenon in immigration accompanied Texas independence—an alteration which would be of utmost importance to urban development. This feature was the difference in character between the old and the new immigrant. Austin's "Old Three Hundred" had been stable, agrarian folk of a type found on almost every American frontier. They were honest peasantry, men and women who believed that their hard work, thrift, and permanency would bring them future reward. Many of the newcomers were quite different.

When the call to arms was sounded by the revolutionary leaders, promises were broadcast throughout the United States of land rewards to be given to those who would come to the aid of the Texans. Thousands of unsettled men hastened to the fray, and when the smoke cleared, thousands more moved in for the spoils. Among these were men who realized that the new influx meant a need for cities. A new breed of immigrant, the urban speculator, built the early cities, and more speculators flocked to settle them.

The urban immigrant often came from an urban setting. He was frequently impetuous, an impatient, eager empire builder, lusting for rapidly acquired money. Newspapers lamented the prevalence of idle men about the towns who schemed for quick wealth and who were general nuisances to the communities.

They encouraged these men to seek their fortunes in the rural districts, advice that was seldom heeded. Not all the newcomers were ne'er-do-wells, but the atmosphere was decidedly speculative and inventive. The new urban immigrant was less permanent than his soil-bound neighbor. Frequent even are the instances where men spent several decades building reputations and fortunes in a young city, only to return to former homes as if they had been away only for a brief interlude.

That there were serious men who came to play responsible roles in the communities is not to be denied; indeed, the majority were of this type. But the distinguishing characteristics of the urban frontiersman were clear and unmistakable. Merchants, mechanics, ministers, or murderers, these men were all intent on gambling with the forces which were rapidly pushing back the wilderness.

Immigration was yet overwhelmingly rural, but the traits which were necessary for the building of cities had been combined. Spain tried to colonize Texas and failed. Mexico was no more successful. It remained for the great American westward migration to populate the lands and build the cities of Texas.

II

THE INLAND SETTLEMENTS:
AUSTIN AND SAN ANTONIO

"The principal Towns are Galveston, Houston, & Austin
—I beg their pardons *cities* I should have said for so they are
called and considered by the Texians."[1] Francis Sheridan, an
unofficial observer for the British government, chided the Texans
on their well-known tendency to exaggerate, yet their boasting
was based on well-grounded optimism. These three towns, no
one of which was yet three years old, and none of which held a
population of two thousand, were to rise rapidly to the full status
of cities. Because of the character and size of the new immigration into Texas, these three quickly reduced the earlier-founded
Spanish and Anglo-American administrative and trading villages
to insignificance.

Commercial vitality and location made it soon evident that the new towns would best fulfill the roles demanded by an aggressively enterprising people who looked to their urban centers for leadership. The coastal communities of Galveston and Houston were, in fact, almost prototypes of the Texan character as it emerged from the Texas Revolution. Economic motivation was dominant, as Mrs. Matilda Houstoun, the wealthy Scottish yachtswoman and authoress, noted: "The Texans are an impatient people; they drive to, and at their end, with greater velocity than any individuals I ever saw or heard of." "Every thought and every idea resolves itself into money . . . dollars, and how to obtain them, seems their one sole and engrossing thought." They are, she added, "extremely apathetic and indolent . . . when there is no present and personal good arising from their exerting themselves."[2] Leisure hours were seldom put to constructive use. Indeed, destructiveness often seemed the prime characteristic of the raw frontier towns; they presented pictures of crude, violent, and bawdy activity during their early years.

Houston was most disreputable, but Galveston did not lag far behind and for a brief period Austin had its share of rough and lawless elements. No man was safe on the streets of early Houston unless armed with a pistol, a Bowie knife, or both. Several killings a day were not unusual, and knife fighting was carried even into the national legislature itself when disagreements occurred among its members. The violent nature of the towns evoked strong condemnation from travelers. One, bitterly annoyed, recorded that never did "such a quantity of rogues . . . populate any corner of the globe."[3]

A major cause of the general lawlessness was the generous use of alcohol. Townsmen gathered at hotels, groggeries, and in their homes to follow their favorite avocation—drinking. Sheridan commented that "the passion for erecting grog shops . . . supersedes the thirst of religious worship & Temples wherein to exercise it, for though we find every town plentifully supplied with Pot-Houses, we see neither a church or signs of building one."[4] Intemperance was a problem in every community, and the local citizenry usually founded their temperance societies before their churches.

The manners of the townsfolk were crude and strange. Swearing was ubiquitous among men and children of every age and was censoriously mentioned by each passing traveler. But the chewing of tobacco provoked the greatest contempt. Francis Sheridan commented that, "Hig[h] & low, rich & poor, young & old chew, chew, chew & spit, spit, spit all the blessed day & most of the night—and as the spitting-box is considered generally speaking a superfluous luxury the floors of the rooms & fire places bear ample testimony to the beastly habits of their occupants. Even before women no sort of consideration is made & they appear from custom to have become perfectly reconciled to this Hoggism." The Bowie knife was indispensable to conversation, having been whipped out at the introduction of discourse to be used to whittle, clean fingernails, cut a piece of tobacco, or, it was even alleged, to pick teeth. No matter how many times daily one met a person, one greeted him, shook his hand, and used "Sir" a "minimum of three times in each sentence, even in the height of anger."[5]

Urban Texans enjoyed a far greater variety of foodstuffs than their rural neighbors, who lived mainly on cornbread, yams, wild game, and honey. Despite the advantages of better dining, the townsmen had yet to cultivate better tastes. They ate with amazing speed. Sheridan described the dinner hour at the Republic's finest hotel, the Tremont House of Galveston: "Dingle, Dingle, Dingle, goes a bell . . . at wh[ich] magic sound the doors of a large room . . . are thrown open, & the crowds of Boarders . . . rush head-long in, & in less than ten-minutes rush head-long out again."[6] As if to compensate for their usual indifference to food, the townspeople grasped every passing excuse, usually a visiting dignitary, to hold a banquet or barbecue.

The theater was a favorite evening pastime, and each of the three towns boasted professional theaters for brief periods. Although one bitter observer announced that "to expect to find a book for sale of any higher character than the illustrated alphabet . . . would be to expect a very remarkable and unusual phenomenon," both Houston and Galveston merchants offered a fair selection of reading materials, and all three communites attempted to establish public reading rooms and libraries.[7] Newspapers, however, constituted the main reading fare of the people. Mrs. Houstoun found the most typical town scene that of men standing or sitting "in every variety of bodily contortion" reading their newspapers. In 1841, there were twenty newspapers in the towns of the Republic.[8]

Following American custom, the Texans were organization-minded. Secret societies were popular, and by 1845 nearly two dozen Masonic lodges enjoyed charters. Houston had a philosophical society, and Austin a patriotic society. Debating groups existed in the three major towns. Merchants organized the "better elements" into volunteer fire departments; women and temporarily reformed drunks organized temperance societies; and tentative efforts were even made to form religious bodies.[9]

Essentially, the customs of the Texans had their roots in the southern frontier of the United States, since the majority of Texans migrated from that area. Yet, as often was true in the South, the townsmen were a more heterogeneous lot than their rural neighbors. Foreign observers noted that most of the country residents were from Virginia, the Carolinas, Tennessee, Alabama, Mississippi, Louisiana, Kentucky, and Missouri, but that the towns were filled with northern, particularly New England, tradesmen and craftsmen. Many of the town builders themselves had lived in northern cities.[10]

A profusion of Europeans immigrated to Texas. Germans, outnumbering other European groups, came individually or with various colonizing societies. The German community of Industry, to the north of Houston, was founded in 1838, and in 1842 a group of German noblemen, led by Prince Solms-Braunfels, organized a colonizing association. Their administrative center, New Braunfels, located between Austin and San Antonio, was one of the major towns of the state by 1850. Many Germans remained in Galveston, Houston, and, later, Austin to become prominent merchants and manufacturers.

A French-Alsatian colony was established north of San Antonio in 1843, with the arrival of three hundred settlers. Although an additional two thousand persons immigrated to the community between 1843 and 1847, the venture was only a slow success.[11] Many who were unable to secure regular employment migrated to San Antonio, adding another ethnic group to that already cosmopolitan center. In addition, large numbers of English, Irish, and Scandinavians settled in the major towns during the early years.

With only rare exception the Negroes of Texas were brought from the United States by their masters. Some traffic in slaves had existed in Galveston, but by 1836 only six thousand blacks were to be found in the Republic. Seven times as many were counted a decade later, but the urban slave numbers remained small. City, county, and national legislation restricted the activities of the city slave, but he generally was better treated than his rural brother.[12]

Legally, the free Negro often was unwelcome in Republican Texas. In 1840 the national legislature passed a law excluding free Negroes from immigration on penalty of being sold into slavery.[13] Many towns passed similar ordinances, but the laws were not always observed and most were soon repealed. By annexation Texas had several hundred gainfully employed free

Negroes, most of whom were urban. They worked as servants, barbers, semiskilled artisans, and laborers. Although Galveston had a Negro dancing master, the Anglo-American towns were often not warmly hospitable to free persons of color. San Antonio, however, with its more heterogeneous population, accepted them.

The Mexican was not yet found in the new towns. Galveston had "a few miserable wretches" who had been taken prisoner from the Santa Anna army; Austin and Houston had almost no Mexicans. San Antonio, of course, was overwhelmingly Mexican. Except for the Mexicans of San Antonio, urban Texans tended to be young men, for the older were reluctant to migrate, and women found the rough frontier centers uncongenial.

Austin, Galveston, and Houston were similar in many respects, yet each had its own peculiar characteristics. San Antonio was still a foreign city undergoing slow transition. Houston, the largest, was the oldest of the newer towns and in many ways the most typical. Austin and San Antonio shared similar problems; both were beyond the frontier of rural settlement and were not, initially, commercially strong.

Austin, President Lamar's "great seat of Empire," was the source of much jealous rivalry between sections and interest groups, both prior to its founding and during its early years. Men from the western sections of the nation were in favor of its establishment as a capital, as were most citizens who envisioned future settlement there. Many speculators in the western lands wished to draw the immigrant to the inland portions of the young nation and to extend the frontier and give it added protection. Also among the supporters of the new capital were men who saw its location as one of unusual beauty, of healthful climate, and on projected crossroads where it might become the financial and commercial as well as the political center of the nation. Too, there were those who had no taste for the rough character and unhealthy situation of Houston, then the capital city.

Opposition came from eastern sections where the main population was centered. East Texans complained of the great distance between the proposed site and the concentration of population and the difficulties in travel, supply, and general communication. Supporters of Houston were, of course, prime enemies, as the withdrawal of the capital from that community meant a loss of prestige, population, and money. Legislators were almost evenly divided, their sympathies depending not only on the sentiments of their constituents and their own personal interests, but also on the outcome of balancing their distaste for mud, excessive heat, and disease with their objection to traveling great distances and their fear of Indians and invading Mexicans.

The Allen brothers, founders of Houston, had wisely realized that the attraction of the seat of government would be a significant boost in the first growth of Houston, and in 1836 they successfully petitioned for the relocation of the capital to their city even before the building of the new town had commenced. In 1837 the Allens built a structure to function as Capitol and rented it to the government for a nominal fee. Houstonians who fought desperately to retain the government continued the campaign even after the loss to Austin in 1839, but they were under no illusion that it would be permanently located at Houston.[14] Citizens of the Bayou City, however, realized that being the capital was not essential for their community's existence, as it was for Austin's, but that it was, nevertheless, a distinct asset. The battle between the two towns was acrimonious. Hence, in 1839, an Austin supporter harangued his colleagues in the House of Representatives: "It requires no other argument . . . than barely to look at this wretched mud hole—*this graveyard*—the city of Houston . . . It would be better to legislate or live in tents or the open air, in a high, healthy section of country, than to inhale the poisonous atmosphere, drink the bad water, and be subjected to the privations and want of comfort incident to a life in Houston . . . Hundreds have been swept from the stage of human action, and consigned to that great reservoir for all the living—*the grave,* by visiting or taking up their residence in this wretched, sickly place . . . And it is not only the diseases that cannot fail to visit and destroy who reside here—but the sickly and poor appearance of the place and the surrounding country immediately adjacent to it—together with the difficulty in getting from it to any other part of the country, drives hundreds from our shores disgusted and disheartened, who came to Texas with the intention of vesting their capital and making their home in it."[15]

After the capital was returned to Houston in 1842, the Austin *City Gazette* chided the departed legislators: "We have understood that the yellow fever is prevailing in Houston . . . Are the people of Austin exposed to greater risk from the possibility of Mexican invasion, then [sic] the people of Houston are from the invasion of yellow and congestive fevers? None but a coward would say so."[16] Cowards or no, the government did not return to Austin until 1845, when annexation was a certainty and when the threat or Mexican invasions had diminished substantially.

Fate had played generously into the hands of the anti-Austin forces in 1842, through the Mexican attacks on San Antonio. When news of the first invasion reached Austin, the entire population fled, excepting about two dozen families and a few single men.[17] After the Mexican withdrawal most returned to their homes, but Sam Houston, leader of the opposition, had found the ammunition he needed. He called the next session of the legislature at Houston because of the "generally unsafe character of Austin." The "City of the Hills" began her darkest days. Almost completely deserted, the streets became obscured by undergrowth; buildings were tenantless; and commerce, non-existent. Between the fall of 1842 and 1845, there were never more than five women residing in Austin at any one time. A passing traveler recorded the scene in 1843: "Lo! Dreariness and desolation presented themselves; few houses appeared inhabited and many falling to decay. The 'Legation of France' empty, its doors and windows open, palings broken down and appearing as if it would be soon in ruins. The President's house looked gloomy, the streets filled with grass . . . The Capitol is the abode of bats, lizards and stray cattle."[18]

In his antagonism to Austin, Sam Houston had sworn to fight until "the time should come when the wild buffalo and the un-tamed savage should alike roam unmolested in the streets." His wish was fulfilled. The largest body of visitors in 1844 was a herd of buffalo which wandered up Congress Avenue from their watering place at the river.[19]

But the remaining residents of the Capital City were a hardy lot, not easily defeated. Because of this small group of frontier men and women the community survived and again became the seat of government. When Houston withdrew the legislature, he left the government papers, temporarily, he believed. Later, when he took steps to remove them, he was faced with opposition by armed force. The unhappy citizens had formed a committee to guard the documents. Houston made several unsuccessful attempts to persuade the Austinites; then he sent a small military detachment to steal the papers away at night.[20] They were discovered, however, while loading the wagons. An alarm was spread, and Mrs. Angelina Eberly, the innkeeper, set off a cannon in the direction of the invaders, putting them to flight with their partially loaded wagons. Soon armed vigilantes over-took the fleeing soldiers, wrested from them the government papers, and returned them triumphantly to the capital. Citizens then buried the papers in metal boxes as a protection against future raids by the Mexicans or the national government. But neither occurred, and the archives remained intact. Convinced at last, Houston and future chief executives found it prudent to leave the papers where they were. The land office was returned to Austin in 1844, and, when prospects of annexation became strong in 1845, President Anson Jones arranged for the convention to meet there. From that date, although controversies would arise, there was never serious danger that another city would be chosen the permanent capital of Texas.[21]

Soon after the government commissioners decided upon the location of Austin in early 1839, President Lamar commissioned Edwin Waller to lay out the city and to construct government buildings with as much dispatch as possible so that the legislature might meet there in the fall. Austin owes much to Waller's abilities and vision. Attractively arranged between two streams flowing into the Colorado, the town boasted ample space reserved for important public buildings. The wide boulevards, which were "an endless morass of mud" to early residents, were blessings to citizens a century later. Two hundred laborers and $113,000 in Texas script were used to erect the temporary nucleus of the capital city. Conditions were difficult and primitive. Stockades protected workers from the Indians, but there was little protection from the elements. Supplies were exorbitant in cost and poor in quality. Much of the timber had to be brought thirty miles by ox cart from the Bastrop pinery.[22]

Despite hardships, Waller was ready to receive the government in the fall of 1839, having completed construction of the major public buildings and a number of private dwellings. Except for the President's house, which was of finished lumber, the structures were built of logs on a double-unit plan with an open run between. Many were enclosed by small log stockades. Large public demonstrations, including a parade, cannon-firing, speech-making, and a banquet and ball in the evening welcomed President Lamar in October. Two and a half months earlier the first sale of lots had been held, which netted the government $300,000.[23] Austin was founded.

The first-comers, including Waller, were charmed with the unusual beauty of the townsite, situated on the river amid rolling, wood-covered hills. It was still a rough little village, yet one English visitor reported in 1840: "The public buildings are not elegant, but very comfortable, and appropriate for a new government . . . A large three-story brick hotel has been commenced, and is to be completed by the fall of 1840. The buildings are generally of a much better description than are usually built in new countries, and the improvement of the city has progressed with a rapidity heretofore unknown, even in this country. It contains about 400 houses and 1,200 inhabitants."[24]

But Austin was also attractive to Indians, who became the young community's primary problem. Because the town was far beyond the line of settlement, raids were frequent and severe, and loss of property and life extensive. Typical was a raid on the night of March 6, 1840. A large party of Indians had divided into squads and entered the town simultaneously, stealing nearly every horse and mule not securely locked up. The next morning it was discovered that two men had been killed, both scalped as well as stabbed, and ten arrows protruded from the body of one. A more serious raid came in the fall of 1842, when over a dozen residents were killed, several kidnapped, and many injured.[25]

Not all Indians were enemies. Several tribes remained close allies of the Texans, while others vacillated between friendly trading and hostile marauding. Some even traded with Austin merchants. A visitor of 1840 noted, "Scattered through the town we discovered a considerable number of Indians, who seem to have visited the place for purposes of trade, as some of their horses carried packs of buffalo and other skins."[26] President Lamar, nevertheless, adopted a policy of extermination and drove the savages from the frontier area by 1842, after which time Austin suffered little.

Indian fighting was probably the most important municipal activity, but it was largely a voluntary affair, as were the other municipal functions. A city government was organized in 1839, and Edwin Waller was appropriately named first mayor. City records prior to the Civil War are no longer extant, but newspapers of the time suggest the scope of government activity. From time to time, the municipal officers hired a cart to carry away dead animals and to fill in washed streets, but generally the care and cleaning of streets was left to individual property owners. Newspaper editors urged the citizens to improve and drain the streets and commended them when they did so. A few thoroughfares were lightly graveled, but most became mudholes during rains. The city fathers established a cemetery to the east of the settlement, but water supply, fire protection, and even policing were, to a large extent, a responsibility left to individual citizens or the county government.[27]

Devoted primarily to national activities and possessing no populated hinterland, Austin developed little commerce and industry other than that necessary for its own needs. A month after the government arrived, a local census indicated nine printers, ten lawyers, three physicians, five merchants, three architects, six hotelkeepers, two auctioneers, three bakers, three house and sign painters, one lime-dealer, one barber, one sundries-dealer, one boarding house operator, seven grocers (saloon keepers), one marble-cutter, one clothing merchant, three livery-stable operators, two restaurant owners, one tailor, one land-locator, and one plasterer. By the following month, "mechanics" had increased to thirty-five, and professional gamblers to twenty.[28]

Merchants received their goods overland, freighted from the coast by ox cart or brought up the Colorado on small barges. Stores were scattered along Congress Avenue in small double log structures. General foodstuffs and liquors were offered on one side, and dry goods on the other. Hotels provided the principal gathering points, though many were merely crude pens or tents. The most prominent and first constructed, Bullock House, was of hewn logs on the lower level and cottonwood plank on its second story. A large log was placed in front of the establishment, and here, each evening, men gathered in general rendezvous to exchange news, to converse, and to debate.[29]

Newspapers were the main sources of information about the outside world. By 1842, the community boasted two weeklies and one sporadic daily. In addition to the news, the journals carried considerable literary material such as that found in the November 27, 1841 issue of the *Daily Bulletin,* where Weber, Diderot, and Marie Antoinette were quoted. An issue of a month later carried several columns on the front page from the works of Whittier and Longfellow. Political controversy heightened competition, and personal squabbles among editors were not uncommon. The publisher of the *Sentinel* referred editorially to his adversary as, "The 'Fat Boy', alias D. W. Wallack, the slick-haired, silly-pated, *gum*-elastic-conscious editor of the *Colorado Gazette.*"[30] Such epithets as "fraud," "blackguard," "idiot," "contemptible and vulgar imposter" were common. The general quality of the newspapers was mediocre, but good enough for the entertainment and enlightenment of the average urban frontiersman.

More erudite enlightenment was attempted by the members of the Austin Lyceum, incorporated by the National Congress in 1841, "for the encouragement of literary and scientific pursuits."[31] A lecture usually preceded a debate on another topic, as at the meeting of October 8, 1840, when a discourse on "the relative merits of the plays of Hamlet and Othello" was followed by a discussion of "the advisability of annexation."[32] Public support was strong. The *Sentinel* urged, "Let's all go, and benefit ourselves, while we give encouragement to those who, in attempting their own improvement, are laboring for the improvement of the public taste." The members organized Austin's first public lending library, which included diverse works of literature, history, philosophy, commerce, and applied science.[33]

Austin merchants handled a small volume of books for local consumption. A variety of periodicals and foreign newspapers were also advertised upon arrival. Moreover, several citizens had reasonably substantial private libraries for so primitive a community. Government officials doubtlessly brought small collections with them.

Much of Austin's intellectual and social life was centered around the French chargé d'affaires, the elegant Count Alphonse Dubois de Saligny. The first legation, although small, was the scene of numerous receptions, banquets, and small dinners honoring visiting dignitaries and entertaining the Austin elite. The Count set an excellent table and supplied his guests liberally with wines and liqueurs. His hospitality was so popular that he constructed a larger legation, which was Austin's most elaborate house. Unfortunately, this activity had an abrupt demise from a cause compatible with the character of a frontier community.

Hotelkeeper Bullock's pigs had repeatedly invaded the stables of the Count, where they consumed an unknown quantity of corn. After exhausting other means of solving the problem, Saligny's servant killed several of the pigs. In the resulting dispute the irate Bullock seized the French diplomat by the collar on the public streets. The Count appealed to the Secretary of State for redress, and when his request was ignored (possibly because of difficulties with a French loan), diplomatic relations were severed between France and the Republic of Texas. The nobleman closed the legation and returned to his native land, much to the distress of Austin society.[34]

Although the city lacked the variety of entertainment found in the coastal towns, balls, public dinners, and barbecues were regular and popular functions when the Congress was in session there. In addition, San Jacinto Day always set off celebrations, parades, speeches, and a barbecue. May Day had its election of a queen and a ball in the evening. During the summer months bathing in the Colorado or at Barton Springs was a common pastime. Hunting was popular, both for food and for sport. Horse racing became the best patronized spectator sport, although cockfighting, a Spanish legacy, had a large following.[35] Bars and gambling rooms were the favorite haunts of Austin men.

Social organizations flourished during Austin's early days. Even before the arrival of the government, a group of citizens had organized a Masonic lodge; in 1841, a second one was founded. The more prominent men of the community organized the Texas Patriotic and Philanthropic Society in 1839. During the same winter military-minded citizens formed the Travis Guards, the local militia.[36] Temperance workers met regularly to combat the rising problem of alcohol, and the Austin Lyceum attracted the public with its bimonthly programs.

Religious activity was as haphazard as elsewhere in Texas. Methodism had more adherents than any other group, and by 1840 the local Methodists had managed to establish a regular pattern of camp meetings. Until 1851 they had the only church building in Austin, a common pine-frame building which they had constructed in 1841.[37] Conferences and circuits were organized from the Austin center as early as 1839. Other groups met in government buildings and an interdenominational Sunday school flourished for a period. Regular religious activity, however, was a rarity.

Despite religious indifference Austin's moral tone was usually high. Except for a brief period at her commencement the town lacked the brawling character of Houston. The local citizenry discouraged unruly behavior. An armed visitor arrived in 1841, and received the following greeting from the editor of the *Sentinel:* "A Rowdie—We noticed, a few days since, a fellow dashing about with a huge Bowie knife protruding from his bosom. We advise him to exchange this weapon for a corn cob; he will find the latter much lighter and more convenient to wear, than the Bowie knife, and just as useful in *respectable* society."[38]

Austin's population was also more stable than others. Few speculators appeared and commercial activity was limited to the immediate environs of the city. Travelers came to Austin to do business with the government, but they seldom lingered because the distances were great and travel was difficult. Moreover, for the same reasons, the swarms of unemployed which plagued Galveston and Houston left Austin unmolested.

If, in the minds of many Texans, Austin was thought too far from the line of settlement to be adequately protected from Mexican invasion and Indian raids, San Antonio was virtually dismissed from their thoughts. That community was eighty miles nearer to the Mexican border, and there was not a single house between the two towns. As the population of the Alamo City was primarily Mexican, its loyalty was regarded as suspect. Because it had no immediate developed hinterland and because war continued with Mexico, its trade was restricted to sporadic smuggling. San Antonio neither prospered nor grew during the early years of independence.

Life there was insecure. Indian attacks were frequent, and although there was no single major foray, the total loss was significant. Most harassments were of the nature of the one which occurred in June 1838, when a party of thirty-eight Comanches approached the outskirts of the town, killed three Mexicans and a German, and kidnapped a boy in a raid that lasted three days.[39] The national government was too poor and distracted by other problems to give effective protection, but the arrival of General

Albert Sidney Johnston in 1838 brought temporary relief. After his departure, the townspeople formed their own militia, which was their only regular protection against the savages until the arrival of Captain Jack Hayes and his Texas Regulars in 1844. In 1840 an effort was made to establish peaceful relations with the Comanches. Tribal representatives met with the local citizens at the court house for a council, but the meeting was disrupted when the white delegation disputed the Indian claim that the Indians held only one captive. In the ensuing massacre, thirty-five Indians and seven whites were killed. This fight destroyed the possibility of friendy relations with the Indians until long after annexation.[40]

Mexican invasions were no less disturbing. The community was in the hands of the Texans until 1842, but twice during that year it suffered invasion. On March 5 an army of seven hundred men under General Antonio Vasquez demanded and received the surrender of the town. All the American families fled. The Mexican army remained only three days but plundered extensively, and withdrew with a number of sympathizers.[41] Again in the fall General Adrian Woll entered the town with a force of thirteen hundred soldiers and captured fifty-two non-Mexican prisoners, whom he sent to ill-famed Perote Prison in Mexico City. Thus, with the loss of its leadership San Antonio merely managed to exist between 1842 and 1844. Trade disappeared, the municipal government declined, and the town again reached a low ebb.

Lacking growth, San Antonio retained its Spanish colonial appearance, which contrasted markedly with other Texas towns. More romantic visitors found its appearance feudal, with "churches and towers, and moats, and bridges."[42] To Prince Karl Solms-Braunfels, the German colonizer, it seemed a "great ruin from Spanish times." Amid its hewn stone structures of "very Gothic" appearance, he felt "like Scipio on the ruins of Carthage." Others earlier saw it as citadel-like, "a system of defence;" the backs of the single-story stone houses making up a fort.[43] Probably the most accurate description was that of the German geographer, Ferdinand Roemer: "From the distance the sight of the city has somewhat of a foreign appearance, altogether dissimilar to any other Texas city. The cupola of a large stone building especially drew our attention, since this was an unusual sight in Texas. This foreign appearance became more pronounced when we entered the city itself. After passing a few miserable huts whose walls were constructed by ramming poles perpendicularly into the ground and binding them with strips of raw oxhide, we came to a street with stone houses. This street led us to a rather large square from which several streets diverged at right angles. The square was surrounded on three sides by one-story, stone houses with flat roofs; the fourth side was occupied by a church built in Spanish style with a low tower above the entrance and a flat-arched cupola over the chancel. The entire place gave the impression of decay, and apparently at one time had seen better and more brilliant days."[44]

The streets were unpaved, irregular, narrow; when wet they were excessively muddy and sticky, and when dry, dusty. At the time of annexation, there was not a house with a floor, including the Spanish governor's palace and the church. But unattractive as most visitors found the town, they were nonetheless uniformly impressed with its site. Even the critical Prince Solms-Braunfels, who saw "in all these ruins . . . nothing but misery," waxed eloquent over the beautiful and well-watered countryside.[45] The town was near the headsprings of the San Antonio River, in the midst of a large and fertile plain, surrounded by low hills, and watered by beautifully limpid little streams. Although the area was devoid of timber, building stone was plentiful and easily quarried.

Particularly impressive was the healthful atmosphere. "Bexar is of remarkable salubrity," noted William Kennedy, an English traveler. "It rarely freezes in winter, and in summer, the heat by the thermometer seldom exceeds 85°. The water is delicious, the sky rarely clouded, and the breezes as exhilarating as Champaigne, and far more invigorating. Many Mexicans, residing in the vicinity of San Antonio, have attained the patriarchal term of one hundred years, in the full possession of health."[46] Its temperate climate, its well-drained land, and its fresh water supply kept San Antonio free of the mortal fevers which ravaged the coastal towns with great regularity.

Observers foresaw a glowing future. The scholarly Roemer recorded: "The thought came to me involuntarily upon viewing the city and the beautiful fruitful valley from a distance, what an earthly paradise could be created here through the hands of an industrious and cultured population. The location of the city in the broad valley, watered by the beautiful streams and surrounded by gently sloping hills is most charming. The climate is delightful and a real winter unknown . . . Figs, pomegranates and all fruits of the warmer parts of the temperate zone grow here out of doors . . . [and] sugar cane was raised extensively in former years."[47]

Frederic Page waxed even more enthusiastic, writing that San Antonio "will soon be the most desirable residence on the American continent." "Considering the facility of obtaining the raw material, and bread-stuffs, and the water power, and the labor, and the market, and above all, the salubrity of the climate, it must some day or other take precedence of all manufacturing cities, and in time acquire a power and wealth unprecedented in the history of America." "The water power and privileges," he wrote, "are as far superior to Lowell as possible, and if $10,000,000 of capital can be employed there, why may not an equal or greater amount be profitably invested in San Antonio?"[48]

Estimates of the permanent population varied, but it is doubtful that the inhabitants ever numbered over a thousand during the years when Texas was an independent nation. A visitor of 1840 allotted the town eight hundred Mexicans and two to three hundred Americans and Europeans, but this figure was probably somewhat inflated. In 1844 an Alsatian of Castroville estimated there were one thousand persons, nine tenths of whom were Mexicans. Roemer's estimate in 1845, undoubtedly more accurate, placed the population figures between seven and eight hundred.[49]

The non-Mexican population was composed of American, French, English, Irish, and German tradesmen and workmen, who were, for the most part, bachelors. The Americans were small merchants who had migrated from the States in pursuit of frontier trade opportunities. The Irish began arriving in San Antonio in the late 1830's, settled in a section behind the Alamo Plaza which came to be known as the "Irish Flats," and engaged in trade and truck farming. The French and Germans comprised a menial laboring class employed as hostlers, cooks, and waiters. Constituting the unemployed overflow of the neighboring German and French colonies, they were often nearly destitute.[50]

The Mexicans were, with rare expection, lower class and predominantly Indian. Illiterate and unambitious, they tended their small farms and contributed little to the economic or cultural advancement of the community. A few educated and propertied Mexicans and descendants of the early Canary Islanders remained and were active in local leadership, but the majority of the upper-class Mexicans fled during and immediately after the Revolution.

Because of its mixed population, lack of prosperity, and isolation, San Antonio lacked the intellectual and social life found in the Anglo-American towns. The Americans and Europeans showed no interest in developing organized cultural activity, and the repeated invasions and Indian attacks undoubtedly lent their discouraging influences. Also, wives among the non-Mexicans were rare, a condition which made them more often transient individuals than settled families.

Education was almost totally neglected. One attempt was made to form a public school when city officials were approached by a teacher who sought municipal support. The councilmen approved, but it was discovered that the treasury could not bear the tariff, and the effort collapsed.[51] The only education available was parental instruction and the infrequent visits of itinerant tutors. Books were scarce, there was no local newspaper, there were no debating or philosophical organizations, as well as no theater or serious music groups. Religious activity was confined to the Roman Catholicism which prevailed among the Mexicans, and there was no Protestant church until after annexation.

The great amusement was the fandango, a quasi-public dance held in various houses nightly. It was so popular that the city, which levied a tax of one dollar per dance on the managers, issued fifty licenses on a single occasion.[52] A visiting Frenchman from Castroville recorded his impressions of the dance:

"We had often heard of the *fandango*. We resolved . . . to go to one, and toward ten o'clock of a certain evening we walked over to Military Plaza. The sound of the violin drew us to the spot where the *fête* was in full swing. It was in a rather large room of an adobe house, earthen floored, lighted by six-tallow candles placed at equal distances from each other. At the back, a great chimney in which a fire of dry wood served to reheat the *café*, the *tamales* and *enchiladas:* opposite, some planks resting on frames, and covered with a cloth, formed a table on which cups and saucers were set out. A Mexican woman in the forties, with black hair, dark even for her race, bright eyes, an extraordinary activity, above all with the most agile of tongues—such was [the] . . . patroness of the *fandango*. At the upper end of the room, seated on a chair which had been placed on an empty box, was the music, which was a violin. That violinist had not issued from a conservatory, but on the whole he played in fairly good time . . . The airs, for the most part Mexican, were new to me. The women were seated on benches placed on each side of the room. The costumes were very simple, dresses of light colored printed calico, with some ribbons. All were brunettes with complexions more or less fair, but generally they had magnificent black eyes which fascinated me. As for the men, they wore usually short jackets, wide-brimmed hats, and nearly all the Mexicans wore silk scarfs, red or blue or green, around their waists. The dance which I liked best was called the quadrille. It is a waltz in four-time with a step crossed on very slow measure. The Mexicans are admirably graceful and supple. When the quadrille is finished, the cavalier accompanies his partner to the buffet, where they are served a cup of coffee and cakes. Then he conducts the young lady to her mother or to her chaperon to whom the girl delivers the cakes that she has taken care to reap at the buffet. The mother puts them in her handkerchief, and if the girl is pretty and has not missed a quadrille, the mama carries away an assortment of cakes to last the family more than a week."[53]

Gaming, particularly monte and faro, was also popular among the men, although ordinances prohibiting it had been passed. Billiards, though taxed, found regular patronage, and the tavern of Dolsen and Locmar was usually filled with Americans and Europeans. When not at the tavern, most local and transient bachelors lived at the boarding house operated by Mrs. Erasmus "Deaf" Smith, wife of the Texas revolutionary hero.[54]

San Antonio's hotel was the former Governor's Palace, and the facilities left much to be desired, as a contemporary patron recorded: "I had no other bed than my own blankets and the hard earth floor; if anything can be harder than such a couch I have yet to find it, and my experience has been rather extensive. A plank really seems to have a 'soft side,' and those who have tried both, as I have, will say that there is a species of 'give,' if I may be allowed the expression, to a stone floor; but a Mexican, hard-trodden earth floor has a dead solidity about it which fairly makes the tired bones ache again."[55]

The American community occasionally staged a ball, as on the occasion when President Lamar visited San Antonio in 1841 and again at the first American wedding in 1844. The few American and European women held social functions whenever possible, but their contact with each other was limited. Mrs. Maverick concluded in 1838 that the only society to be held was with the Mexicans, "only two Irish families being here, and the women homebodies."[56]

All inhabitants bathed in the river, but, for the Mexicans, bathing was a particularly pleasurable activity. "It was quite a startling spectacle to see here just above the bridge in the heart of the city, a number of Mexican women and girls bathing entirely naked. Unconcerned about our presence, they continued their exercises while laughing and chattering."[57] Not all was pleasure and indolence for the San Antonians, however. The community suffered through isolation, invasions, Indian harassments, and caravan robbers.

Some trade did exist sporadically for San Antonio merchants. There was commercial activity between the coastal towns and San Antonio until 1841, when the Mexican government successfully renewed its efforts to curtail smuggling. A Houston paper noted, in June 1843, that there were thirty-one wagons at Port Lavaca loaded for San Antonio, with twenty more expected.[58] This flowering was shortlived, however, and it was not until late 1844 that serious commerce revived. The trade of late 1844 and 1845 was brisk and profitable with Mexico, but, because of difficult transportation, almost nonexistent with the rest of the

Republic. Cattle, hides, fruits, vegetables, sugar, cotton, and tobacco were exchanged for silver bullion from Chihuahua.[59] The contrast between early 1844 and the revival of trade later that same year is shown in the commentary of two visitors. Bollaert, arriving in the early months, found "little or nothing to be done at San Antonio at the present moment in really a mercantile line. The very few picayune shop-keepers supply the smugglers who come in from the Rio Grande, these bring seldom more than 3 to $500 and the talking and chicane to be used and heard is perfectly disgusting."[60]

By the time of Roemer's visit, trade had revived and was thriving: "A long train of more than one hundred pack mules wended its way through the streets . . . This was a caravan of Mexican traders, a so-called 'Conduta,' just arrived from the Rio Grande. Their object was to carry goods back to Mexico. Such caravans come annually to San Antonio in great numbers, and this trade with Mexico, has given the city its only importance. The chief articles which these traders obtain here are cotton goods and tobacco, which are usually paid for with Spanish silver dollars, because the articles of trade, which they bring along, consisting of Mexican woolen blankets and other things, are not usually in demand. A single caravan sometimes carries with it five to eight thousand dollars in cash. Mexico imposes such high import duties on articles of this kind that the Mexican traders, by smuggling them into the country, make a handsome profit despite the long, tedious journey of several hundred miles through the wilderness."[61] This revival of smuggling was the foundation of commercial San Antonio, which, within a decade, became permanently established as a major entrepôt of Texas.

The Law of June 2, 1837 established San Antonio as an incorporated municipality of the Republic of Texas. The first elected council was composed entirely of Mexicans, with the exception of John W. Smith, a longtime San Antonio merchant and the husband of a Canary Island descendant.[62] The responsibilities facing the city fathers differed from those of the younger Texas communities in two ways. First, San Antonio officials were spared the necessity of creating extensive public improvements. Their Spanish and Mexican predecessors had long before established the market place, laid out streets, constructed bridges, jails, and meeting houses, and had plotted the cemetery, then in use for over a century. Secondly, unlike the aldermen of Houston and Galveston, the San Antonio fathers were faced constantly with the major problems of defense against the Indians and the invading Mexican armies.

After the city council conducted a census to ascertain the number of men able to bear arms and the supply of horses and mules which could be used to repel invaders, a militia was organized. A strict account was demanded of all who were found within the city limits, and ordinances were passed requiring tavern keepers to supply a daily list of all persons remaining in their houses. Noncitizens registered with the mayor upon entering the city, and failure to do so was punished by heavy fine and by expulsion. The city handled vagrants, who were generally deserters from the Mexican armies, by putting them to work on public projects or by hiring them out to private individuals. When, however, the problem became too severe, the city banned vagrants from its limits. The census of relatively permanent residents having been taken, the government made a citizens' collection in 1842, for the purpose of paying spies and volunteers in the militia.

Normal revenues were obtained from head taxes, fines, and particularly from license taxes. An Ordinance of September 1837 levied a tax of fifty cents or four *reales* per month on dry goods stores and warehouses, and twenty-five cents or two *reales* a month on grocery stores. Each beef butchered brought twenty-five cents, and each billiard table operated cost the owner five dollars per year. Dogs were not exempt. Fifty cents was assessed for every "mail" and two for every bitch. A head tax on every resident was in effect for six years, but it met with serious resistance. Funds for maintenance of bridges were derived from a tax of two dollars on every wagon and one dollar for every ox-cart entering the city.

Individuals who paid none of the designated taxes gave or paid for two days' work each year to the corporation. Revenues were also raised in special cases, such as for the erection of bridges by the sale of public lots. Despite the complicated tax system, collection was irregular and undependable and collapsed with the municipal government in 1842.

At its first meeting the city council faced the problem of sanitation, discussing the importance of cleaning streets and plazas. An ordinance was soon passed requiring all persons to clean the streets before their houses and business establishments and to remove all filth which might be injurious to the public health. In 1840 the corporation assumed the responsibility of hauling away the refuse and of cleaning all public places. Wandering swine were prohibited on the public thoroughfares, and owners of cows were ordered to keep them confined at night.

The marketplace received regular inspection. When it was re-established after the Texas Revolution, an ordinance prohibited the butchering of animals within the city limits except at the marketplace itself. Yet, despite efforts of the city administration, the town was too poor and too plagued with other problems to maintain good sanitary conditions.[63]

Indeed, both San Antonio and Austin faced seemingly endless problems. Neither made marked progress until the 1850's, although influences were at work suggesting important changes.

The coastal towns, on the other hand, were a direct contrast. Houston and Galveston were, from their inception, vital, aggressive, and flourishing communities, and their early growth was a marvel to many.

III

"THE GREAT EMPORIUMS":
HOUSTON AND GALVESTON

In April 1836 two enterprising New Yorkers, A. C. Allen and J. K. Allen, had witnessed Santa Anna's destruction of Harrisburg, temporary capital of the Revolutionary Government of Texas. They knew that the title to the town's land was snarled in what promised to be endless litigation. They believed that the time of its rebuilding would be remote, if, indeed, the town revived at all. They also realized that within a small radius around Harrisburg a commercial city for the new nation was a virtual necessity. With these thoughts in mind and the substantial financial resources of A. C. Allen's wife in pocket, they hastened to purchase a league of land five miles up the bayou from Harrisburg. They hired the Borden brothers, Gail Jr. and

John P., to lay out a town to be named for the nation's foremost citizen, Sam Houston.

Hurrying to the government, then in temporary quarters at Columbia, they promised inducements of free public buildings and grounds for the new republic to relocate in the planned city. Their petition succeeded. Even before receiving the government's affirmative answer, however, they announced their plans in the Columbia *Telegraph and Texas Register:* "Situated at the head of navigation, on the West bank of Buffalo Bayou . . . , the City of Houston is located at a point on the river which must ever command the trade of the largest and richest portion of Texas . . . making it, beyond all doubt, the great interior commercial emporium of Texas . . . Tide water runs to this place . . . vessels from New Orleans or New York can sail without obstacle and steam boats of the largest class can run down to Galveston Island in eight or ten hours, in all seasons of the year . . . The City of Houston must be the place where arms, ammunition and provisions for the government will be stored because, situated in the very heart of the country, it combines security and the means of easy distribution and a national armory will no doubt very soon be established at this point. There is no place in Texas more healthy . . . Nature appears to have designated this place for the future seat of Government . . . It combines two important advantages: a communication with the coast and foreign countries, and with the different portions of the Republic."[1]

Six weeks after this advertisement the town was so undeveloped that Francis Richard Lubbock, who was to be a Confederate governor of Texas, passed the townsite without realizing it. But speculation was rampant; lots sold at exorbitant prices, and within a few months Houston became a boom town crowded with an estimated seven hundred active inhabitants. It rose with such rapidity that much of it was makeshift. Since the building of houses could not keep pace with the demand, Houston was filled with tents. Many of these were large; Kesler's Round Tent, a saloon, measured more than a 100 feet in circumference and thirty or forty feet in height.[2] When the *Telegraph and Texas Register* moved from Columbia, the best available building for it was a small log structure full of gaping holes "without a roof and without a floor, without windows and without a door."[3] Laborers were scarce, and most of the lumber was rapidly and crudely sawed from the local pineries.

The Allens made immediate efforts to consolidate their achievement by incorporating the community, but the first charter of 1837 granted the new corporation few powers. The brief act permitted the election of officials and enumerated their responsibilities, which included keeping peace and order by means of a police force and a system of fines, levying taxes for the removal of nuisances from the streets, keeping public improvements in order, and securing revenues from taxes levied on an ad valorem basis. They could also require citizens to keep fire-fighting equipment on hand, and the municipality, should it wish to do so, might establish a school.[4] As the town grew and became more complex, the city government accepted new responsibilities and demanded new legal privileges from the national government. Municipal functions broadened significantly during the first years to include not only the activities undertaken initially, but also new ones related to the public health, issuance of money, control of the public market and the port, construction and fire regulations, licensing of occupations, erection of public improvements, and the protection of citizens against fraudulent or tainted merchandise and services.[5]

The governing body was composed of nine elected officials: eight aldermen, from among whom would be selected a mayor and a secretary-treasurer; and a collector, who was to be chosen by the voters. The system was altered in 1840, when the town was divided into four wards, from each of which were to be selected two representatives, a system which increased neighborhood representation. Aldermen were required to be property owners and citizens of Texas.[6]

One of the growing town's first needs, which had not been recognized by the national legislature, was the establishment and control of marketing facilities. The council met these problems in December 1838 by appointing a market inspector and permitting a private individual to erect a market house on the market square. Permission had been given previously to butchers to erect stalls of council-approved dimensions and composition. Fees for use of the market ranged from twenty-five cents per day for a butcher to twelve and a half cents per day for vegetable- and poultry-venders. In 1839 the city marshal assumed responsibility for the market, but in 1840 a market-master was reappointed. His additional duties included regulation of scales and testing of weights, and keeping brand books of slaughtered livestock. Butchers complied with regulations which required them to present the hide and head of every animal slaughtered. Those who sold unsound food found themselves subject to twenty-five dollar fines. Moreover, for the benefit of consumers the market-master graded the products into categories of superfine, fine, good, and condemned.[7]

Within a year the old facilities were adjudged inadequate, and the council authorized an expenditure of between ten and twelve thousand dollars for the erection of a new market house and stalls. New regulations were added, restricting to the market the sale of beef in sections of less than a quarter and prohibiting the location of slaughterhouses within a mile of the court house. It became illegal to sell poultry, fresh fish, fresh meats, and other designated articles on sidewalks in front of stores.

A great abundance and variety of cheap, fresh vegetables in season were to be found daily at the market house. During the year between January 25, 1842 and January 25, 1843, citizens purchased 1,124 beefs, 345 hogs, 165 pigs, 128 calves, 36 sheep, and large quantities of fish, fowl, wild game, dairy products, fruits, and vegetables.[8] No other Texas community could boast such variety and quality of foodstuffs.

Although the municipal government made extensive efforts to protect its citizens through food inspection and sanitary measures, Houston had a major health problem. The coastal climate was hot and humid, and the plains drained badly. Epidemics of yellow fever occurred almost annually and, at times, almost decimated the population. Cholera, influenza, pneumonia, and malaria along with numerous minor ailments plagued men, women, and children. Visitors to Houston invariably commented on the unhealthy conditions and bad climate.[9]

Newspapers were reluctant to admit the extent of illness, and little mention was made of it unless an epidemic was full-blown. Nevertheless, the repute of Houston's unhealthfulness was widespread. In 1841, the Boston *Nation* contended that Houston, though only five years old, had four thousand inhabitants and six thousand graves. Houston papers angrily retorted that this was "the most paltry yankee notion, that has ever been retailed by a Boston pedlar, bass-wood hams, wooden nutmegs, and clay indigo, not excepted." The fact remained, however, that an appalling number of deaths did occur. To combat the recurring menace, the city fathers established a hospital and a board of health, purchased vaccines, improved sanitation, and appointed two city physicians and a health inspector.[10]

The Texas government had erected a small structure as a military hospital soon after the founding of Houston. Within a few months, the city assumed its control and administration. Free to all and basically a charity institution, the hospital was entirely supported by local tax funds. Houstonians soon became annoyed, however, by the extensive use of the hospital by nonresidents. The editor of the *Morning Star* complained, in October 1839, that the hospital had eight patients, of whom only three were local inhabitants. The *Telegraph* joined in the protest, estimating that the town cared for three fourths of the paupers in the Republic. The city council continued to make sizable appropriations for the hospital until 1840, when it was leased to a private physician.[11]

Early in 1839 the city council appointed from its members a board of health which operated sporadically for several years, but the problems it had to deal with were overwhelming. The worst epidemics occurred while the town was still young. Temporary dwellings afforded imperfect shelter; the bayous were choked by refuse timber and vast accumulations of vegetable matter in various stages of decomposition. Moreover, the town attracted transients who were often destitute, intemperate, and subject to exposure day and night. Many died of alcoholism and disease. Swine ran loose in the streets, and when the board was not active in inspection, considerable filth accumulated.

During one such period in 1839 the editor of the *Telegraph* protested that an epidemic was raging, and he blamed the board of health for neglecting its duties. The town had remained unattended, carrion were lying about, and the rotting washings of kitchens and backyards thrown into streets and gutters filled the area with a disgusting and poisonous stench. He accused the board of palpable, if not criminal, neglect of duty. In 1843 a report of the board itself concluded that before the establishment of the board the condition of the city was quite bad, with the resultant "fearful mortality," but that now conditions had improved and epidemics were less frequent and less destructive.[12]

In addition to the city's health efforts, there were the efforts of responsible physicians who were concerned about the community. Numerous charlatans flooded the frontier, presenting themselves as trained physicians and surgeons. To deter this activity, the Medical and Surgical Society of Houston was founded in 1838; it set a schedule of prices and a standard of competence for its members. Some of the physicians were well trained. Ashbel Smith was a graduate of Edinburgh and Paris, and Robert A. Irion had taught at Transylvania Medical School in Kentucky. But most were poorly trained and often incompetent. It is likely that as many people died from maltreatment as from disease itself. The national government tried to help by establishing a Medical Censor's Board, of which Smith was the Harrisburg County Censor. But both the Censor's Board and the Medical and Surgical Society were short-lived. The public resented government regulations; hence, quacks infiltrated the ranks, and the physicians themselves became apathetic.[13] When all else failed, the city assumed a final role. From the time of its establishment, the municipal government had maintained a cemetery. Certain sections were allotted to private organizations, but the bulk of the property was under city administration. In certain years over half of the burials were at public expense. The graveyard was a primitive affair, as in most frontier communities, and no record was kept of interments.[14]

Another problem of the city government was the maintenance of the thoroughfares. The streets were carefully laid out in rectangular blocks with the principal avenues fronting on Buffalo Bayou. The major difficulty in their care was proper drainage. The Gulf Plains on which Houston is located are table flat, and water from heavy rains turned the streets into quagmires. Mud, in fact, was a common complaint of visitors, who found moving about difficult and unpleasant. One legislator referred to Houston as "this detested, self-poluted, isolated mudhole of a city." Another who wished to change the location of government said his argument needed no other basis "than barely to look at this wretched mud hole." Samuel Maverick, San Antonio's most prominent citizen, wrote his wife praising the growth of Houston's commerce but added that the town itself was a "wretched mud-hole."[15]

The council worked toward a solution of the drainage problem through a system of fines. Owners of property were required to keep sidewalks and gutters or ditches in front of lots open and clean. If, after notice, they did not conform, they were fined ten dollars. The city also did ditching work, but the situation remained bad. The small bridges placed over the gutters were usually broken, and it was dangerous to drive horses over them for fear of breaking the horses' legs. Gullies and ravines continued to develop in almost every part of the city despite the construction of small dams.[16] Gradually, the streets were cleared of the trees and stumps that had been a hindrance, and the general condition somewhat improved.

Sidewalks in the business areas aided the pedestrians, and as early as 1839 brick ones had been completed on Main Street. Ordinances appeared requiring sidewalks of certain dimensions and composition and regulating the height of awnings and the condition of draining apparatus.[17]

Bridges over the bayous were originally in the hands of private owners, but service was so poor and crossing so hazardous that the county government decided that spans, like streets, should be a public responsibility. The county constructed substantial structures over Buffalo and White Oak Bayous, and the city began to assume certain liabilities for those within the corporation limits. When a storm destroyed the bridge over Buffalo Bayou in 1843, it was replaced by a new one, the largest and most substantial to be found in Texas.[18] The town elders could easily come to grips with the material municipal challenges, but the thornier human problems created by urban life often baffled them.

Houston's brawling and chaotic character exerted a detrimental effect on the young. Visitors to the frontier were amazed at the behavior of small boys who roamed the streets undisciplined, chewing tobacco, swearing, fighting, and tormenting passersby. Juvenile delinquency was no minor matter; grand juries deliberated on the problem; editors lamented the "false attitudes" of child-rearing, protesting against the Southern concept of the indignity of work, which encouraged idleness and mischief. They did not overstate the problem. The editor of the *Telegraph and Texas Register* was particularly concerned. "Verily what are we coming to, when the rising generation exhibits such instances of gross depravity?" His complaint had been incited by seeing two boys scarcely ten years old cursing and fighting on one of the main streets of the town. The conflict terminated when one of the tots drew a small pistol from his pocket and shot at the other.[19] Education and discipline were an obvious necessity, and citizens sought to provide them.

Private schooling was available within two months after the town was founded. A Mrs. Andrews opened a school primarily for young ladies, but she also accepted a few boys under twelve for instruction in "various branches of English education." Three months later more versatile instruction was to be had when Mr. F. Lamky announced that he would give lessons in music, German, and French. Numerous other small, single-instructor private schools were attempted during the first years. By 1842 pedagogy became more strict and formal. The Reverend H. Reid accepted students in his Select Classical School for five dollars a month, assuring parents that "all immorality and profane language [would be] strictly prohibited."[20] The wealthy either hired tutors or sent their children to the United States.

Schools for young ladies were popular during this period. These academies emphasized not only reading, computation, and writing, but also "natural, mental and moral philosophy," and the "female arts" of ornamental needlework, music, drawing, and painting. Enterprising young men often taught part-time as private tutors. One of these was George Teulon, editor and publisher of the *Morning Star*, who frequently advertised his services in his newspapers.[21] When private instruction seemed insufficient for the needs of the community, residents turned to cooperative efforts to provide instruction for their young.

The first city school was in operation in 1838, and a year later the council provided a school building. Further improvements were made in 1840, with the addition of a heating stove, a privy, and shade trees. The operation of the school was under the jurisdiction of the city fathers, who gave individual franchises to directors. Most of the students were required to pay fees, but one of the conditions under the franchises was that a designated number of children from poor families be admitted free. Selection of these students was left to the discretion of the mayor. The progress of the public school was uneven, and in 1845 it closed and the schoolhouse was sold.[22]

Tutors and schools offered subject matter beyond the basic limits of reading, writing, spelling, and arithmetic. Young Houstonians labored over philosophy, geography, history, advanced mathematics, and sciences, and aspiring linguists could choose among Latin, Greek, Hebrew, Spanish, German, and French.

There was no shortage of books. Early in 1838 a merchant offered for sale nearly three hundred spellers, three hundred grammars, and a large assortment of histories, mathematic and scientific texts as well as numerous readers. From 1840 onward, such merchants as Gazley and Robinson had large stocks of school books. In one early advertisement alone, this house offered for sale twelve hundred spellers, six hundred primers, six hundred *Juvenile Libraries,* and one hundred and twenty *Practical Grammars.*[23]

Nor was education restricted to the young. Adults attended the city school in evening classes and private schools, and they employed tutors in a variety of subjects. The evening sessions offered arithmetic, surveying, and mathematics. Private tutors in Spanish, French, and music were always available, and the day city school had mathematics and commercial departments, the latter empha-sizing stenography. As the town became more sophisticated, courses in art flourished, and "Louis from France," described as a perfect master of his profession and a polite and intelligent gentleman, opened a fencing school![24]

The denizens of Houston did not stop at classroom instruction in their pursuit of knowledge and enlightenment. To be certain, the number of citizens who were avid for such activity was small, but they comprised some of the most prominent citizens of the town. Early in 1838 the Philosophical Society of Texas was orga-nized with Mirabeau B. Lamar, second President of Texas, as president of the society, and Anson Jones, last President of Texas, as one of the vice-presidents. Dr. Ashbel Smith, undisputed intel-lectual leader of the Republic, was a vice-president, along with such other local notables as Robert A. Irion, Secretary of State under Houston, and Alcée La Branche, American chargé d'affaires to Texas. In the first meeting, the society formed its constitution, stressing Bacon's maxim: "Knowledge is power." The group met regularly to discourse and to debate; it began a collection of "mineralogical, geological and natural history specimens."[25]

Regular debating groups were popular even before the Philo-sophical Society was formed. The Franklin Debating Society met regularly beginning in October 1837. This organization was joined with the Houston Young Men's Society in 1838. Both societies regularly involved their members in learned debates on such topics as "Have theatres an immoral tendency?" "Has the use of tobacco a more injurious tendency, morally and physically, on mankind, than the use of ardent spirits?" "Was Bonaparte a bene-factor of mankind?" "Was Queen Elizabeth justifiable in her con-duct toward Mary Queen of Scots?" "Would it be advantageous to Texas to annex herself to the States of the North if practi-cable?"[26]

For self-improvement, circulating subscription libraries and reading rooms were especially popular. By the middle of 1839, two of the former were in operation, one boasting thirteen hundred volumes on a wide variety of topics. Although both closed their doors in 1840, 1844 saw a revival of interest, and a new commercial athenaeum, supported by liberal contributions of the citizenry, offered several thousand works. The new library especially concerned itself with the "interests and conveniences of the ladies."[27] In addition, several of the hotels had reading rooms where newspapers and periodicals were available. The Star House advertised that "a good glass, an interesting paper, and a pleasant cigar may always be found at the Star."[28] Private libraries were not extensive, although a few men had fairly large collections. Probate records indicate, for example, that John Scott possessed two hundred and twenty-one volumes; D. H. Fitch, John R. Sleeper, Abram Gazely, George DeStockfleth all had smaller technical collections listed in their estates. Dr. Ashbel Smith kept a small, but well-selected library during his residence in Houston.[29]

One of the problems facing bibliophiles was the twelve and a half percent ad valorem tariff on books. Newspaper editors fought the discriminatory tax, which, oddly enough, allowed many luxuries duty free. Commenting on the rejection of a bill to remove the provision for the book tax from the law which exempted ice, the editor of the *Telegraph* wrote that "one might infer from this, that the Legislators consider *Mint Juleps* more important than *mental* improvement."[30]

Nonetheless, Houston book dealers offered a large selection. The bulk of these were reference or technical works, but advertisements often included the writings of Shakespeare, Byron, and other literary greats, as well as solid historical and philosophical studies. Merchants offered a variety of foreign newspaper and magazine subscriptions, but the favorite pastime of Houstonians was reading their local journals, the *Telegraph* and *Texas Regis-*

ter, brought to Houston by Gail and John Borden in 1837, and the *Morning Star,* which began publication in 1839.[31]

Art, music, and drama also diverted the city's pioneers. Young ladies studied painting and drawing with considerable zeal, but professional artists were occupied almost exclusively with portrait and miniature painting. Jefferson Wright followed the legislature to Houston, where he opened his Gallery of National Portraits to display his likenesses of major political figures.[32]

Music found its following mainly among women. Pianos were brought in on the first steamships up the Bayou, and advertisements for teachers of piano, flute, guitar, violin, and clarinet were frequent. Germans were the principal participants in the regular concerts, which usually emphasized classical works. But many elements of the rough frontier community enthusiastically supported performances of works by Mozart, Brahms, Rossini, and Verdi, and occasional traveling performers found large and responsive audiences.[33]

Houston's best patronized art was the theater. Henri Corri arrived in Houston in the spring of 1838, and announced that he had secured a company of a dozen persons who had all had previous experience in the theaters of New York, New Orleans, Boston, Mobile, Philadelphia, and London. He established himself as the "founder of the legitimate drama in the glorious Republic of Texas." He later constructed a large theater on Main Street, and the public flocked to see such productions as *Romeo and Juliet, Othello,* and *The Milesian,* a play in five acts written by a citizen of Houston. Corri continued his theater for about three years until misfortune overcame him; his leading man committed suicide, and financial difficulties forced him into bankruptcy.[34]

Corri's rival was John Carlos, a promoter who often played to a wider audience by lowering the calibre of dramatic selections. A typical performance was held on May 6, 1839, offering: "Miss Hamblin, Lewelen, and Timour in 2 spectacles. This evening Mazeppa. A Tambour major jig performed by Mr. and Mrs. Bennie. 'Does your mother know you are out?' by Mr. Farrell. 'Come dwell with me,' 'Love was once a little boy' and 'On yonder rock reclining,' [performed] by Madame Thielman."[35] The usual dramatic fare was chosen from the favorites, *The Rent Day, The Robber's Wife,* and *The Dumb Belle—or I'm Perfection,* but Shakespearean drama was played, too.[36] Carlos's audiences were often lively. A contemporary patron reports a scene: "The [Milam Guards] escorted the President [Houston] to the Theatre . . . to witness the performance of Belvidere. The orchestra was discoursing sweet sounds when a peal of three cheers proclaimed the arrival of the President and suit was speedily followed by a hissing, the discharge of pistols, the glistening of Bowie-knives, while many a knight proclaimed his prowess by a volley of profanity, some leveled at the President, some at the Mayor, some at the police; when at length all seemed exhausted, the field of battle was examined and three reported wounded; killed none."[37]

Although the arts may have been somewhat neglected, more plebeian entertainment certainly was not. In the early years, when women constituted only a small part of the population, amusements were crude. Drinking was probably the most common leisure-time activity. Edward Stiff, the deputy constable, listed the public buildings of Houston in 1838: "a market house, an arsenal, court-house, jail, two small theatres, the president's house, and the capitol or state house, . . . twelve stores of assorted merchandise, six mechanics' shops . . . and last, forty-seven places for selling intoxicating drinks, most of which are gaming dens."[38] Townsmen enjoyed a broad choice of liquors, unlike their rural neighbors who usually had to drink red whiskey or nothing. Wine and liquor dealers advertised varieties of Scotch, Irish, and American whiskey, French, German, and Italian cordials and liqueurs, brandies, absinthes, and rums. Wines of every description were available. The hot Gulf climate, however, made mint juleps the favorite summer beverage. Ice, although often costing over fifty cents per pound, was always to be found at hotels and saloons.[39]

Drunkenness soon became a major problem. The editor of the *Telegraph* insisted that Houston's reputation for unhealthfulness was almost exclusively due to illness induced by imbibing and that the graveyard held "scores of young men who died from intemperance." Abstinence societies appeared, the first of which held its initial meeting in February 1839, recruiting ninety-eight drunkards who signed pledges. Sam Houston, known frequently by his Indian name, Big Drunk, led in the making of resolutions.[40]

Concern about the problem was seasonal. The *Telegraph* editor who lamented the large number of drunkards in 1840 happily announced two years later that "drunkards in Houston are almost as rare as snowbirds"; and in 1843 he protested against the great number of transients crowding the city, many of whom "died of drunkenness." But permanent residents also contributed to the problem. Sam Houston, for instance, was notorious for his intemperance, and a diarist's note in 1838 refers to "a serenade and much carousing. The Vice President, Attorney General, Commonwealth Attorney and others arraigned for riotous conduct."[41]

Although the taverns furnished the main spots of entertainment, the hotels were more often the central informal meeting places. Travelers and newcomers brought news from the outside world and furnished variety to routine frontier life. The first hotels were rude affairs with several lodgers assigned to each room, but merchants realized the need for desirable accommodations and early in 1837 they petitioned the legislature for a charter for an exchange hotel and bath house with banking privileges. A dozen others sprang up by 1839, but local citizens still envied Galveston its plush Tremont House.[42]

Improvement began in 1841, when the Houston House constructed a "broad and easy flight of stairs," converted the billiard room into a gentlemen's parlor, and "established a Ladies' Parlor [with] volumes of costly engravings [and] embroidery hangings."[43] Luxury services such as shoe cleaning, clothes brushing, clean sheets, and warm shaving water were added.

The City Hotel was the chief gathering place of politicians. Little more than a "spacious wooden shack," it often served a hundred and fifty persons at dinner on ordinary days. DeChene's Hotel, near the steamboat landing, was a favorite with travelers who found it convenient and well kept. It also boasted the best food and wines. The Mansion House, with the notorious Pamela Mann in charge, catered to women, offering "beds, building and furniture of best quality." A woman superintended the "female branch of the house," and "order and decorum . . . [were] strictly observed in the bar." Numerous boarding houses fed and housed more permanent guests, but boarding houses were not popular: "For the *poor beef, musty bread, and miserable coffee* that we get here, we have to pay from $18 to $25 per week."[44]

Travelers and single men found that the quality of commercial food improved as the community matured. The Restaurant of the Four Nations was patronized, as was the City Hotel. There were several coffee houses which served food, and Thomas House's Confectionary offered such delicacies as cakes, pies, tarts, jellies, custards, ice cream, ice punch, and assorted candies.[45]

There were regular public dances and dinners which the populace eagerly anticipated. Cotillion parties brought out the "respectable folk" almost weekly between 1839 and 1842, with prominent citizens serving as managers. Private lessons were given in the waltz and in the fashionable steps of Europe. Decorated hotels and public rooms were used for dances which often lasted until morning. Little incentive was needed to stage a ball, which would be either a masquerade or a more formal occasion in honor of some dignitary. Sam Houston delighted in these affairs. A French visitor writes that he saw Houston, then President, going to an ordinary ball "in a superb suit of black velvet lined with white satin, and a large hat ornamented with waving plumes!"[46] Houston felt that the balls had a decidedly high quality. In one of his letters to Anna Raguet of Nacogdoches, he wrote that there were some forty or fifty ladies in attendance at a dance which would have shown well in Washington society.[47] Many others did not share his enthusiasm, for, as the evenings wore on, rioting among the men was common.

Public banquets honored every passing dignitary, and frequently the christening of a community improvement, either public or private, would be accompanied by a dinner ball. The English importing house of Ruthven & Power entertained almost a hundred at a "bountiful and splendid supper" commemorating the erection of a large, two-story brick building on Main Street in 1842.[48] But barbeques, Austin's pride, were not yet commonly known in Houston.

Second only to drinking, gambling was the favorite informal activity. Many of the bars, ten pin alleys, and billiard establishments had gambling rooms. Permanent residents fought gambling, which enjoyed its greatest boom during the sessions of the national government in Houston. One commentator noted: "Games of hazard were forbidden, but nevertheless the green tables were occupied by the gamblers for whole nights. What is more, these blacklegs even formed a regular guild, against which any opposition was a risky matter. The resident citizens, however, who were intent on the peace and good reputation of their new dwelling place, checked with all their might the nuisance that had gained ground."[49] Another observer recalled: "When 'Houston' was founded it became for a time the resort of all the gamblers in the country, until the citizens decided . . . to turn Congress adrift, and make them seek some other place upon which to inflict their concomitant nuisances."[50] Despite such warm praise of the local citizenry, gambling remained a part of the local scene.

Horse racing also satisfied the gaming urge. A fine course was constructed at Post Oak, featuring mile and repeat races. The Houston Jockey Club was in existence by 1837, and track owners found their investments profitable.[51] But tracks bred violence. Gustav Dresel recounts an unusually destructive scene: "the wealthy planter Walker made a bet with the gambler Vance, the stakes being the horses on which they were mounted. Walker lost. He contested the bet. A dispute ensued. Walker shot a bullet through Vance's heart. The latter's friends drew their pistols, and in a few minutes seven of the shooters were more or less seriously wounded."[52]

The community was also divided on another form of male amusement—that of the "Houses of Ill-Fame." Protests were based not so much on morality as on the violence and general disturbance which characterized these establishments. The city fathers vacillated as to what to do about them. Unsuccessful in banning the women, they tried imposing fines. Then the councilmen contented themselves with insisting that the women not display themselves obviously on public streets and not maintain their businesses within two blocks of a family residence. One "fair cyprian . . . of the *cassa blanca*" was fined $10 and costs for her disorderly conduct, and finally, in 1843, the council agreed that no lewd women would be permitted within the city limits after September 1.[53] It is likely that the ordinance was ignored or, at best, that the ladies temporarily moved their residences beyond municipal jurisdiction.

Fraternal organizations were also popular. The Freemasons had constructed a hall by the end of 1838, and within eight years, three lodges, Holland, Grand, and Temple, were active. These and the International Order of Odd Fellows, presided at funerals, parades, and cornerstone layings for the entire community. In addition, the local militia companies and the volunteer fire companies served social as well as functional purposes.[54]

Excursions by horse, buggy, or on foot into the countryside were regular pleasures. Often a party would make the steamboat trip to Galveston for oysters, shrimp, crab, and other Gulf delicacies. Bathing never reached the popularity it enjoyed in Galveston, but local citizens dipped in the bayous to escape the summer heat. The men fished and hunted, and women found time to cultivate the ornamental gardens which would one day achieve national fame.[55]

Religious activity was not young Houston's forte. Three years before the erection of the first church, the editor of the *Morning Star* complained: "It is a source of much astonishment, and of considerable severe comment . . . that while we have a theatre, a court house, a jail, and even a capitol in Houston, we have not a single church."[56] He was, no doubt, too shame-ridden to admit that there were over half a hundred bars and liquor dealers. In 1840 only the Presbyterians had a regular minister. The Methodists, Episcopalians, and Baptists had circuit riders and occasional itinerant preachers, and an interdenominational Sunday School operated intermittently.[57]

The American Methodist Missionary Society sent workers and literature to the frontier town, as did the American Tract Society, which operated through its local organization, the Texas Bible Society. Charlatans among the newly arrived preachers were so common as to be a caricature of the "Gone to Texas" reputation. Qualified ministers finally organized the Ecclesiastical Committee of Vigilance for Texas, which insisted that nonresident preachers present testimonials for the committee's perusal.[58]

Although Houston was predominantly Protestant, Catholics were numerous, and the two groups maintained cordial relations. The Bishop of Galveston preached at the Capitol in 1839; his interdenominational audience, including several Protestant ministers, received him warmly. When the construction of Protestant churches lagged, the editor of the *Morning Star* praised the vigor with which the Catholics were building their church and announced that he and other citizens would attend it, if it were finished first.[59]

Not until 1842 were churches actually in use in Houston. The Catholics and Presbyterians consecrated their churches in that year and the Methodists joined them in 1844 with a church which had been constructed largely by funds from the United States. For the time being, Episcopalians remained contented with the Court House, and German Protestants continued to hold their meetings at the schoolhouse.[60]

Religious activity in Houston served a social as well as religious function. Ministers often complained that people showed little interest in activities which would not aid them economically. And one bitterly recorded, "With Job it was principle not lucre, with others it is otherwise."[61] "Otherwise" it was indeed, for Houston's dominating interest was economic growth. The confluence of White Oak and Buffalo Bayous proved an ideal natural point for a break in transportation. The Allens' prophecy that Houston "must ever command the trade of the largest and richest portion of Texas," making the town a "great interior commercial emporium," was not in error. Houston rapidly became the "grand focus of the Republic." Steamships plied Buffalo Bayou immediately, bringing in immigrants, adventurers, and consumer goods of almost every variety and returning with cotton, timber, hides, and general agricultural exports. The town builders had seen Houston as a rail center, and by 1839 serious efforts began to bring a railroad to the Bayou City.[62] Although poor roads made land transportation difficult, the streets were crowded with ox-carts and wagons bringing in produce and returning to the hinterland with consumer goods from the nation's major wholesale market.

Newspaper records show that within nine months of the sale of the first town lot, eighteen mercantile establishments were flourishing; thirty-six commission merchants advertised their services regularly between September 1837 and January 1842. The major problem for merchants was not selling goods but obtaining them. Demand was great and prices were exorbitant. Laborers received between three and four dollars per day, a wage considered grand, but flour, when available in 1838, sold for forty dollars a barrel. Cloth which retailed in the United States at between five and six dollars brought between fifteen and twenty in Texas. Hats, wholesaling at between two and three dollars, commanded ten to fifteen dollars; and boots which were normally worth from five to six dollars could not be had for less than eighteen in Houston. Immigrants were urged to bring at least a six months' supply of provisions because of the scarcity and high prices. Houston suffered slight recessions when the government was moved and during the Mexican invasions in 1842, but even three years later there was complaint of the high cost and shortage of goods.[63]

When the ships did arrive, they brought a wide variety of goods. A wholesaler, George Fisher, advertised a stock received on the brig "Sam Houston" in 1837 of groceries, liquors, general provisions, dry goods, clothing, shelled almonds, New Orleans sugar, brown, white and marbled paint, starch, sweet oil, ginger, sweetmeats, honey, Havana leaf tobacco, beans, lard, pork, mackerel, blankets, grass and gunny sacks. By 1840, larger lots appeared. Black and Thompson, located on the upper end of Long Row, the center of the commercial houses, offered seventy thousand pounds of prime Tennessee bacon and leaf lard. Their competitors, Miller and Dexter, boasted ten thousand Cuban oranges, a *bonne bouche* of the period. In 1844 over $23,000 in sugar was handled by Houston dealers. And it was not staples alone that were sold. Pickled oysters, anchovies, guava jelly, brandied fruits, and other delicacies were often on merchants' shelves, and fine wines and liquors were ever present.[64]

While trade boomed, industry (other than construction) did not. Lumber-, brick-, and cotton-processing necessitated several mills, and a few tailors and blacksmiths were to be found. But practitioners of other crafts were rare. On the other hand, services were numerous. There was an overabundance of lawyers and physicians of questionable competence, and land-dealers swarmed over the community. But Houston's existence was squarely based on commerce.

The central artery for this nascent entrepôt was Buffalo Bayou. Although it was the best inland waterway of the Republic, it was by no means comparable to the open channels that had facilitated the settlement of the Atlantic Coast and the Middle West of the United States. At its lower end, two sandbars, Red Fish and Cloppers, were serious hazards on which ships regularly foundered. The upper part of the bayou was winding, filled with snags from overgrowth, underwater roots, floating logs, and debris. Its entire length was shallow and so winding that the water route was almost twice the length of the land route. The bayou had so little current that a fallen tree or log might lie in the same position for weeks. A traveler has left an account of the unpleasant and hazardous trip in 1838.

19 January 1838. *Embark on the Sam Houston* [steamboat] a small filthy, horribly managed concern, for Houston, seventy-five miles distant . . . Ground on Red Fish bar, seventeen miles distant.

20 January 1838. Get off bar. Venison stake for Breakfast, the remnants of the buzzards & feast.

20 January 1838. Attempting all day to get off, succeed at night. Fare distressingly bad, Crackers, potatoes (ind.) & Beef (tough) Coffee (very bad).

21 January 1838. We proceed to Clopper's Bar, seventeen miles further and stick. Work all day unsuccessfully to get off. Passengers dissatisfied; some speak of going ashore and walking up forty miles, but decline.[65]

The first sailing ship and the first steamship arrived by the spring of 1837, but not until 1839 was serious action taken by a committee of citizens to improve the condition of the water route. Two years later the city received a charter from the national government to incorporate the Port of Houston, and thereafter the municipality aided in improving the channel as well as the port with funds obtained from wharfing charges.[66]

During its first eleven months of activity the Port of Houston exported 4,260 bales of cotton, 72,816 feet of lumber, 1,803 hides, and 480 barrels of sundries, principally deer skins and hides. Within six months, exports also included moss, shingles, brick, buffalo skins, and "sundry boxes of wild animals." The year 1844 saw eighty steamboats and sloops docked at the wharves, taking on, among other products, 6,893 bales of cotton and 6,486 hides.[67]

At the other end of Buffalo Bayou and across the bay on a small island lay Houston's sister city, Galveston. Competition between the two existed from the beginning, but cooperation was also a strong force. Both ports were initially important, because Galveston served as the break in transportation from sea to river craft, and Houston from river to land carriers. Not until Houston began lightering cargo from ocean vessels in the bay and bypassing the Port of Galveston did the rivalry become intense.

The two communities shared many characteristics. Both were commercial centers with water advantages; both were of an age;

both were by-products of Texas independence. There was even a connection in the town builders. The Allen brothers, Houston's founders, were also original investors in the Galveston City Company.* Both cities suffered the same unhealthy and unpleasant summer climate, and both had the compensating advantage of not being subject to Indian attacks.[68]

Galveston's early years were full of great troubles. Michel B. Menard and his associates had purchased a league and a labor of land in 1834, with the thought of founding a city. The War of Independence intervened, after which their title was of questionable validity. Finally, by offering the Texas Congress fifty thousand dollars in clothing and provisions for the army, they secured confirmation of the claim, and the Galveston City Company was born.[69]

During the summer and fall of 1837, Galveston began her first serious growth. McKinney and Williams, the nation's foremost merchants and the financiers of the Revolution, moved their business from Quintana and built a large store and warehouse. Michel B. and Pierre (Peter) J. Menard opened a merchandising house, and Paul Bremond, who later became a leading Texas railroad magnate, opened a store. Gail Borden, who was Collector of Customs, broadly announced that "nature has designed [Galveston] as the New York of Texas."[70] But in October of that year the first of the great storms that were to plague Galveston for over half a century, and that were finally to contribute to her decline, swept the island clear of its proud new improvements. Recovery began immediately. Several ships had been swept ashore and Borden claimed one of these for his new customs

---

* Houston's founders initially believed that the island city would be the primary economic center. In an advertisement to sell Houston lots in 1836 the following was included: "Galveston harbor being the only one which vessels drawing a large draft of water can navigate, must necessarily render the Island the great naval and commercial depot of the country" (*Telegraph and Texas Register* [Columbia], November 16, 1836).

headquarters. Another, the "Elbe," served as a hotel for a short time and a jail for a much longer period.[71] By the spring of 1838 Galveston was booming again. Numerous business houses had been constructed and the town boasted a two-story hotel. Tragedy struck again, however, in the following year. Yellow fever reached epidemic proportions, wiping out between a tenth and a quarter of the population. Fever recurred in 1844, taking off nearly four hundred persons more.[72]

Despite these misfortunes Galveston thrived. By 1839 it boasted two hotels in operation and three more under construction. There were three large warehouses, fifteen retail stores, several lumber yards, six licensed taverns and coffee houses, two printing offices, drug stores, confectionaries, fruit stores, bakeries, slaughter and oyster houses. The crafts and professions included lawyers, doctors, consuls, notaries public, carpenters, painters, glaziers, cistern-makers, turners and cabinet-makers, ship-joiners, plumbers, sail-makers and riggers, tin and sheet-iron manufacturers, blacksmiths, armorers, watch and trinket menders, harness-makers, tailors, milliners, dressmakers, and barbers. One business official wrote that in 1837, Galveston had only three houses and that in 1840, it boasted six hundred, "many of them elegant." And there were six hotels as well as numerous business houses.[73]

Shipping boomed. In 1836 there was hardly one arrival a month, but in May 1839 there were thirty vessels in the harbor at one time. Three steamers plied regularly between Galveston and New Orleans, and the same number made the Galveston-Houston run. The two wharves constantly serviced the two hundred and twenty-eight arrivals from United States and European ports.[74]

Texas ratified a commercial treaty with France in 1839 and regular commerce between the two nations followed. English merchants eagerly tapped the new trade, and by 1840 three Galveston houses, Charles Power, Frankland & Jones, and Alexander Eadson, handled English goods. The German concern of

Kauffman & Company was founded the same year to handle the German trade.[75] These establishments received European manufactured imports, acted as agents for the shipping firms, and handled the return cargo, usually cotton. Trade with the United States was extensive, and local merchants penetrated remote portions of the Republic with their wholesale dealings. Cotton was the major export, and numerous factors busily handled this commodity, which grew on the rich river lands above Galveston Bay.

The lack of roads was a major problem facing Galveston merchants. Barges and small steamboats carried most of the cotton downriver and returned with general merchandise. But where no navigable water existed, there was little trade, for roads were scarce and notoriously poor. Local merchants urged the private and governmental building of highways, and combined with Houston merchants, they even organized to finance roads and railroads.[76]

There was also considerable monetary instability, one great cause of which was the lack of faith in the credit of the national government. Currency did not exist, and merchants discounted the military scrip and treasury warrants heavily. Scarce foreign money circulated at a premium. To meet the need for currency for small transactions, the Board of Aldermen issued change notes in small denominations until annexation. Since banks were illegal, larger merchants assumed many financial responsibilities such as issuing notes and credit, particularly on cotton advances. A department of the firm of McKinney and Williams became the McKinney and Williams Bank, and the notes of the Mills brothers circulated throughout the Republic on a par with specie.[77]

As in Houston, industry was negligible. In 1838, Galveston had only one iron foundry, a few mechanics shops, and three cotton presses. Construction flourished, however, and buildings rose with remarkable rapidity. Carpenters controlled the craft and built entirely of wood. Not before 1845 did a brick house appear, and when one was built the materials were brought in as ship's ballast.[78]

A variety of loosely defined groups assumed municipal responsibility in early Galveston. The Galveston City Company controlled much of the physical development of the town and continued to wield local power until late in the century. A group of merchants, known as "The Committee," functioned as a board of trade, and its influence kept commercial activities organized and more or less responsible. Many individuals, however, arbitrarily assumed leadership and control without legal sanction. Gail Borden, the Port Collector, threatened personal punishment for those not careful with fire, a constant threat to the infant town. Others found their own pet projects to direct.[79]

Not until 1839 did the national government grant a municipal charter. At the first meeting of the council the aldermen immediately set themselves to the task of selecting minor town officials, establishing salaries, and levying taxes. Revenues henceforth came from a head tax of two dollars on all white males and of one dollar on all slaves between the ages of ten and fifty. A business license tax ranged from one hundred dollars on bars and billiard tables to twenty-five dollars per year for boarding houses. The council, itself largely composed of traders, showed obvious sympathy for merchants, for while stores and shops paid only twenty-five dollars, the council taxed competing peddlers and auctioneers fifty and one hundred dollars respectively. Ordinances prohibiting the throwing of filth in the streets and forbidding the shooting of carrion crows recognized the problem of sanitation. An attempt was made to control free Negroes by requiring them to register with the mayor, by prohibiting them from being on the public streets after ten in the evening, and by forcing them to contribute an impossible seventy-five dollars per month to the city when they rented houses.[80]

This government lasted little over a year. In May of 1840 the national legislature granted a new charter, which gave additional privileges to the town government but which also tightened suffrage requirements. No one could hold public office who possessed less than five hundred dollars in local property. The incumbent mayor and much of the population disenfranchised by the new charter refused to recognize the document, and a local "charter war" broke out. The incumbent mayor, John B. Allen, a professional revolutionist who had been with Lord Byron when he died in Greece and who had been a military hero at the Battle of San Jacinto, was a dedicated democrat. He refused to surrender the office of mayor on the legal grounds that he had been elected and could not be evicted from office until his term expired, even by the issuing of a charter by the national legislature. Galveston thus found itself with two "official" governing bodies during the summer of 1840. Armed violence threatened on several occasions, and only after prolonged negotiations and several elections and court decisions was order satisfactorily restored. The new council won; from that time until after the Civil War Galveston was without universal white manhood suffrage.[81]

Although the original government had been far from liberal, the monied groups now in power found the old acts insufficiently conservative, rigorous, or protective of their interests. The new aldermen immediately launched strict enactments against vagrants and disorderly persons, regulated the sale of alcohol, and passed Sunday "Blue Laws" which prohibited gambling, and billiard and tenpin playing. A measure limiting the amount of charges which could be demanded by lightering craft and dray vehicle owners favored local merchants. Councilmen continued to issue small currency notes to facilitate exchange. Rigid ordinances on fire control and the establishment of a volunteer fire department protected property owners. Stealing was regarded with abhorrence, and culprits were unhesitatingly and severely flogged.[82]

Other areas of the public welfare received less attention. Water on the island was unusually bad, and the individual citizen relied on rainwater barrel cisterns for his personal supply. Most of the streets remained simply "wide passages between rows of houses, . . . ankle deep in fine sand during dry weather, and almost deeper still in mud during wet." The neglected cemetery horrified visitors who found bones lying about and graves in disarray.[83] Francis Sheridan's description was particularly vivid. The cemetery was, he said, "unenclosed on either side & is entirely deficient in 'Storied Urns or animated busts.' . . . [It] is far from being romantically situated, or indeed judiciously inasmuch as part of it merges into a swamp & some of the graves in consequence are filled with & destroyed by water . . . I marked several large . . . Buzzards in close consultation round a grave that had just fallen in."[84] The city hospital, used largely for paupers, was completely abandoned.[85]

Galveston lacked a satisfactory public market house until 1846, although butchers and greengrocers had earlier held a daily market. Beef and fish were plentiful and cheap, but pork was high, and mutton very expensive and rare. Truck farmers had difficulty raising produce in the sandy soil of the island, and there was a dearth of green vegetables from outside sources. The council controlled the market through a clerk who enforced the strict slaughter and sale ordinances.[86]

The legislature passed a law in 1846 permitting the government of Galveston to levy a tax for the support of free schools, and the Galveston City Company constructed a two story building to be used as a schoolhouse. But neither of these efforts was sufficient to provide incentive for supporting a permanent public school until long after annexation. Private schools functioned even before the town's incorporation, and continued to offer education to those who could pay. The wealthier families often hired tutors or sent their children to schools in the United States.[87] Intellectual activity was no more extensive than in Houston. No records exist indicating sizeable private libraries, nor, apparently, was there a public reading room or circulating library. As to music, Hooton speaks of a woman offering musical training: "But what Texan barbarian could be found who would attempt to 'soothe his savage breast' by learning music? I know not. An election drum, or a . . . [Negro's] fiddle, makes up about the only orchestra ever heard in Galveston."[88] The dearth of musical activity continued until the arrival of large numbers of Germans in the mid-1840's. Serious theater appeared only in amateur productions and an occasional traveling troupe from New Orleans or elsewhere.[89]

Newspapers constituted the main reading matter in Galveston, as in other Texas cities. Mrs. Houstoun noted of them that "as entire liberty of the press is . . . allowed, their contents are often amusing enough."[90] The first newspaper, the *Commercial Intelligencer,* a small five-column folio, appeared weekly for about a year beginning in 1839. The *Civilian and Galveston City Gazette* succeeded it.[91] The Galveston *News,* currently the oldest newspaper in Texas, commenced publication in 1842. Advertising constituted much of the contents of early papers, but each took a strong editorial stand on the issues of the day. Editors published world news, accounts of activities on the local scene, and occasionally a literary item.

Social organizations were numerous. Women had their sewing circles and men strongly supported fraternal orders. Two Masonic and one Odd Fellows lodge were in regular session by 1840.[92] The Galveston Artillery Company, founded in 1840, was from the beginning a social as well as a military organization.

Patriotic groups organized two other military companies before annexation. As in many frontier communities much social activity centered about the churches.

When speaking of Galvestonians' church activities, visitors would often comment on the lack of "feeling of devotion, and the respectful upholding of religion," and Mrs. Houstoun was one who thus commented. Nevertheless, Galveston was far ahead of other Texas towns in religious organization. The Presbyterians constructed a church in 1841, and the Episcopalians and Catholics had their own buildings the following year. The Methodists joined this group in 1843. By 1845 Galveston boasted five churches, with two more soon to be added by the Baptists and German Lutherans.[93]

Informal amusements occupied the leisure hours of the men, women, and children. Men sought escape in the numerous bars, billiard rooms, and tenpin alleys as well as at the race track. The beach attracted frequent excursions by Galvestonians and mainlanders alike. Hot summer weather drove the population to these areas daily, and a year-round pleasure was a ride or carriage drive along the thirty-mile stretch of beautiful, hard-packed white sand beach. While Christmas was neglected, national holidays were celebrated with gusto. Parades, speeches, balls, and banquets drew the entire populace to honor Texas Independence Day, San Jacinto Day, and even the Fourth of July.[94]

These festivities often centered about Galveston's hotels, which were the best Texas offered. McKinney and Williams celebrated the opening of their Tremont House, an ornate three story structure, with an elaborate reception and public dinner which attracted people from throughout the interior. The choicest wines, confectionaries, and rare fruits were obtained in New Orleans for the christening of what would remain Texas' largest and finest hotel for many years. Monsieur Alphonse, a widely known

French caterer, operated the San Jacinto Hotel, Bar, and Restaurant in a manner which honored the traditions of his native land.[95]

Such men as Monsieur Alphonse began arriving in Galveston during the early 1840's and contributed much toward taming its raw frontier nature. Anglo-Americans continued to predominate, but representatives of nearly every nation were found among the citizenry. Between 1843 and 1845 thousands of Germans landed in Galveston on their way to settle the interior. After seeing the prosperity of the city, many remained to become the most industrious and stable element of the community, with some individuals rapidly rising to the stature of major merchants and civic leaders.[96]

By 1845 Galveston boasted over five thousand citizens, a prosperous economy, and the beginnings of enlightened social activity. Rapidly overtaking Houston as the major city of the Republic, it faced annexation unwillingly, for fear of losing its new-found primacy. But optimism and cooperation prevailed over skepticism, and the islanders looked hopefully toward future greatness.

The republican decade had been a formative one for the Texas cities. Each had begun to develop its own peculiar characteristics. San Antonio and Austin, both lying beyond the settled frontier, suffered from privation and attacks by Mexicans and Indians and decayed temporarily between 1842 and the eve of annexation. Austin, the planned capital, with its Anglo-American orientation, was an eager, young community, aggressive for political power and determined to survive. San Antonio, already over a century old, continued along its lethargic way, but subtle undercurrents worked to establish the base on which it would soon achieve economic significance.

While Austin struggled for mere existence and San Antonio did well to hold its traditional character and relevance, the coastal towns boomed. Houston flourished from its inception, holding the title of "Grand Focus of the Republic" for seven years. Not only was it a major inland port and the nation's capital for two brief periods, it dominated, along with Galveston, whatever cultural and intellectual currents existed during the early years. Houston and Galveston were essentially twin cities. Each was a major port in its own right, and, until the economic need for two breaks in transportation disappeared, cooperation prevailed. Both towns grew rapidly and extended their trade into far-reaching areas.

As these towns began to outgrow their lawless crude youth and to develop economic stability, another characteristic emerged: the decline of the frontier spirit of cooperation, camaraderie, and equality, and the rise of class distinctions and pretensions. While urban services expanded in the over-all, they diminished or disappeared in areas of social responsibility, particularly in Galveston. Public schools were not simply badly supported, the school houses were closed and sold. Hospitalization for paupers and the medically indigent ceased, and the hospital buildings were abandoned or sold. The towns became unwilling to do more for the unfortunate than to bury them and they did that grudgingly. New suffrage restrictions at times cut the electorate in half. At the same time new harbor improvements, currency issue, fire and police protection were developed to aid the emerging merchant class. Often, the communities grew at significant cost to large groups of their citizens.

On February 19, 1846, while lowering the Lone Star flag at Austin, Dr. Anson Jones, last president of independent Texas, intoned: "The final act in this great drama is now performed: The Republic of Texas is no more." Annexation to the United States ended the first phase of life for Texas towns. Having completed their early youth and having established the bases for future dominance, they were now ready to begin their transformation from towns to cities.

IV

OX-CARTS AND

STEAM ENGINES

At the time of their state's annexation to the United States, Texans were dependent for transportation on the waterways and the crude roads which traversed the state and tied the urban centers together. The terrain offered certain natural advantages; most of the land was flat and few barriers protruded from the treeless coastal plains. The major disadvantage of land transportation was that drainage was poor and the roads were frequently muddy for months at a time. In 1858, for example, roads leading from Lavaca to San Antonio were so bad for several weeks that an empty stagecoach could not go five miles without becoming hopelessly bogged. Two years earlier Frederick Law Olmsted, the great urban planner and designer of New York's Central Park, described the same road as "a mere collection of straggling wagon-ruts, extending for more than a quarter of a mile in width, from outside to outside, it being desirable, in this part of the country, rather to avoid the road than follow it."[1] The state did little to improve the highways, for the legislature held that road building and upkeep were the responsibility of the counties. As the antebellum county governments were generally impoverished, they accomplished little. Occasionally county commissioners would lay out roads, cut down obstructing trees, and, more rarely, arrange for ditching to assure proper drainage. Texas had no graveled or macadamized roads until after the Civil War. Many people hoped to build plank roads across the prairies. In 1852 Houstonians began one from their city to the Brazos River, but abandoned it with the coming of the railroad.[2]

Houston, Galveston, and San Antonio, as wholesale centers, were hubs for the crude road system that did exist. Their hinterland markets stretched great distances and travel was slow. Freighters, usually drawn by oxen, required weeks, and sometimes months for the trip from interior markets to the coast with their cargoes of cotton and other raw materials. About the same time for the return trip was required to bring the foodstuffs and manufactured goods procured at the wholesale centers.

The most common freighting vehicle was the ox-cart, a crude affair generally made without benefit of iron or other metal. Rawhide ropes and wooden pegs held the parts together; a method which was perhaps best, for when it broke, the parts could be repaired with easily procurable materials. Two to ten oxen pulled each cart, depending on the size of the load. Nearly as common as the ox-carts and by far the most picturesque freight vehicles of the time were the Conestoga wagons, each of which could carry an average of seven tons of goods. Strongly built of *bois d'arc*, with iron axles and wheels five and a half feet high with tires six inches wide, each wagon required twenty to thirty oxen or ten to twenty mules or horses to pull it.

Both the cartmen and wagoners traveled in caravans, and it

was not rare to see a hundred or a hundred and fifty carts or wagons creeping along their way to San Antonio or Houston, laden with goods.[3] By the beginning of the Civil War, at least ten thousand teams were covering the trails of Texas, and the teamsters represented a powerful and vocal group. Edward Cushing, editor of the Houston *Telegraph and Texas Register* summed up their role: "Ox teams and teamsters have been the pride and glory of this city for many years. Whatever else might have been dispensed with as instruments of its prosperity, they are indispensable, for they form the connecting link between the merchant and the planter, without which both merchant and planter could do nothing. They have a position in this great and growing state second to no other interest, and they stand in the same relation to the general prosperity that railroads, canals and steamboats do in New York and Pennsylvania. Not less than 4,000 bales of cotton have arrived in this city in the last two weeks on ox-wagons giving employment to 4,690 yoke of oxen and 670 wagons and drivers. Besides the above there have been at least two hundred arrivals of wagons freighted with other produce than cotton."[4]

Stages transported the mail, men, and light freight. By 1860 thirty-one lines connected the various towns, cities, and forts of Texas.[5] Important for the urban centers because they were communication as well as transportation lines, the stages also filled the important function of tying the country to the city in the prerailroad era. During the 1850's, stage companies charged fares averaging ten cents per mile and covered an average of six to ten miles an hour, assuring passengers of relative speed, if not comfort, in their travels.[6]

Most of the lines were local, such as the run between Houston and Austin, which opened in 1841 and which extended to San Antonio in 1850. The major stage firm of Sawyer, Risher, and Hall controlled sixteen of the Texas lines. This prosperous concern ordered coaches of the latest design from Philadelphia and employed over three hundred men and a thousand horses and mules in its operation.[7]

The most important stage in Texas was the San Antonio–San Diego Mail Route, said to be the first American transcontinental mail and passenger line. Operations began from San Antonio in June 1857, with four-horse Concord stages covering most of the relays. Passengers paid two hundred dollars for a one-way fare and arrived at their destination in about twenty-seven days, after traveling 1,476 miles. The Civil War terminated the line's life, but San Antonio had the prestige of being the major antebellum southwestern tie with California.[8]

The telegraph offered the final means of land communication prior to the railroads. The first line in Texas was a crude affair built in 1850, between Houston and Galveston. It rapidly disintegrated because of faulty materials and delinquent repairs. In 1858 a second wire-laying, begun in 1853, reached completion. Financed by Houston and Galveston, the Texas Telegraph Company's wires stretched between those two communities along the right of way of the Galveston, Houston, and Henderson Railroad, which was also being constructed at that time. On the eve of the war, the Texas Telegraph turned east from Houston with the ultimate aim of reaching New Orleans. Completed as far as Orange, the line proved an important military as well as commercial asset.[9]

Water was the main source of coastal transportation and communication during early statehood. On the map, rivers along the Texas coast appear to be promising for navigation, for they go deep into the interior and often flow through the highly productive bottom-land which their waters nourish. In actuality, river traffic in Texas is fraught with problems. During the brief rainy season the rivers flood and develop hazardous currents; during most of the year the water is shallow and filled with shifting sand- and mudbars. The bays and harbors of the coast, too, are obstructed as an almost continual sandbar follows the entire coastline of Texas, partially built by the action of rivers emptying against the tide of the Gulf and partially formed by the pressures of the prevailing southerly winds.

Nonetheless, Texans dreamed of establishing major water routes as the core of their transportation network. America was in a period of enthusiasm for water transportation improvements when, after the initial triumph of the Erie Canal, every community felt impelled to imitate the New York effort. River steamers, increasing in size and efficiency yearly, attracted the attention of the Texas settlers. Each of the early empresarios located his administrative town on the rivers. Surveyors placed Austin on the spot where they thought the major land-routes of the state would cross on the Colorado, then believed navigable. And, somehow, at least one steamboat did manage to get to Austin during the forties, before silt from the bankside farms finally made it entirely impassible.[10] Galveston and Houston were both placed with a major view to their importance as breaks in navigation.

Because of unstable conditions and the scarcity of credit, Texans did little during the Republic to improve river or harbor conditions. By the early fifties, however, the state government began work on plans to improve the waterways, since such responsibilities were then considered a state, not a national problem. Legislators appropriated over two hundred thousand dollars in 1852, and a larger sum again in 1856, for dredgings and improvements. Most of this work was done on the Brazos, Trinity, lower Colorado, and San Jacinto Rivers, and in Galveston Bay and Buffalo Bayou.[11]

Private enterprise invested money for further improvements. The Galveston and Brazos Navigation Company, incorporated in 1854, offered regular steamer service on the Brazos, on Buffalo

Bayou, and in Galveston Bay between Houston and Galveston. The company dug and operated a canal connecting the Bay and the Brazos River, but shifting tides soon made it unnavigable and it was abandoned.[12] In due course each of these waterways, save Buffalo Bayou and Galveston Bay, were abandoned to all but occasional barge traffic, although for another decade or so flat-bottom steamboats did navigate the lower Trinity and Brazos Rivers, bringing rich cargoes of cotton and sugar into the Gulf of Mexico.

Ultimately the two major waterways for the state were Buffalo Bayou and Galveston Bay, and upon them centered the rivalry between Galveston and Houston for the role of entrepôt of the Texas Gulf coast area. Trade in articles of export and import were almost entirely confined to these two communities. New Orleans furnished the Texas ports with the majority of articles for local consumption and took most raw materials from them, but the Texas ports carried on considerable trade with both the older states and Europe.[13]

Buffalo Bayou is unlike most of the other Texas streams in several advantageous ways. First, it runs in an almost exact east-west direction, in contrast to the generally north-south flow of most of the rivers. This places the head of navigation on the Bayou within twenty miles of the heart of the richest agricultural area of the state—the lower Brazos River bottomlands. Second, although originally shallow and winding, with numerous bars and log jams, the Bayou was deeper and straighter than other Texas waterways and required few alterations for year-round river traffic. It was, from the beginning of exploration, regarded as the best year-round waterway on the Texas coast.[14] By the eve of the Civil War it was handling the overwhelming majority of internal water traffic in Texas. All Houston required was a point of contact with ocean vessels. For a decade after annexation Galveston provided that break.

Although Galveston boasted the finest harbor on the Gulf of Mexico between Pensacola and Vera Cruz, the competition was not great. Galveston harbor, located on the landward side of the island, was blocked by a sandbar across Bolivar Roads over which there was at best only twelve feet of water. Thus, no sizeable ocean vessels could enter the port.[15] Lightering of most deep water craft was consequently necessary, and business in the Gulf was often brisk. "No less than 23 square rigged vessels are now in the roadstead outside Galveston bar, discharging their freight or taking freight," the *Telegraph* announced at the end of 1858.[16] The lighters, shallow-draft barges or small sailing sloops or schooners, did a steady business with the ocean traffic. Yet even smaller vessels which could cross the bars often could not reach the shorter wharves because of the shallowness of the water near the island. Negro slaves unloaded less bulky and weighty items from these ships by wading out to them.[17]

River craft, barges, flat-bottomed steamboats, shallow-drafted barks, and other small sailing vessels did reach the island, however, as could be attested easily by the appearance of the town's bayside, which was lined with wharves. Between 1839 and 1855 ten wharves were constructed along the waterfront, most by independent warehouse owners and shippers. Some serviced only the particular merchant-owner, but others were open to public use, functioning as profit-making enterprises. A few men permitted their properties to decay or fall into disuse but held on to them for speculative purposes.[18]

In 1853 and 1854 Galveston business leaders worked secretly and successfully on a project which was to prove disastrous for Galveston's future. Through purchase, combination, and absorption these men joined together in acquiring the several wharf companies of Galveston and tying them into a monopolistic unit, legally named the Galveston Wharf & Cotton Press Company, but popularly known as the "Octopus of the Gulf." M. B. Menard and other owners of the Galveston City Company were among the directors and associates of the Wharf Company. They arranged for the city to own one third of the stock, the remaining two thirds to be owned by Menard, his associates, and the major merchants of Galveston. By involving the city in ownership, the wharf-owners established it as a semipublic corporation, relieved of the usual burden of taxation, and granted legal as well as actual control over all the usable water front area. These advantages were in no way diminished by the city's participation, since the merchants also dominated the city government and the city owned only a minority of the stock.[19]

Citizens of the bay area soon realized that the port had been turned into a monopoly and in various movements unsuccessfully tried to wrest part of the port property from the Wharf Company for either private or true public control. Popular antipathy might have been lessened if the monopoly had not abused its power, but from its inception the Wharf Company incurred the wrath of shippers in the entire bay area. Charges for wharf use were the highest of any on the Gulf throughout the 1850's, and it was obvious that the owners were primarily interested in acquiring personal wealth rather than in developing the city for the future.[20]

Merchants and shippers in Houston looked for possibilities of avoiding Galveston altogether. They hoped to achieve access to the open seas without the obstacle of the island. The earlier cooperative spirit between the two cities was destroyed by the Galveston Wharf Company. Houston merchants decided to eliminate Galveston as the second break in transportation. Since it was in any case necessary to lighter from the island to ocean vessels in the Gulf of Mexico, why not eliminate this step and transfer goods directly from river barge or steamboat to ocean vessel in the Gulf? Houston merchants began this process in the late fifties. Immediately after the Civil War Houstonians claimed

that "three-fourths of the freights and products of the interior
... [are] borne upon the waters of Buffalo Bayou, and freight ...
[is] carried direct to and from the Gulf of Mexico on barges,
avoiding the charges and losses incident to handling at Galveston" at an estimated saving of a million dollars per annum.[21] This
temporary expediency gradually gave way to the more reasonable and economical process of deepening the Bayou to accommodate ocean vessels.

In 1853 Houston leaders secured money from the state for
minor improvement of Buffalo Bayou. After the war Houston
leaders organized the Buffalo Bayou Ship Channel Company in
order "to construct, own, and maintain a Ship Channel from
any point in the corporate limits of the City of Houston through
Buffalo Bayou, deepening, straightening, and widening the same
and through the waters, connecting the Bayou with the Gulf at
Bolivar Channel."[22] Meanwhile, Commodore Charles Morgan
dredged through two bars in the Bayou to enable his deep draft
ships to navigate as far as Clinton, only eight miles from Houston.
When the first steamer plied through the Bayou, Houston papers
gleefully shouted, "Galveston's cuttle fish—its Wharf Company
flanked and checkmated! . . . The merchants who receive this
freight get it free of the extortions of Galveston *bête noir,* its
hideous Wharf Monopoly."[23] The editor of the *New Orleans
Times* observed that the Galveston "Wharf Monopoly has thus
killed the goose that laid the golden egg. Moral: Other close
fisted monopolies should take warning and avoid her errors."[24]

Galveston had indeed erred. Her postannexation trade had
been significant. In addition to her regular and sizeable New
Orleans trade, twenty-two packets ran regularly to New York and
Boston. Sailing ships carrying large cargoes and passengers came
frequently from Liverpool, The Hague, Bremen, and other European ports, and returned with cotton and other raw materials.[25]
Galveston's existence was based on the premise that it would

become "the New York of Texas." The community had the best harbor on the Texas Gulf but it let opportunity for greatness slip from its grasp. Greed for immediate profits and shortsighted caution consigned it to mediocrity and set the course of greatness for its rival, Houston.

What Galveston leaders failed to realize was that Houston and the interior were not dependent on the island's harbor, but that Galveston was dependent on Houston's trade. As late as 1857 over eighty percent of the cotton shipped out of Galveston still came from Houston and its suburb-to-be, Harrisburg. Driven by high charges, aggressive Houston merchants refused to yield permanently to these abuses when they could develop other alternatives.[26] Houstonians eliminated Galveston as a break in transportation by lightering directly in the Gulf of Mexico, by deepening the Bayou channel, ultimately to a depth which would receive all ocean going vessels, and by their greatest antebellum coup—the capture of Texas railroads.

When Texas achieved her independence from Mexico in 1836, there were no railroads west of the Mississippi and scarcely over a thousand miles of track in the entire United States. Steam railroads had not yet proven to be an efficient, economical, and safe means of transportation, and one frequently encountered outright hostility to them. Yet many early Texans were hit with railroad fever. General Sidney Sherman, credited by most chroniclers with first having uttered the cry, "Remember the Alamo, remember Goliad," wrote his home-town newspaper, the *Louisville Journal,* on the day after the Battle of San Jacinto that Texas was particularly well adapted to railroad communication, having the best of construction materials abundant and easily procured. Sherman later built the first railroad in Texas.[27] Three years earlier, Stephen F. Austin had said, "Texas is susceptible of great internal improvements by rail," and the founders of Houston, A. C. Allen and J. K. Allen, were also early converts.[28]

Texas boasted the first charter granted for a railroad west of the Mississippi. The Texas Railroad, Navigation and Banking Company counted among its organizers Stephen F. Austin and other political leaders. Violent opposition to the company immediately sprang up among those who believed that the people were being betrayed into the hands of a monopoly. Jacksonian Democrats flocked to the banner carried by Anson Jones and Sam Houston, attacking mainly the banking features of the charter, rather than the railroad. Despite this substantial opposition many subscribed for the stock. However, the Panic of 1837, not political opposition, put an end to outside sources of capital and the organization died.[29]

Urban rivalry accounted for three more charters issued by the legislatures of the Republic of Texas. Galveston business leaders hoped to seize some of Houston's rich river valley trade by their proposed Brazos and Galveston Company, but Houston's A. C. Allen was not far behind with the charter of the Houston and Brazos Valley Railroad. Great festivities, monument laying, and other gala preparations were made for the beginning of the latter line in 1838. Harrisburg, still struggling to rise from the ashes of its destruction by Santa Anna, secured a charter for the Harrisburg Railroad and Trading Company, whose first stage was to lead it to the Brazos Valley to compete with Houston and Galveston. Successive stages in the wild surveys and plans of its proprietor extended the line to San Diego, California. The line was to be financed by the sale of town lots in communities planned along the route.[30]

None of these early railroad projects materialized but they generated much interest and aired controversies which would dominate transportation thinking throughout the forties and fifties. Texans favored the rapid development of the railroads. An editorial in 1855 by Edward H. Cushing of the Houston *Telegraph and Texas Register* reflects this enthusiasm with a strong economic argument.

Let us calculate the amount of capital and industry employed in handling the cotton alone. Last year, with a short crop, the receipts at this point were in round numbers 38,000 bales. The loads average from 3 to 10 bales according to the roads, but, say, an average of 6 bales to the wagon, which is probably over the mark, then there were 6,333 trips required for last year's business. Many wagons make from four to six trips per year. At an average of four trips there were 1,566 wagons, giving employment to an army of teamsters twice as large as the number of men engaged in whipping Mexico at San Jacinto.

Each of these wagons require on an average, seven yoke of oxen, which with regular teamsters, are changed for fresh cattle several times each year. Wagoners tell us that it requires a fresh team as they are almost exclusively fed by grazing along the road. At this rate it requires, in round numbers 25,000 yoke of oxen for the year's business. Oxen are worth an average of $50 a yoke. Wagons, complete, $150 each. The capital engaged was as follows:

25,000 yoke of oxen at $50 a yoke	$1,250,000
1,566 wagons at $150 each	234,900
	$1,484,900

. . . The cotton transported last year was fully 40 per cent less than the whole transport engaged in the trade. In fact the up-freight from this point required much more than 40 per cent greater transportation than the cotton, to say nothing of the corn, sugar, and molasses, hides, skins, etc. brought to this market. There must be considerably more than two million dollars invested in transportation to and from Houston, two-thirds of which would be unnecessary if we had about 200 miles of railroads; or in other words, here is $1,300,000 that might be invested in railroads to great advantage.

We can have no sort of transportation without capital, and delay investment in railroads as we may, a similar investment must be made in wagons and oxen, which means that in about three or four years more instead of 2,000 wagons we will require 8,000, at a cost of about five million dollars. Wagons and oxen last about five years and when worn out are a total loss. Railroads can be constantly repaired and the cost of repairs in twenty years is only equal to the original investment. These figures are merely estimates, but they are approximately correct and they serve to show what large sums of money are being thrown away each year on present means of transportation.

We hope the day is near at hand when railroads will be one of the "peculiar institutions" of this city and the state, when the ox shall give way to the iron horse which travels with twenty times the speed of the ox and carries a thousand times its burden.[31]

The differences of opinion arose over the geographical orientation of the roads and the means of financing, owning, and operating them. The geographical problem focused on two conflicting propositions. The proponents of the transcontinental idea insisted that Texas should be a link in a great east-west chain of railroads, the local lines of which would mainly converge on the interior town of Houston. Texas would prosper because of its land communication with the rest of the nation. Houston merchants strongly favored this plan in the knowledge that the railroad builders would become important consumers of local products and the railroads themselves would make Houston the center of rail and, thus, commercial activity in Texas.[32]

Willard Richardson, editor of the *Galveston News*, led the proponents of the competing Galveston Plan. He argued that not only Galveston, but the entire state would flourish if all railroads in Texas led to Galveston. This north-south fan-shaped funneling of the Texas production into the port of Galveston would assure the state of control over her own merchandising. With the transcontinental system, he argued, Texas would become subservient to New Orleans or St. Louis.[33]

Richardson also warned Galveston merchants that if the transcontinental system won, the island would lose control of its economic future. His greatest opponent, however, was the economic reality of attracting independent financial backing, which was impossible unless the Texas system was linked with transcontinental projects. In the mid-fifties Richardson realized that his system had to join with the state ownership plan if it were to be realized. Galveston merchant leaders supported private financing, regardless of geographical orientation, and this support eventually caused the demise of the Galveston Plan.[34]

The geographical controversy was highly charged, but the dispute over ownership and operation was equally heated. Galveston and Houston were also the focus of this latter controversy. From independence in 1836 until the late 1850's, substantial support for state ownership of railroads flourished throughout the state, reflecting nationwide attitudes. Numerous politicians, newspaper editors, and a diversity of prominent individual citizens supported the movement. In 1853 the gubernatorial nominee, John W. Dancy, ran on a platform supporting state-owned railroads, and Governor Elisha M. Pease became a convert to the plan of state construction, ownership, and operation before he successfully ran for re-election in 1855.[35]

Not all advocates of state ownership supported state operation; many preferred leasing the government properties to individual concerns. Some believed in a limited series of roads, but the majority of those who flocked to this cause sought an extensive system of internal improvements with the railroads as a central feature of the system. The most comprehensive plan called for the digging of canals and the improvement of harbors to connect the coastal areas and the extension of railroads into the interior where rivers were too shallow for navigation.[36] These improvements were to be financed by the sale or mortgaging of the public lands. The entire project became more plausible after 1850, when the federal government paid the state debt for the settlement of the New Mexico Territory dispute in the Compromise of 1850, and there were five million dollars in United States bonds left over in the state treasury. The public ownership enthusiasts advocated putting this money into the railroad construction, harbor improvement, and canals scheme.[37]

The staunchest supporter of the state system was a Galveston lawyer, an old New York Loco-foco and a man of considerable persuasive abilities and extensive financial knowledge. Lorenzo Sherwood threw himself into the fray with a fervor appalling to the interests behind the corporate plan of ownership. Sherwood attacked private ownership as being uneconomical and inimical to the public welfare.

Many of the rank and file of Galveston citizenry strongly supported Sherwood's ideas. Almost everyone recognized that railroad building in Texas required some governmental participation in financing. Sherwood saw the corporate system in the 1850's as one of "disorder and conflict," and he insisted that if the public lands, money, and credit were not used in some major enterprise for the state as a whole they would be exhausted piecemeal and would benefit only those who exploited them. Sherwood addressed audiences throughout the state, wrote numerous articles, attended railroad conventions, and enlisted the support of political candidates and office holders. He found popular support among many of the voters on the mainland who were Jacksonian in political persuasion and were hostile to any corporate form as well as to charters offering banking privileges, which most people erroneously believed the railroad charters contained.[38]

Old-line leaders in Galveston disapproved of Sherwood's concepts, however, and they were frightened by his successes with the electorate and his logic in the courtroom. Besides, as William Pitt Ballinger, legal counsel for most of the city's merchant elite, sniffed, "He [didn't] act like a gentleman."[39] In the end, his opponents apparently were driven to abandon rational arguments and to apply the devious technique of guilt-by-idea association. To defeat his proposals, they tagged Sherwood with abolitionist tendencies. The method was successful to the point that Sherwood finally was forced to resign his seat in the Texas legislature, editor Richardson abandoned him, and the movement for state ownership fell apart.[40]

Railroad construction began in neither of the great rivals of the fifties, Houston and Galveston, but at Harrisburg, located on Buffalo Bayou, nine miles below Houston. Harrisburg had been a thriving village in 1836, before the founding of either Houston or Galveston. During the war for independence Harrisburg citizens fled before Santa Anna's army and the invaders put the buildings to the torch. The townsmen returned and made a valiant but unsuccessful effort to revive the community in the 1840's and 1850's. Harrisburg became only a small railroad center and was incorporated into its erstwhile rival's borders in the early twentieth century when Houston began swallowing its suburbs, but in the early 1850's some yet hoped Harrisburg might become the state's major city.

The Harrisburg owners represented a combination of Texas enterprise and Boston finance. General Sidney Sherman, credited with being the father of Texas railroads, joined with Boston capitalists led by Jonathan Fay Barrett of Concord to buy lots, and chartered the Harrisburg City Company. The purpose of the company was to rebuild the town by the use of a railroad to tap the rich Brazos valley's cotton and sugar.[41]

On February 11, 1850 the Buffalo Bayou, Brazos and Colorado Railway officials, the same men who controlled the Harrisburg City Company, secured a charter. Actual construction of the road began in 1852. The company began its efforts without expectation of state financial aid, but later the legislature made direct grants. From the beginning the government permitted condemnation, but it limited the line's acquisitions to fifty yards in width for right of way and small sites for depots and stations. The state set maximum rates for mail and maximum charges for freight and passengers.[42]

Barrett earnestly tried to interest Texas capital in the project. He first concentrated on Robert Mills of Galveston, the major merchant-banker of the state. For a brief time Barrett apparently had Mills convinced that any land traffic into Galveston Bay at Harrisburg would be beneficial to Galveston, and that a railroad terminal at Harrisburg would deter traffic from Houston. Mills, however, discussed with Horace Greeley the problem of whether Galveston would be served best by using Harrisburg as a terminal or having lines run directly to Galveston. Greeley's lack of enthusiasm for the Harrisburg project decided Mills against investing in Texas railroads at that time.[43] Thus, a major source of local financing was lost. But other Galvestonians, believing their city would benefit, took small blocks of stock. Major Houston merchants, like W. M. Rice, John H. Stevens, and B. A. Shepherd, took some stock probably from fear that Galveston merchants might later attempt to dominate the road. The major financing, however, was from Boston.

In August of 1853 the first twenty miles of the Buffalo Bayou, Brazos and Colorado opened with a great celebration of barbecue and speeches. Houston newspapers ignored the event. Houston had shown a decided hostility to the railroad after the company directors issued a report in 1853 lauding the advantages Harrisburg would have over Houston once the road was built. The report falsely stated that no Houston merchant owned his place of business because all were skeptical of Houston's future and planned to move to Harrisburg when the railroad was completed.* Houston was soon to rise to the challenge.[44]

Meanwhile the Buffalo Bayou, Brazos and Colorado continued to grow. Building costs were low because of the level land and few streams or rivers. The line reached Alleyton on the Colorado River in 1860, boasting over eighty miles of track. Among its rolling stock were two locomotives, twenty-four freight cars, and five passenger cars. The company soon replaced the passenger cars, since they were originally intended for street cars and often had difficulty staying on the railroad track.[45] John Dancy, later a vice-president of the road, described another of its many perils: "A temporary bridge was built across the [Brazos] River six feet above low water state. The Brazos had a tendency to go on a rampage and overflow the whole country. The train could not always get across this low bridge and there was another drawback to this drawbridge—steamboats had to pass occasionally. An opening of fifty feet was left for them. This span was floated on a large flat boat. On account of the steep incline the engine had to hit the bridge at full speed and the long span of the flat boat did not always hold up under the strain. It was quite common for a whole train to be dumped into the River. For this reason it was customary to stop the train just before it reached

---

* The 1850 census proves that contrary to the assertions of the director's report, Houston's merchants did hold considerable investments in real estate, as shown in the following contemporary evaluations: B. A. Shepherd, $30,000; W. M. Rice, $25,000; Paul Bremond and T. W. House, $15,000 each; and Cornelius Ennis, William J. Hutchins, and William Van Alstyne, $10,000 each. Most of these holdings were increased by 1860. See Census Schedules for Harris and Galveston Counties, Census Records, RG29, National Archives, Washington, D.C.

the River and give the passengers the choice of taking their chances with the train or getting off and taking the ferry."[46]

Despite these hazards, the Buffalo Bayou, Brazos and Colorado was a thriving road and Houstonians lost no time in countering its threat and turning it to their advantage. Deciding literally that if they could not beat the Buffalo Bayou, Brazos and Colorado, they would join it, the Houston fathers, after winning approval of the city voters in February 1856, secured permission from the state legislature to build a line, seven miles in length, to be known as the Houston Tap, connecting Houston with the Buffalo Bayou, Brazos and Colorado Railway. Excited members of the Harrisburg Company agitated to block this move legally but discovered that this was impossible because an amendment to the original Buffalo Bayou, Brazos and Colorado charter permitted the tap.[47]

Houstonians voted almost unanimously in favor of issuing bonds for the tap. City fathers then provided for an ad valorem tax and license tax for the dual purpose of providing for interest and creating a sinking fund to retire the bonds. Work began two weeks after the election and was completed within eight months when the tap met the Buffalo Bayou, Brazos and Colorado at Peirce Junction.[48] The Houston City government was not in the railroad business for long, however. The Buffalo Bayou, Brazos and Colorado furnished transportation for the interior counties along the Brazos, but the Gulf counties, rich in sugar cane and cotton, were without service. The planters of Brazoria, Matagorda, and Wharton Counties joined together in constructing the "Sugar Railroad," which connected with the Buffalo Bayou, Brazos and Colorado and the Houston Tap and reached south as far as Columbia. The "Sugar Railroad" owners purchased the Houston Tap from the City of Houston for $172,000 and merged the two systems into the Houston Tap and Brazoria Railroad in 1858. Houston had spent $130,000 in the construction of the tap and made a direct profit of over thirty percent in less than two years. The indirect profit is, of course, incalculable.[49]

During this same period Houston again outdistanced Galveston in another major transportation coup. In 1848 the legislature chartered the Galveston and Red River Railway, which was to run from Galveston Bay into northeast Texas and connect the Galveston market with the rich timber and cotton producers of that area. Ebenezer Allen of Galveston was the entrepreneur behind this project, but he was unable to develop any interest among the Galveston business elite. In fact, it was said that he was met not with simple indifference, but with ridicule and active opposition from many.[50] Nothing was done for seven years until a group of farmers northwest of Houston at the small trading town of Chappell Hill decided that a railroad into Houston would be their salvation. This rich center was cut off from its markets during much of the year by the prairies, which were impassable when wet. Houston merchants led by Paul Bremond had begun a plank road in their direction, but with the invitation of the Chappell Hill farmers to meet with them, Bremond and his colleagues discontinued the plank road construction and took up serious consideration of the proposed railroad. This new road, the Houston and Texas Central, added more to Houston's early significance than any other rail line, for in the prewar years it reached eighty miles into the rich heartland of the state, and after the war it was a major link in the transcontinental Southern Pacific system.[51]

With Ebenezer Allen's permission the Houston and Texas Central took over the charter of the Galveston and Red River. Bremond worked tirelessly to develop the road. Only two miles were completed during the first three years, but such major Houston merchants as William Marsh Rice, B. A. Shepherd, A. S. Ruthven, and T. W. House lent their prestige and money for the road. The editor of the *Telegraph,* Dr. Francis Moore, enthusiastically put his weight behind the project. By 1858 the road was racing across the prairie northwestward, founding as it went the towns of Cypress, Hockley, Waller, Hempstead, and finally reaching Millican, which was the terminus until after the Civil War.[52]

One of the most important roads of the prewar period connected Houston and Galveston. The Galveston, Houston and Henderson Railroad was originally a belated effort by Galvestonians to check the burgeoning growth of their inland rival, but it was actually advocated and supported from its earliest days by Houston interests, too. At a meeting held in Galveston in May of 1855, Houston and Galveston each agreed to subscribe for $300,000 of the stock. The new line was to extend from Galveston Island to the northeast Texas agricultural center of Henderson via Houston. Construction finally began in 1856, at Virginia Point, on the mainland opposite Galveston Island and reached the outskirts of Houston in October of 1859. Texas now had a railroad reaching the seacoast.[53]

Initially, passengers and freight were taken across Galveston Bay by ferryboat, but shortly after the road reached Houston, Galvestonians completed a magnificent railroad bridge connecting the island with the mainland. Boasting that the 10,000 foot bridge was the longest in America, Galvestonians could laud themselves on this one feat of cooperation. The citizens voted almost unanimously for city bonds in the amount of $100,000 to build the bridge. The road was not profitable in the beginning and was sold at execution sale, but its postwar history is a story of prosperity.[54]

The Texas and New Orleans was the longest, the most rapidly built, and the last of the railroads constructed in Texas before the Civil War. The line was built and managed under Houston direction. Abram M. Gentry, a Houston merchant, served as president of the road. The Texas and New Orleans proved to be yet another example of Houston's taking over where Galveston had failed. The line was originally chartered as the Sabine and Galveston Railroad and Lumber Company in 1856. Nothing was done until 1857, however, when construction began and track was rapidly laid to Beaumont, where it was completed in May 1861.[55]

In 1859 New Orleans leaders persuaded the Louisiana legislature to issue charters and to urge the Texas legislature to follow suit, enabling the construction of a line connecting New Orleans with Houston. New Orleans merchants feared that their Texas markets, now connected by water, would be lost when the great inland railroad centers of St. Louis, Memphis, and Chicago made contact with the rails leading out of the Texas centers. In 1859 Houstonians complied in taking over the charter of the Sabine and Galveston Railroad and Lumber Company, renaming it the Texas Division, Texas and New Orleans Railroad. The line failed to reach Orange, its planned terminus, before the Civil War erupted. Even though the road did not then connect with the Louisiana branch, itself incomplete, it did see extensive service, both civil and military, during the war years, and became a major link in the Southern Pacific lines after the War.[56]

Thus, Houston captured the coastal rail network during the fifties. Driven by an enterprising and optimistic spirit and by the challenge of Galveston's port monopoly, Houston's early commercial leaders assured their city's future greatness by establishing it as the hub of rail activity and the major break in transportation for the state.

During the 1850's tiny Austin seemed to be content to sit back and wait for the railroads to come to it. San Antonio, however, bestirred itself when it apprehensively learned of railroad activity in southeast Texas. San Antonio's relative prestige began to decline with the increase in settlement along the rivers to the east and the rise of new coastal towns, particularly Houston and Galveston. The city continued to control most of the trade with

Mexico, but the total was small in comparison with that which came to her rivals from the other states and foreign countries. When the port cities began to stretch their railroads in the direction of San Antonio's ever diminishing hinterland, the town's merchants became alarmed and laid plans to connect their community to a coastal port by rail.[57]

In 1850 the San Antonio and Mexican Gulf Railroad was chartered to run from San Antonio to the thriving little coastal ports of Port Lavaca and Indianola, ten miles apart on Matagorda Bay. San Antonio's business elite, including S. A. Maverick, J. A. Paschal, B. Callahan, and John Twohig, served as directors of the company, but they had trouble selling stock. Many donations of land were offered along the right of way, and in 1854 the state legislature offered land grants of eight sections to the mile, a move which revived interest. In 1851 the city fathers of San Antonio had passed an ordinance permitting the mayor to subscribe for $50,000 of the bonds.[58]

After many difficulties, the road was begun at Port Lavaca and reached the town of Victoria on the eve of the Civil War, giving temporary prosperity to the latter community, but leaving San Antonio out of the state's railroad pattern until after the war.

Thus, in the antebellum period, Texans largely limited their railroad building to the Gulf Coast area, where the production of cash crops and the existence of heavily populated counties created markets demanding advanced transportation facilities. The bitterest urban conflict during early statehood was between Houston and Galveston for the control of transportation routes, the lifelines of their growth. It was a fight for survival, for few believed that they could remain equal. One would ultimately triumph, and the key to that victory lay in the story of transportation by road, by water, and by rail. It was a story of the search for security and frequently of personal greed but often, too, of creative enterprise and of high hopes for future greatness.

V

QUEEN COMMERCE

Cotton was the major cash crop in the Texas economy, as it was elsewhere in the lower South. The Lone Star State held the advantage over its neighbors, however, for by 1850 its fertile lands averaged more fiber per acre than any other state, surpassing its nearest competitor, Arkansas, by an average of fifty unginned pounds. Moreover, millions of acres of virgin land remained to be opened to cotton cultivation, and optimistic Texans saw no limit to future expansion. Cotton production had risen dramatically from the five hundred bales produced in 1826 to 431,463 bales in 1860.[1] Sugar and wool, too, were important cash crops grown in the young state. These three products formed the foundation of the urban export trade.

Galveston and Houston fought vigorously for the business of the farmers and planters along the rich river bottomland of the

Texas Gulf coast, and particularly for that of the seven richest counties of the state, Brazoria, Austin, Colorado, Fayette, Washington, Fort Bend, and Wharton, which stretched along the lower Brazos and Colorado Rivers. As early as 1848, for example, Brazoria County yielded over five million pounds of sugar, or ten times the production of all other Texas counties combined, plus ten million pounds of cotton, or twice that of any other Texas county. In 1860 these seven out of one hundred and fifty-one counties produced a quarter of the cotton and fourteen percent of the corn and livestock. Brazoria and Fort Bend counties produced nearly eighty-five percent of the total sugar for the state.[2]

Before the Galveston Wharf Company began its abusive policy of high charges, most cotton brought into Houston was sent down Buffalo Bayou to the port of Galveston. In fact, most of Galveston's business in the white staple came directly from this source. As late as 1857, for example, over eighty percent of the cotton shipped from Galveston wharves came by way of Houston and Harrisburg. The next largest source of supply, that which floated down the Trinity River, amounted to only nine and a half percent of its total.[3] Before 1860, only one Houston factor, T. W. Whitmarsh, operated a compress, so Houston merchants shipped the raw, unginned, unpressed cotton to the Galveston wharves, where twenty cotton factors arranged for transshipment.[4] Meanwhile, three steam presses, capable of compressing 1,500 bales a day, condensed the cotton into four hundred pound bales and placed them in storage to await shipment. Along the wharf-front, storage rooms, enclosed and covered, could accommodate 20,000 bales, and inland warehouses held another 25,000. In 1860 Galveston factors shipped over 250,000 bales of cotton from their wharves to buyers in Europe, in the North, and in New Orleans.[5]

Sugar was second in importance to cotton in the Gulf economy. By the early 1850's, the coastal counties with their warm climate, rich soil, and plentiful water were producing more than enough sugar for local needs, and thousands of hogsheads were sent to northern cities. Galveston acted as the major Texas market for the sales, although no southern city except New Orleans supported a sugar trade to justify the establishment of a regular market. Men who were primarily cotton factors doubled as sugar brokers when the need arose.[6]

The great prewar year for sugar was 1852, when planters brought over eleven million pounds to Texas markets. Several conditions, including bad weather and invading insects, brought a temporary decline in production. What inhibited further growth most of all, however, was the scarcity of capital, for sugar, unlike cotton, required substantial monetary outlay. Small farmers and great planters alike might grow cotton, but sugar was not profitable unless grown on a large scale. The average sugar plantation for Brazoria County, for example, averaged over five hundred and eighty acres of improved land. Negroes, too, represented a major investment, but most costly was the sugar-making equipment. The twenty-nine sugar plantations of Brazoria County represented an investment of $392,000 in sugar houses, over five times the value of their land![7] Most planters could ill afford the capital required in a shift from horse power to steam in their mills, but the improvement was necessary if they were to continue to compete successfully in the market. Sugar planters, then, were major agricultural capitalists.

Cotton and sugar represented two major cash crops for Texas markets. The third agricultural export item was wool, which was largely handled through San Antonio. The state produced nearly 1,500,000 pounds of wool in 1860, the major portion finding its way to San Antonio. A tiny woolen factory there transformed a fraction of this into cloth, but middlemen sent the majority either overland by ox-cart into Northern Mexico or to the coast for shipment to New Orleans and eastern points.[8]

Cotton, sugar, and wool represented major cash crops for

Texans, and they were the only significant export articles. Yet agricultural production was by no means limited to these items, and the cities were centers of significant local trade. The maddeningly monotonous diet of cornbread and sweet potatoes, of which Olmsted and other travelers so bitterly complained, was locally produced. In 1860 Texas farmers and planters gleaned 1,846,612 bushels of sweet potatoes from their soil, along with 16,500,702 bushels of corn, much of which was for human consumption. At the same time, they produced less than one tenth that amount of Irish potatoes and wheat, which were more popular dietary items elsewhere.[9]

Neither Galveston nor Houston was in agriculturally productive counties. Of the million acres in Harris County, farmers and planters improved less than 50,000. The entire county produced less than one hundred dollars in market-garden crops in 1860.[10] San Antonio and Austin were surrounded by somewhat more diverse and productive agricultural activity, which included Bexar County's nearly twenty-thousand pound annual honey crop. Yet none of the early urban centers was immediately located in high yield agricultural areas but profited rather because of its general proximity to regions of great agricultural significance.

Slaves represented a significant investment for many whites in the coastal cities. By 1860 there were over a thousand slaves more or less permanently located in both Houston and Galveston.[11] In addition, the domestic slave trade of Texas centered its activity in the two cities. Agitation for the revival of the African slave trade often dominated the political life of Houston and Galveston, and the latter city was known to be a focal point for considerable illegal importation of slaves. The economy of both communities was solidly based on the cotton and sugar trade, and profitable cotton and sugar production and trade depended on cheap blacks.

Colonel John S. Sydnor, a plantation owner and one-time mayor of Galveston, operated the largest slave market west of New Orleans in the heart of Galveston, and Houston always had a substantial slave mart.[12] A prime slave often sold for as high as $1,500, and many of the incoming Negroes passed over Sydnor's and his competitors' blocks. Slaves poured into Texas during the 1850's, on an average of twelve thousand per year. Most arrived with plantation owners from the Old South, but many were imported independently from the South to be sold in the new virgin cottonland. Not a few were smuggled from Africa.[13]

The exploitation of the rich bottomlands lying uncultivated in Texas was deemed by most citizens as the basis for the state's future economic greatness. That exploitation necessitated an ample labor supply. By 1850 it was known that more cotton was being produced per acre on virgin Texas land than in any other state and that cheap land was available. The only problem was labor, scarce and expensive since the closing of the slave trade. Thus the coastal cities were hotbeds of agitation for the reopening of the African slave trade. The major newspapers of both cities steadfastly advocated the reopening of legal importation of blacks. Hamilton Stuart of the *Galveston Civilian* argued "that the products of slave labor sustain the commerce of the world, civilization and Christianity." "The whole continent of South Texas is going to waste for want of white intellects and Negro laborers." Furthermore, he said, the Negro could never achieve a better status than that which he knew under a mild system of slavery. Willard Richardson of the *Galveston News* heartily agreed and added that the legal restrictions on the trade were cruel, since the trade would continue regardless of the law and the circumstances of smuggling caused unnecessary suffering to the Negroes. E. H. Cushing of the Houston *Telegraph* noted that African Negroes were being "apprenticed" for ten years in the British sugar islands and that "apprentices, if not nominally slaves, are really so and it will be no cheating, if once we get them, to make slaves of them." The editor further argued: "Let us take those black barbarians and make good Christians of them and raise them to the level of our Negroes. The work is one of philanthropy and patriotism."[14]

These editors represented the opinions of a substantial proportion of the citizenry of Houston and Galveston. Yet, despite Frederick Law Olmsted's biased comment that Galveston was remarkable for "the bigoted devotion of its inhabitants to African slavery as the social ideal," not all were of such persuasion.[15] The urban Germans were largely hostile to slavery expansion. Ferdinand Flake, editor of Galveston's German-language newspaper, *Die Union*, regularly denounced the idea of reopening the slave trade. Adolph Douai, editor of the San Antonio *Zeitung*, was such an outspoken abolitionist that he was finally forced to leave the South.[16] And many native-born Americans strongly supported Sam Houston's militant stand against the reopening of the slave trade.

The urban slaves worked largely in domestic service. Occasionally, a bondsman learned a trade or assisted on the wharves or in the storerooms of a merchant. Such performance was rare, however, for educated and ambitious immigrants, particularly Germans, could be cheaply hired. Most urban masters kept two to three adult Negroes and rarely had more than six. In 1850 only three Galvestonians owned more than a dozen slaves; a decade later this number had only doubled. In 1850 no one in Houston owned twenty slaves; ten years later only a half dozen exceeded this number.[17]

The inland cities had proportionately fewer slaves. San Antonio, the most populous Texas community, had less than six hundred bonded servants on the eve of the war. Austin masters owned nearly a thousand, but many of these were field hands of the large number of planters who lived in the city. The many

Germans in both communities and the majority of Mexicans in San Antonio not only did not own slaves, but also were hostile to the institution. Geographical and climatic reasons also account for the smaller slave population for the inland cities.

The growth of cotton, sugar, and other argricultural products, largely with the labor of Negro slaves, formed the foundation of one major aspect of the urban mercantile trade. The other factor was the supply of the urban and rural dwellers with finished goods. The same concerns that controlled the cotton and sugar trade also handled the merchandise exchange. Nor were they restrictive as to clients, for all these businesses participated in both wholesale and retail negotiations. Neither did they specialize in the type of goods sold. The same merchant might deal in items as diverse as sewing needles, railroad ties, champagne, and miller's stones.

After carpenters and laborers, merchants composed the largest urban occupational group in Texas.[18] The majority of these were no more than tiny shopkeepers, often joining their trading activities with some other occupation. Many of the newly arrived Germans who brought small reserves of cash became tradesmen, but few could be classified as major merchants until after the war. The origins of the larger merchants contrasted sharply with their fellow citizens, for nearly ninety percent of native-American Texans on the eve of the Civil War were of southern birth or ancestry, but a sizeable proportion, perhaps even a majority, of the larger merchants came from the Middle Atlantic or New England states. Several of Texas' most prominent merchants were European-born. North Americans composed the wealthy merchant class in Galveston, Houston, and Austin, but San Antonio's merchant elite was Irish in the 1850's.[19]

Three of the four richest men in the Alamo City, John Twohig, James Vance, and B. M. McCarthy, were Irish-born merchants, and the town's wealthiest woman was the widow of Irishman Edward Dwyer, who had also been a merchant. They all maintained agencies on the Rio Grande for their large, open, and often illegal trade with Mexico. Joined by several smaller French, German, Mexican, and American traders, they supplied the needs of the nearby thriving immigrant communities, particularly German Fredericksburg, New Braunfels, Comal, and Boerne, French Castroville, and Irish San Patricio.[20]

The transportation of merchandise by ox-cart formed the principal support of Mexicans, who constituted the majority of the Alamo City's population. Primarily brought to San Antonio from the Gulf ports of Indianola and Port Lavaca, goods often commanded high prices but were subject to variation depending on the state of the roads and actual supply. San Antonio merchants specialized no more than their counterparts in other Texas communities. Olmsted noted, for example, that "each of a dozen stores offers all the articles you may ask for . . . Silk shawls, Windsor chairs, Ambrosia tobacco, hides, German hardware, livestock feeds and champaign."[21]

Much of the prosperity came to San Antonio during the Mexican War, when the government disbursed payments to merchant-contractors for the army. This activity alerted the business leadership to the possibilities of a permanently lucrative military market and began the process of luring military installations to the community, thus establishing the major foundation of the city's twentieth-century economy.

San Antonio in the 1850's lacked the local wealth or developed hinterland to rival seriously Galveston, Houston, or even nearby Austin. Not only were there fewer actual merchants, despite the community's larger population, but also the more important merchants failed to amass holdings comparable with their counterparts in other Texas towns. Prior to the Civil War no San Antonio merchant controlled property worth as much as two hundred thousand dollars.[22] San Antonio, the most populous of the four communities, was, by all standards, the poorest.

Austin recovered slowly after annexation. By 1850, the population still had not reached six hundred and fifty people. A decade later, however, the community claimed nearly thirty-five hundred residents, with a proportionate growth in wealth.[23] Commerce in Austin meant primarily supplying its citizens with goods, rather than attempting to create large hinterland markets. The central plains surrounding the Colorado hill country in which Austin is located were as yet only lightly settled. The town's commerce, however, was substantial. Luxury goods began flowing in early. On March 18, 1848, John Wahrenberger announced the arrival of four thousand excellent oysters, which could be procured in "quantities to suit purchasers at the bakery, two doors below the Post Office."[24]

Goods were brought in from Houston and Indianola, primarily the latter, by ox-cart. Occasionally, as in the drought years of 1855–1857, tradesmen sent for foodstuffs from as far distant as Monterey and New Orleans. Merchants waxed wealthy with this trade. In 1850 not one owned property valued at over fifty thousand dollars, but a decade later, three estimated their wealth at over a quarter of a million dollars.[25]

One of these was S. M. Swenson, a Swede who had come to Texas in 1838, become an Austin merchant after annexation, and later branched into finance and land speculation. After the Civil War his West Texas speculative lands were merged to form the SMS Ranch, one of the half-dozen largest in the state. Swenson's Union sympathies were similar to those of his friend, Sam Houston, and although Austin voted to oppose secession, Swenson's views were so extreme that he went to Mexico in 1863. After the Civil War he moved to New York to found S. M. Swenson and Sons, one of the major banking houses of nineteenth-century America. His uncle, Sir Svante Palm, remained in Austin to man-

Samuel A. Maverick,
an early San Antonio leader

John K. Allen,
a founder of Houston

View of Austin

Alamo Fire Association No. 2 of San Antonio

Ox-carts on a San Antonio street

State Gazette.

TRI-WEEKLY.

MARSHALL & OLDHAM.   AUSTIN, MONDAY, DECEMBER 3, 1855.   STATE PRINTERS.

HOUSE JOURNALS.

Nov. 26th, 1855.

State of Texas and the territories of the United States ; read second time and referred to the committee on Finance.

A bill to authorise the Commissioner of the General Land Office ....

Middleton, Sayles, Smith, of 44th, Stedman and Worsham—14.

And so the amendment was la d on the table.

Mr Cleveland, of Liberty, offered the following amendment.

San Antonio-Zeitung.

Ein sozial-demokratisches Blatt ... Deutschen in West-Texas.

Eigenthümer: A. Forst, M. Niebner.   Redacteur: Dr. Adolf Douai.

San Antonio, Sonntag, den 24. Februar 1855.

2. Jahrgang. Nr. 35.   Laufende Nr. 87.

Newspaper mastheads from San Antonio and Austin

J. M. Brown house, Galveston

Powattan House Hotel, Galveston

The Governor's Mansion, Austin

Mission San Antonio de Valero (the Alamo)

A fandango in San Antonio

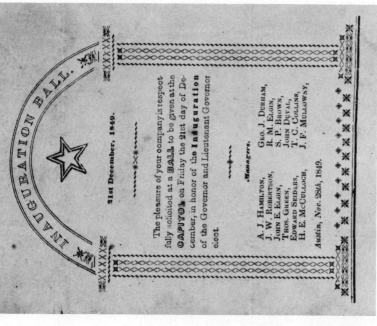

Invitation to the Inaugural Ball, Austin, 1849

Theater playbill, about 1839

The Confederate recapture of Galveston

Many merchants amassed wealth rapidly. James H. Stevens arrived in Houston in 1845 and obtained a position as clerk with a salary of twenty-five dollars a month. He soon opened his own establishment, and when he died eleven years later, his estate was valued in excess of $300,000.[30] William Marsh Rice's career paralleled that of S. M. Swenson of Austin. At the age of twenty-two, in 1838, Rice arrived in Houston with a small stock of goods. On the eve of the Civil War his property was valued at $750,000. During Reconstruction he moved to New York, but continued in Texas business affairs. At the time of his death in 1900, his holdings had grown to $8,000,000, which he bequeathed for the founding of Rice University.[31]

Stevens and Rice were significant, but they were not exceptions. William J. Hutchins built his real estate from $10,000 in 1850 to $300,000 in 1860, and estimated his total wealth, all from merchandising activities, at $700,000. Cornelius Ennis listed his assets at over $400,000 in 1860, and half a dozen other merchants valued their taxable possessions at over a quarter of a million dollars that year.[32] Merchants unquestionably dominated Houston's economic life.

Galveston's commercial activity is more difficult to ascertain than Houston's, for through Galveston's port came not only the inventories of the city's merchants, but also the goods sent directly to mainland tradesmen, particularly those of Houston. Without question, however, Galveston retail and wholesale sales climbed steadily throughout the fifties. An official report for 1857 placed the total value of imports through the Galveston port at $2,163,504. Block, Ware and Company took $75,000 of that merchandise; Ball, Hutchings & Company and J. C. Kuhn over $50,000 each; and three other firms over $40,000 each. In 1860 nearly $200,000 in coffee alone was brought to the island.[33]

As in Houston, the merchants controlled much of the wealth of the city, and their individual possessions grew during the fif-

age the Swenson interests and became a major entrepreneur a prominent citizen.[26]

Merchants in Austin did not control economic life as co pletely as their counterparts in San Antonio and the coas towns. Lawyers, physicians, planters, and contractors ran merchants a close race for economic dominance. As the st capital, Austin attracted numerous and able lawyers who own substantial real estate as well as personal property. George Glasscock, a contractor, owned $150,000 in real estate, a la sum for the pioneer community. But the wealth of their fell citizens merely enhanced the market for the merchant class. T capital city's wealth sharply contrasted with San Antonio's. the basis of the personal property and population listings of 1860 census, Austin boasted over eight times the per cap wealth of the Alamo City.[27]

The major points of distribution of goods, however, were coastal towns. On the eve of the Civil War, Houston was w established as the major wholesale depository for the state. D ing the mid-fifties Houston merchants imported ever increasi inventories. The amount of goods in 1854, $918,175, nearly d bled to become $1,719,194 two years later. In 1856 one merchs brought in $282,956 in merchandise.[28] A breakdown of groce imports over a two-year period attests to the volume and grow of this form of traffic alone:

Article	1858–1859		1859–1860	
Flour	23,758	barrels	31,385	barrels
Pork	1,541	barrels	3,852	barrels
Whiskey	8,143	barrels	7,894	barrels
Salt	27,938	sacks	30,604	sacks
Coffee	12,656	sacks	15,847	sacks
Sugar	2,937	hogsheads	4,113	hogsheads
Molasses	4,156	barrels	6,953	barrels
Bacon	1,420	casks	2,458	casks
Corn	1,721	sacks	38,060	sacks[29]

1

ties. By 1860 the Mills brothers, Robert and David, whose enterprises centered in Galveston, held property valued at between $3,000,000 and $5,000,000. Another dozen merchants valued their taxable property at varying sums over $50,000.[34]

The success of Texas merchants depended to a considerable extent on reliable systems of exchange. During the period of the Republic the coinage was chaotic and of every type imaginable, and the paper of the government fluctuated wildly. After annexation the coinage difficulty was largely solved, but the transfer of larger sums continued to pose problems.

From the time of the Texas Revolution through the Civil War, banks and the issuance of paper money were illegal in Texas. The majority of Texans, being good Jacksonians, regarded banks with deep distrust, believing that they benefited the few and brought misery to the many. Not a few Texans flatly maintained that banking charters and democratic constitutions were incompatible.[35] Texans first legalized this view at the time of independence and incorporated it into the Constitution of 1845, which admitted the state into the Union. Legal banks were not to come to Texas until after the Civil War, when provided for by the National Bank Act of 1863.[36]

The absence of banking services created an economic void that was bound to be filled by indirect means. Two major Galveston concerns reduced the problems considerably by functioning as banks, even if denied the name. In 1835 Samuel May Williams and Thomas McKinney had obtained a charter from the Mexican state of Coahuila and Texas for the *Banco de Comercio y Agricultura*.[37] On the basis of the Dartmouth College case, the owners regarded the charter as inviolate, but even this institution did not openly operate by name, but as a branch of the merchandising house of McKinney and Williams. The other major "bank" of Texas was the R. & D. G. Mills and Company, which was also the largest commission house in the state. The paper of these two concerns circulated on a par with specie throughout Texas and in much of the lower South. A branch of Watson Brothers of Liverpool in Galveston offered British exchange, and the island firms of E. Kauffman and W. D. Lee sold German and French bills of exchange. Swenson and Swisher of Austin, B. A. Shepherd of Houston, and a number of smaller commission merchants also extended credit to planters on a significant scale, handled checks on American banks, dealt in domestic and foreign exchange, and issued various forms of paper.[38]

The issuance of printed paper was, of course, quite as illegal as the open operation of a bank, yet it was not until the late 1850's that any serious litigation threatened the existing illegal system. Both Samuel May Williams, the senior partner of McKinney and Williams, and Robert Mills, the senior partner of R. & D. G. Mills and Company, were highly respected businessmen, and sharp traders rather than wild speculators. They maintained large deposits of specie in Galveston to back their paper. Their strength was verified during the Panic of 1857, which destroyed many northern financial institutions. Runs on both Galveston houses occurred on October 19 and 20, 1857, and although between them they had over a million dollars in demand notes circulating throughout the Gulf Coast area, and much of it in Texas, they were able to meet the demand for specie redemption and keep their doors open.[39]

The stability of these two companies was never in question, but criticism did center around the problem of availability of money for loans and the open violation of the laws and the constitution of the state. Both the Williams and the Mills firms could make advances to their customers and furnish Texans with substantial sums of money, but they lacked the resources to make really sizeable loans for speculative purposes such as railroad building or the development of industry. Thus, many Texans urged the enactment of banking laws which would permit the operation of commercial banks in the state. The scarcity of money for loans drove the rate of interest up to an average of twelve percent, double that of New Orleans or New York at the time.[40]

During the mid-fifties frontal attacks on "Williams paper" and "Mills money" began to increase. The Williams concern was first taken to court in the spring of 1853, on charges that by issuing certain promissory notes, intended to circulate as money, it was violating the constitution and, particularly, the act to suppress illegal banking passed March 20, 1848. First, Williams' lawyers argued on their traditional stand that the government of Coahuila and Texas had issued the charter for the *Banco de Comercio y Agricultura* and the legal tradition of sanctity of contract required the Texas government to uphold the agreement. The government countered this argument on the basis that the bank was not in actual operation when the Republic's laws against banking were passed. The Williams' lawyers then argued that his enterprise was not a company or association or corporation, and thus not within the meaning of the banking code and the restrictions of that code could not be applied to his private operations. Again this failed, and after Williams' death in 1858 the Texas Supreme Court upheld the decision of the state's lower courts, and the "bank" was closed and liquidated immediately.[41]

Robert Mills was more astute. Instead of issuing paper himself, Mills used the devious method of endorsing the bank notes of the Northern Bank of Mississippi, located at Holly Springs.[42] By countersigning the notes of this "wildcat" institution, he created sound currency yet avoided the letter of the law in not issuing currency himself. Mills' signature was as sound as gold itself, most Texans believed, for the magnate and his brother not only operated the commission house in Galveston, but also owned the major partnership in Mills, McDowell and Company of New York, served as a second partner in McDowell, Mills Company of

New Orleans, and held substantial interests in several European and Mexican commission firms, all of which combined were estimated to be worth between three and five million dollars. In addition, they held title to four major sugar and cotton plantations embracing in improved and unimproved acreage over 100,000 acres of land. Until the end of the war they owned over eight hundred slaves. Because of this sound backing, "Mills money" circulated on a par with specie.[43]

Extensive court action continued throughout the fifties, with political considerations often weighing heavily. Businessmen argued that even though Mills might not be operating within the spirit of the law, he was furnishing an invaluable economic service to the state, and should be permitted to continue until the legislature enacted responsible banking laws. The Supreme Court of Texas eventually agreed to this argument or, at any rate, found loopholes in the law permitting Mills to continue his banking activities.[44] The "Mills money" only disappeared with the advent of the war, when Confederate and state money flooded the Gulf Coast. Apparently the courts wished to use the Williams and Mills enterprises as test cases, for the dozens of smaller commission merchants who indulged in issuing various forms of currency went unchallenged throughout the decade.

Williams and Mills kept the coast supplied with paper money, specie was brought in aplenty from New Orleans and New York, and the Gulf Coast never lacked for exchange except in the case of that required for large, speculative loans. S. M. Swenson's firm along with others in Austin kept that small community largely supplied with paper.[45] San Antonio and West Texas, however, had no banking facilities and cash was extremely scarce throughout the fifties, although the trade with Mexico brought in considerable silver. The government bought some of its army supplies in San Antonio, and some hay, corn, and other supplies were contracted for in the region; from this source and from the leavings of casual travelers and new immigrants, merchants obtained hard money for circulation.[46] D. and A. Oppenheimer opened their merchandising house in 1857, and their credit system and that of the older Irish merchants eased the problem somewhat. But there was little money for speculation and, as in other Texas cities, almost none to finance industry.

None of the antebellum towns could be considered industrial centers. Few men invested capital, production was small, and employees were few in the occasional industrial firm. The iron foundries at Houston and Galveston were the largest industrial employers, and neither employed more than forty men.[47] Much creative effort was actually craftsmanship but, for want of greater things, often was included in the more impressive category of manufacturing.

The only industries in San Antonio in 1850 were a brewery, a woolen manufactory, and a number of minor craftsmen. The Alamo City's three bakers did produce the impressive sum of 163,400 loaves of bread annually. A decade later San Antonio claimed two printers and publishers, two soap and candle manufacturers, several harness-makers, wagon-makers, iron- and silversmiths, and the infant Menger Brewery, San Antonio's largest industrial concern, which employed ten skilled Germans, who brewed 8,000 gallons of beer each year.[48]

Austin's total "industry" in 1850 was a bakery, employing one baker, whose monthly wages were fifteen dollars and whose total annual product was estimated to be three thousand dollars. By the beginning of the Confederacy, the capital city had increased its industry to a total of fifteen concerns, whose annual product was nearly $230,000. The grist and saw mill employed twenty-five workmen alone and had an annual product of $182,000. Twenty men worked at the brick kiln, the two wagon-makers and the carriage-maker employed additional laborers, but Austin's economy was no more industrially based in 1860 than it would be a century later.[49]

Soon after annexation Houston boasted more manufacturers, higher wages, and greater annual production than any other Texas city. The last and blind plant employed eight men, but most other "manufacturers" were self-employed craftsmen such as the ten coopers and smiths, eight wagon-makers and wheelwrights, four shipwrights, two bakers, two boot and shoemakers, two cigar-makers, the confectioner, the hatter, the saddler, and the upholsterer. The saw mills employed several men each, but all except one of Harris County's eight mills were outside Houston's municipal limits. In 1860 the census-taker was more moderate in his classification. Houston had only fifteen manufacturers, he maintained, but these included the thirty-employee iron foundry, which produced over $50,000 in goods yearly, and the three brewers and distillers who brewed nearly 70,000 gallons of wine, ale, beer, and porter annually.[50]

Galveston's industry paralleled that of Houston, except that control was concentrated in the hands of a few rather than more widely distributed as in Houston. In 1860 the Close Iron Foundry employed between forty and sixty men, occupied an entire block, and yielded a $50,000 annual production. Two publishing houses employed fifteen men each, a sash and blind producer utilized twenty workers, and the dried biscuit factory engaged eight in its operations. The rope factory used six hundred pounds of cotton daily, producing a quantity of finished goods marketed in New York.[51]

The only real possibility for genuine industrial greatness in antebellum Texas centered on Gail Borden, an inventive genius, who was Galveston's and the state's most interesting and promising industrial entrepreneur. One of Galveston's original settlers, Borden arrived on the island in 1837 to act as customs collector for the Republic. His successes in this position and in personal business activities soon enriched him enough to allow turning his major efforts to inventing and experimentation.[52]

The Terraqueous Machine was his first invention to draw public notice. The machine was a large wagon with sail attached which Borden intended to function both on land and water (when in water the wheels served as paddles). A demonstration involving several friends and neighbors proved almost disastrous when the Terraqueous Machine overturned in the Gulf. The effort was abandoned. Borden's second most notorious machine was one designed to rid the island population of yellow fever epidemics. Borden observed that the disease disappeared with the first frost. Thus, he set about designing ice boxes wherein he would place each Galveston resident for a period of temporary winter lasting one frosty week and thus destroy the mortal fever. This project, too, soon collapsed.

His most consuming interests, however, were in preserving natural food and developing synthetic foods, and he spent the 1850's creating several food-preserving and synthesizing systems. He served the results of his first major experiments to neighbors immediately before the first wild ride of the Terraqueous Machine. Guests received the midnight supper of bread made from finely ground bones, jelly from horns and hoofs of cattle, cakes make from hides soaked in acid and cooked in syrup, and butter made from lard churned in milk. The guests were understandably somewhat less than enthusiastic. Immediate success in food processing was not to be his, yet he persevered.[53]

The problem of food supply for mobile groups such as westward migrants, explorers, marine and military personnel disturbed Borden. During 1850 and 1851, he worked to develop, promote, and distribute a dehydrated meat biscuit. The biscuit was an easily portable, nonspoiling food item. The manufacturing process involved the separation of meat fibers from broth, with the latter distilled into a dehydrated extract. Workers then kneaded the extract into wheat flour and baked the concoction. The result was a small biscuit which could be baked, fried, made into a pudding or a meat pie, or melted and used as a syrup.[54]

Early in 1850 the United States Army showed interest in the invention, and the American government granted him a patent. This same year he gave his occupation to the census-taker as a manufacturer of meat biscuit. He claimed eight employees and forty thousand dollars in finished products annually. The highly mechanized factory was located near the center of the city in a two-story brick structure with a smaller one-story frame penthouse attached. It boasted a ten-horsepower steam engine and two cylinder boilers which drove the biscuit machines involved in kneading, rolling, and cutting the dough. A fan raised the fire in the blast furnace for heating the oven, and the "guillotine" severed the meat into small bits to speed up the cooking process. Great wooden caldrons could boil seven thousand pounds of meat in twelve to sixteen hours.[55]

Borden desperately needed a promotional figure, as he was too much involved in the production of his invention to be able to devote the time necessary to make the world aware of this dietary improvement. The promotional expert was near at hand. Dr. Ashbel Smith was then living quietly at his plantation, "Evergreen," across the bay from the island. Restless for activity, he struck a bargain with Borden and set to work immediately, preparing a series of letters, sending meat biscuit samples to the American Association for the Advancement of Science, and preparing to address the American Medical Association, then meeting in Cincinnati.

Promising first results of the army's testings and praise from several important private investigators encouraged Borden and Smith to procure agents in St. Louis, New York, New Bedford, San Francisco, and New Orleans. The flourish of activity continued, but no biscuits sold and Borden went deeper into debt.

When Ashbel Smith went to London as Texas representative to the 1851 World's Fair, Borden decided to investigate overseas market possibilities. He instructed Smith to show the biscuit at the Great Council Exhibition. It ranked high among an unimposing array of American offerings, won a gold medal, and attracted worldwide comment.[56]

During the winter of 1851 the Galveston factory produced thirty-four thousand pounds of biscuits, and the *Scientific American* called the product "one of the most valuable inventions that has ever been brought forward." Yet Americans were still not buying, and at the height of praise and production the army's board of inquiry issued its report. It was a death knell. The officers found that the biscuit failed to live up to its claims of nourishment and palatability. Stunned, Borden denounced the report as "a plot" and "villainous," but the truth is that the taste of this processed food disgusted most people and the product was thus always doomed.[57]

Deeply in debt, separated from his family and abandoned by his friends, Borden, after agonizing effort, managed to sell thirty-six hundred pounds of biscuits in England and twelve hundred pounds in France, and to dispose of the rest of his stock in the United States. While closing the biscuit business, he was actively at work on another project, the condensing and preserving of milk by canning. At last his inventive genius succeeded. By 1863, Gail Borden's condensed milk factories were processing fourteen thousand quarts of milk per day and were unable to keep up with the demand.[58]

Galveston was not to reap the benefits. Borden located his factories in New York State near the major sources of both supply and consumers. He moved there shortly before the outbreak of the Civil War, and although during Reconstruction he began spending several months yearly on the Texas mainland, he never returned to Galveston. The city had lost its most creative citizen and Texas its only antebellum hope of a nationally recognized industry.[59]

The primary economic effort of the Texas cities during early statehood was to supply themselves and their hinterlands with finished goods and to attract raw materials, particularly cotton, sugar, and wool, from those hinterlands. Commerce, then, rather than agriculture or industry, dominated these communities, although some infant manufacturing developed in each during the 1850's. In these years after annexation the coastal towns vied vigorously with one another for markets. The competitive-cooperative spirit which had characterized their relationship in the era of the Republic gave way to fierce competition. San Antonio, largest of the four towns, sought army contracts, supplied its hinterland, traded with Mexico and the North, but remained comparatively poor. Austin, still near the frontier, strove to preserve its status as capital, but in economic matters appeared content to grow proportionately with the rest of the state.

VI

SOCIAL PATTERNS AND
CULTURAL ASPIRATIONS

On the eve of the Civil War, San Antonio was the largest city in Texas, with over eight thousand people composing its cosmopolitan population. Galveston ranked next with above seven thousand, Houston followed with nearly five thousand, and Austin had grown during the 1850's from a village of nine hundred to a bustling community of thirty-five hundred.[1] The character of their social and cultural pursuits and institutions was now well established.

One of the major social transformations in the period from 1845 to 1860 manifested itself materially. Merchants, professional men, and planters began to demonstrate their social status and aesthetic sensibilities by constructing elaborate and ornamental business and residential buildings. This was in sharp contrast to the purely functional structures erected during the period of the Republic. The change was striking and abrupt, for formal residences were often built next to rude log cabins. Each town offered its own peculiarities in architecture, which were major keys to understanding the geographic, economic, social, and cultural character of the community.

San Antonio was not only the largest of the four, but also it was the most diversified ethnically and the most attractive to the tourist. Frederick Law Olmsted, visiting the town in 1855, asserted: "We have no city, except, perhaps, New Orleans, that can vie, in point of the picturesque interest that attaches to old and antiquated foreignness, with San Antonio. Its jumble of races, costumes, languages and buildings; its religious ruins, holding to an antiquity, for us, indistinct enough to breed an unaccustomed solemnity; its remote, isolated, outpost situation, and the vague conviction that it is the first of a new class of conquered cities into whose decaying streets our rattling life is to be infused, combine with the heroic touches in its history to enliven and satisfy your traveler's curiosity."[2] Olmsted was particularly impressed with the variety of architectural forms, most of which had appeared within the previous decade. In 1846 San Antonio was a century-old town of low, rude stone or adobe structures, usually roofed with straw or rough tiles. With the exception of two recently erected American-style dwellings, not a house had any other than a dirt floor.[3] These ancient buildings lined unimproved, narrow streets whose frequent, irregular bends were caused by the San Antonio River, which curves so repeatedly that it almost returns to itself in a dozen places.

During the fifties Germans began building neat, single-story houses of creamy, white limestone, adding an occasional balcony or gallery for ornamentation, thus beginning a trend in style that was to reach its apogee in the seventies in the lavish mansions on

König Wilhelmstrasse. Alsacian influences arrived with the over-flow of immigrants from nearby Castroville. The most impressive residential architecture created, however, was for the business elite, primarily the Irish. Most lavish of these mansions was that designed by the capable architect John Fries, for James Vance. Recognized immediately as one of the more elegant dwellings in the state, Vance House, erected between 1857 and 1859, followed the basic Greek revival plan. A central hall twelve feet wide extended through the rectangular form. Porches for both stories stretched both front and back enclosing the sixteen rooms of the interior. Builders decorated the large, elegant reception rooms with ceiling cornices, wooden entabletures over the doors, etched glass windows, and other finished work brought from New Orleans. All water fixtures were of solid silver. The hardships of army life on the frontier must have been softened for the Virginia aristocrat, Colonel Robert E. Lee, by his frequent visits to Vance House, whose rich hospitality he enjoyed.[4]

Other houses vied with that of James Vance. Nat Lewis built on the river bank an imposing two-story, cut-stone mansion with ornate porches, double windows, and high ceilings, and with kitchens and slave quarters in the rear. John Twohig began his residence on the river in 1841, and he continued enlarging it until secession. This eccentric bachelor filled his small but elegant home with elaborate furnishings imported from Europe. Another large mansion of classical form, the "Argyle," boasted cured cypress floors and woodwork carved and brought from New Orleans. Located on a land grant of nearly one hundred thousand acres adjacent to the town's limits, the house combined many of the best elements of functionalism and aestheticism.[5]

Although San Antonio claimed several Greek revival mansions, most authorities considered Austin as the end of the South in terms of the antebellum classical expression. Among the four Texas towns Austin's appearance changed most radically during the period between annexation and the Civil War. Its rise in population brought with it a significant improvement in physical structures. Clean masonry and frame commercial buildings took the place of the ugly log shacks of the earlier years. Governmental buildings proliferated, led by the new capitol and governor's mansion, built in the mid-fifties. In residential architecture, saltbox frame cottages and little temple-fronted dwellings rose among the log huts. Houses of distinctly German style appeared behind the capitol to be used not only by Germans, but also by citizens who let German artisans use their own discretion in design. Builders constructed the small houses of pine from the nearby Bastrop Pinery or the forests of East Texas. Finishers and cabinetmakers used pecan, cedar, and oak, the local hardwoods, for more elaborate woodwork and floors. Lamar Moore opened a commercial brick kiln in 1851, but brick and the peculiar light sandstone quarried near the town cost too dearly for the average house; thus they were reserved for business buildings and the more ornate residences.[6]

The mansions in which Austinites took justifiable pride were largely the result of the efforts of one man, architect-contractor Abner Cook. Arriving in Austin in the early fifties, Cook spent the rest of the decade designing and constructing most of the big houses built during the era. Woodlawn, the Raymond home, Swisher House, Shelly House, Edgemont, Hill-Neill House, and the governor's mansion all followed the same general pattern. The severe formal arrangement rarely varied. Each structure formed a two-story rectangle with a center hall running on both levels, containing the main staircase. Each side of the main level was divided into two rooms, a parlor occupying both sides of the entryway. The second level held four equal-sized bedrooms. Each of the eight rooms contained a fireplace and four large windows reaching from near the floor to a height of eight feet or more.

The exteriors followed a wide diversity of style within the classical motif. Some porticos, for example, merely covered the main entrance, most extended the entire front length of the house, but others ran also to the sides. Despite the order, however, the number of columns seldom changed from six on one side. As transportation conditions on the frontier restricted the use of imported ornate pillars, many builders, including Cook, frequently used square in place of rounded columns with Doric capitals, and probably not one Corinthian house appeared in Texas until after the War. Cook preferred Ionic capitals, but these costly imports came only from the East, and Doric usually sufficed by necessity. Most colonnades stood free, although occasionally the architect inserted a balcony on the second level.[7]

Owners attended equally well to the interiors of their homes. Furniture, rugs, tapestries, crystal chandeliers, and other interior decorations were collected in New Orleans, eastern cities, and in Europe. S. M. Swenson made the long journey from Austin to New York to select furnishings for the new governor's mansion. Most popular styles ran to American "Jacksonian," but some preferred revivals of eighteenth-century or Empire French models. The new Victorian taste attracted a few, and occasionally a locally manufactured piece appeared. For example, a Seguin cabinetmaker designed and made the bed Sam Houston used in the governor's mansion.[8]

The merchants, professional men, planters, and politicians of Austin prided themselves on the houses which they built in the capital city and believed that they enhanced its beauty and prestige. Fortunately, Cook's presence assured that this effort would be crowned as an artistic achievement. Greek revival was passing from vogue in most of the older states by 1850, but its success in the interior towns of Texas was assured by the simplicity of its construction and by the population's isolation from the latest trends in architectural fashion.

Galveston, in contrast, had much intercourse with the rest of the world. Into its ports came ships carrying immigrants, cargoes, and knowledge of life from far beyond the confines of the Texas border. The city's leading citizens were intrepid travelers who returned home with urbane notions and educated tastes. Residential and business architecture reflected this cultivated, cosmopolitan character. Numerous three- and four-story brick buildings rose in the downtown area, most ornamented with elaborate wrought iron workings. More than their counterparts in any other Texas city, the Galveston aristocracy poured its money into elegant housing and furnishings. J. M. Sauters' establishment carried a regular line of fine English carpets, French china, Bohemian glassware, rosewood pianos, and northern and European furniture. Sauters traveled in Europe selecting and shipping articles to Galveston to fill the homes of the elite. Many home owners traveled abroad themselves to select their household effects.[9]

Sumptuous mansions began to fill the streets of Galveston soon after annexation. Captain J. M. Brown built his Italian-styled, three-storied, sixteen-room Ashton Villa of brick brought in ballast from Philadelphia. Brown bought delicate wrought-iron balcony railings, fences, and gates from England and hand-carved walnut valances for the windows in Paris as well as other materials from Europe. He brought in French artisans to decorate Ashton Villa's ceilings and walls with friezes, panels, and medallions in gold leaf. The specially designed dining table could seat forty people. Brick for Thomas League's house came from England. Galleries, doors, and windows were faced with white marble, the exterior was ornamented with medallions of hand-wrought copper in leaf designs, and the finely proportioned white fluted columns reached to the third floor. Henry Rosenberg's house, topped by a large captain's cupola, boasted eight Italian marble fireplaces and rosewood cornices etched with gold leaf over every door and window. Everywhere one turned in the Third Ward one encountered lavish residences.[10]

Unlike the mainland's upper classes who usually dispersed themselves throughout their towns, Galveston's elite created an island for itself in the Third Ward. These American families whose money came from mercantile, shipping, professional, and plantation sources and who ruled the town during the fifties moved in a closed, cosmopolitan social circle. Their affluence contrasted strikingly with that of their neighbors. The census breakdowns for 1860 clearly show the sharp disparity in wealth between some of this group and their nearest neighbors. For example, twenty-four contiguous households controlled wealth estimated at over $880,000. The next twenty-four households, except for one prosperous carpenter, owned real and personal property valued at only $8,000.[11] Except for this one family, the first two dozen households were one hundred times wealthier than their equivalently numerous neighbors. Open conflicts between the monied elements and other classes rarely occurred prior to the Civil War, yet by sealing itself away from the main body of the community the elite began to undermine the cohesiveness of the city.

Houston, although richer per capita than Galveston, was more democratic and more egalitarian. Houstonians put their money into business investments rather than into architecture. No tourist really found Houston a terribly appealing place, but they did find it economically aggressive. Downtown buildings were functional and residential architecture unostentatious. True, William Marsh Rice's house was a large classical mansion, with hand-carved window frames and wrought-iron hardware, but he had bought it inexpensively from General Ebenezer Nichols when the latter decided that Galveston better suited his tastes. Houston, bitterly competitive with its island neighbor in the economic sphere, was quite content to let its rival spend its way to dominance in the realm of lavish architecture. Moreover, Houston's leaders seemed to realize the political value of egalitarianism. Scattering themselves throughout the four wards, they more easily maintained their positions of political as well as economic leadership in the community.[12]

Next to the home the most important social institution in the antebellum towns was the church. Religious affiliation revealed much of the nature of the municipality. The four communities varied considerably in their religious characteristics. All, however, took their religious duties more seriously than they had during the period of the Republic, and all four boasted substantial church property and membership.

Galveston spurned fundamentalism and evangelicalism in the fifties and embraced the formality and ceremonialism of the Episcopal and Catholic faiths. Most of the social elite, led by General Ebenezer Nichols, Henry Rosenberg, John Hutchins, and Thomas League directed the affairs of the Episcopal congregation, largest Protestant sect on the island. Trinity Church, completed in 1859, could seat eight hundred worshipers and was the most elaborate religious building in Texas. The Catholics, piloted by Bishop Oden and Michel Menard, the founder of Galveston, erected the impressive St. Mary's Cathedral, which could accommodate over a thousand parishioners, and St. Joseph's, a smaller building which seated five hundred and ministered primarily to the Germans. Lutherans, Presbyterians, Baptists, and Methodists all operated regular services and Sunday schools, but they attracted fewer converts, and their influence was slight. The latter two sects built especial buildings for the Negro adherents, each accommodating three hundred and fifty members. Galveston's few Jews founded a cemetery during the decade, but they worshiped in private homes until 1871, when they constructed a temple. Whatever the affiliation, Galvestonians improved their outward moral and religious appearances during the period of early statehood. Many travelers were impressed. Melinda Rankin, a New England woman of missionary bent, believed that in Texas generally, the standard of piety should become more elevated but she found the religious character of Galveston highly respectable. She stated that "in respect to morality, Galveston is superior to many other places whose pretensions have been greater than a Texan city has been permitted to claim."[13]

In Houston, as in Galveston, the Episcopal Church tended to attract the wealthier citizens. Christ Church of Houston cost twice the amount of any other religious building in the city. Despite the social prestige of the Episcopalians, Methodism was the religion of Houstonians. No less than five Methodist churches were scattered throughout the small city. The French missionary Domenech found, to his disgust, that Houston was "peopled with Methodists and . . . ants." Baptists and Presbyterians tied for a poor second place in terms of adherents among the Protestants, and Lutherans came in last. Roman Catholics now played only a small role in the religious life of Houston; they were few in number and support for their church was not substantial.[14]

Austin's religious configuration was more varied than other Texas cities, in large part because of the drawing of politicians and government employees from various areas of the state. During the 1850's nine organizations built churches, the smallest accommodating a hundred, and the largest but four hundred. Austin's Presbyterians split into the Cumberland and the Old Style sects, but the Episcopalian congregations united to form St. David's congregation and to build Austin's finest church building. Methodists and Baptists tended to attract the largest membership, but they by no means held a monopoly on the religious affiliation of Austinites.[15]

The element in San Antonio which participated in religious association was overwhelmingly Roman Catholic. Virtually all the

Mexicans worshiped regularly at the renovated and enlarged San Fernando Church. St. Mary's Church, newly built, was used largely by the Germans and Irish. These two edifices cost more than all the Protestant churches combined, although, by 1860, the Presbyterians and Episcopalians were building large and elegant churches. Both the Methodists and Lutherans had small congregations holding regular church services, and after 1854, when they founded the cemetery, Jews met regularly in members' homes.[16]

Many urban churchgoers believed that the theater had no place in their communities. "That baleful nuisance to public morals" intruded its "demoralizing effects upon the youthful," and, indeed, did the work of the devil.[17] Many of their fellow citizens, however, disagreed with them, found the theater amusing, and often a basis for cultural uplift. Although many enthusiastic patrons could be found in each of the communities, they were too few in number anywhere to support a regular theater of good quality. Both coastal cities had theater buildings or opera houses: Perkins Hall, an ornately handsome three-story brick dwelling built in Houston in the mid-fifties, housed performances for several decades. In Galveston, Sydnor Theater opened in 1845, followed by Neitch's Varieties in 1854.[18] The fare was bad and apparently the season of 1857–1858 was finally enough to drive one correspondent to the *Civilian* to distraction. He wrote, "The performances at this resort have been a libel on the town and an insult to intelligent people." The only "legitimate drama that we have had was Donnetti's 'Acting Monkeys,' and they were bad enough, God knows." Galvestonians must learn "to frown upon these clap-trap clowns, and cease patronizing every humbug announced in flaming hand bills."[19]

Theaters showed light comedies and, occasionally, serious pieces like *Hamlet* or *Macbeth*. However, there did seem to be an unusual number of circuses, including sideshows offering fares like "a fat girl who would yield about three barrels of No. 1 soap," a giant Indian, and fire-eaters. In 1858, one circus troupe performed in a tent which seated twenty-five hundred persons. Individual small shows came with their Swiss bell-ringers, mountain minstrels, musicians, dancers, dogs, monkeys, goats, and, last but not least, lecturers. Once an abolitionist lecturer even dared to approach the Galveston stage. Pseudo-scientific demonstrations flooded the boards with their electro-biology, science of animal magnetism, and phrenology.[20]

Local impresarios usually managed the theaters, hiring traveling companies coming, as did Joseph Jefferson, from New Orleans, or occasionally New York, Boston, or Philadelphia. Houston and Galveston often had the same fare. Rarely, a troup would go on to Austin.

San Antonio had no regular theater during the forties or fifties, but Pudding Stanley, operator of a barroom, a fandango, a keno-table, and a faro bank, was a former actor and theater manager. When he learned that Joseph Jefferson and his colleagues were playing in Houston, he sped there to try to persuade them to come to San Antonio. San Antonio, despite Stanley's dazzling descriptions, was too far and too dangerous a journey for the taste of the thespian society. However, as the company was on hard times, and as Stanley claimed that his popularity in Texas was second only to that of the late Davy Crockett, he was easily persuaded to give a public rendition of Shakespeare's *Richard III* with the cast. Jefferson's description of the performance and the audience show that Houstonians had yet to go some to reach cultural maturity.

At the rise of the curtain the expectant audience were on tiptoe to meet their comrade . . . After bowing low . . . he began his soliloquy. The performance proceeded quietly for a time, the silence being broken now and then by expressions of approval in complimentary but rather familiar terms. During the love scene with Lady Anne, her ladyship was warned by someone in the audience, who claimed to have an intimate knowledge of Richard's private domestic affairs, that the tyrant had already two Mexican wives in San Antonio.

[At one point], being overstimulated by excitement and applause, he nearly stumbled into the private box. Straightening himself up, his ostrich plumes became entangled with a . . . chandelier and set him in a blaze . . . He glared with indignation at the convulsed audience . . . until the unmistakable odor of burnt feathers warned him that his diadem was in danger . . . In the death scene, just as *Richard* expired, a voice, signifying that the game was over, shouted "Keno!" This allusion to Pud's commercial pursuits brought him to life, and as the curtain was descending he sat up and warned the interlocutor that he would "keno" him in the morning.[21]

Perhaps the theater as a cultural effort had yet to reach its apogee or even materially improve. Education, however, became a stronger issue with the urban populace in the postannexation era. Despite the generally anti-intellectual attitude of the frontier, few citizens opposed education itself. The two leading statesmen of the period made unequivocal pronouncements on the need for an educated populace. Sam Houston believed that "the benefits of education and of useful knowledge, generally diffused through a community, are essential to the preservation of a free government." His political opponent, Mirabeau B. Lamar, agreed with him: "Cultivated mind is the guardian genius of Democracy, and while guided and controlled by virtue, the noblest attribute of man. It is the only dictator that freemen acknowledge, and the only security which freemen desire." Noble sentiments these, and Texans established dozens of institutions of learning, but they were mostly private, for few men were yet ready to tax themselves for the education of other men's children and free public education in antebellum Texas was largely limited to the poorest of the cities.

In 1854 the legislature set aside a sum of two million dollars to be used to establish a public school system throughout the state. The administration of the money and the schools was to be under county control, with the allocation of money on the basis of a census of all white children between the ages of one and sixteen years of age living in the county. State funds paid salaries only; the county provided equipment and buildings for the schools.[22] As Texas county governments were notoriously poor during the fifties, few took advantage of the benefits of this law.

San Antonio could boast of its public education as an unquestioned first. This community, whose per capita wealth was far behind the others, was alone in enthusiastically supplying the money necessary for the education of its young. Over two hundred students regularly attended the City Free Schools, one for boys and one for girls, which opened in 1853. Several decades earlier the Mexican Congress had granted certain lands to the city for the support of free public schools, and the municipal government derived the $2,300 per year budget largely from this source.[23] Admittedly, the student-teacher ratio of one to eighty was far behind the average of one to thirty or forty found in the private schools, but it was an education for the poor, which was more than wealthy Galveston or Austin were providing for their underprivileged. Houston's two public schools of sixty students ran a poor second to San Antonio's, although it again pointed up the more democratic and enlightened spirit which pervaded Houston and was often found lacking in its island neighbor.[24]

The best schools of the cities were the Roman Catholic institutions. In 1847 a group of Ursuline nuns from New Orleans established an academy for girls in Galveston. Four years later this same order founded the Ursuline Convent School of San Antonio. The nuns accepted students of any faith as day or boarding students, and many Protestant, as well as Catholic, families took advantage of the superior education offered and sent their girls. In 1860 over three-hundred and fifty students studied under the supervision of the nuns in these two schools.[25]

In San Antonio, St. Mary's College, founded in 1852 and located on Military Plaza, taught boys from the primary grades through university preparation. St. Mary's left an indelible mark on the area because for several generations it educated the sons of most prominent families of southwest Texas and northern Mexico.[26] By the eve of the Civil War nearly two hundred lads worked under the dedicated and disciplining Brothers. Young boys who sought the advantages of a Catholic education in Galveston and its vicinity attended the school under the direction of the Oblates of Mary Immaculate. If they were competent enough, they graduated to the only school of higher learning in the coastal area, the University of St. Mary. This school, founded in 1854, and incorporated by the legislature in 1856, was empowered to grant degrees. The curriculum included both the classical and the practical. Latin and Greek opened the list of offerings, but not of secondary emphasis were courses in surveying, mechanics, and mathematics. The editor of the Houston *Telegraph and Texas Register*, E. H. Cushing, long a critic of education in Texas, recognized its good reputation for scholarship and gave it his stamp of approval.[27]

The other urban schools often were established for profit, snob appeal, or the preservation of cultural identity, and usually placed quality of scholarship far behind these other purposes. Cushing, a Dartmouth graduate and former teacher, lashed out at the "humbuggery" of the Gulf Coast schools. This gadfly of elementary education was particularly enraged by the tendency of one-man private academies to call themselves universities. He pointed to schools in Houston and Galveston in which "the president, the board of trustees, professors, and tutors were all comprised on one person, and he having no right to attach an A.M. or even A.B. to his name." He admitted that there were a few qualified teachers who were performing their jobs adequately, but he insisted that many schools had teachers who were too ignorant or indolent to teach well and who fawned over parents rather than teaching children. Many believed that the problem would not be rectified until the profit motive was eliminated from education.[28]

Private schools increased in number in San Antonio and Austin during the fifties. San Antonio's private institutions grew from five teachers and one hundred and fourteen students in 1850, to thirty teachers and nearly a thousand students in 1860. Austin education scarcely existed in 1850; a decade later Austin and Travis County boasted twenty-seven teachers and over five hundred students. Galveston had only one more teacher than Austin and fewer students although its population was more than twice as great. Houston's private schools lost one teacher during the decade, but the reason probably lies in the opening of the public schools.[29]

Most of the private institutions were elementary schools for girls, boys, or common schools for the two. Galveston, Austin, and San Antonio Germans sponsored German-English schools for their children. Austin, Houston, and Galveston all had academies, presumably to prepare young men for university admission, and, of course, the Catholic men's schools offered this same fare. With the exception of the free public and Catholic schools, teachers usually numbered one per school. San Antonio's ten private male and female schools employed a total of eleven teachers. Galveston's nine private schools had nine teachers in 1860. That education was not totally inadequate with such competition and shoestring budgets is a small wonder.[30]

Most of the early urban instructors came from New England, but as sectional tensions grew, the Texas cities became increasingly reluctant to accept northern scholars who were "not to be trusted with institutions such as ours"; nor were the Yankees often willing to come.[31] Texas had few satisfactory schools of higher learning to train teachers, and, here too, the 1850's brought with them problems of faculty recruitment similar to those experienced by many southern universities a century later.

To improve adult education, townsmen renewed efforts to begin public libraries, but most of these trials were unsuccessful. However, there were several private libraries of substantial size in each community. Many were primarily professional. As early as 1850, thirty-five attorneys and physicians in the coastal cities averaged over three hundred works in their personal libraries.[32]

Galveston's Lyceum, a private organization of thirty members, housed a library of six hundred volumes. William Pitt Ballinger had some two thousand books, mostly classics, in his personal collection by 1860. Sir Svante Palm already had two thousand tomes in Austin, the beginning of a collection ultimately to form the nucleus of the library of the University of Texas. Two San Antonians possessed fifteen hundred volumes of natural history and twelve hundred volumes of philosophy, respectively. The Germans of both Galveston and San Antonio established circulating libraries for themselves, the one at the Alamo City offering fourteen hundred volumes on German literature and science. The State Library at Austin had built up a collection of over four thousand by the eve of the Civil War, which were available to the denizens of the capital city, and Sunday schools everywhere had substantial collections of religious literature in their Sunday school libraries.[33]

Newspapers remained Texans' favorite reading matter. Hundreds sprang up between 1845 and 1860, and over seventy were operating on the eve of secession.[34] The giants of the urban press were the now-venerable *Telegraph and Texas Register* of Houston and the *News* and *Civilian* of Galveston. Closely following were the *State Gazette* and *Southern Intelligencer* of Austin and the *Herald* of San Antonio. Subscribers to these major journals multiplied many times over during the decade. Widely divergent philosophical and political viewpoints were argued on their pages. Readers could take their pick of papers professing Whig, Calhoun Democratic, Houston Democratic, independent Democratic, and Know-Nothing sympathies. The journalistic quality improved with time but was never high. At least, however, editors no longer indulged in the sophomoric personal attacks which characterized the papers of the Republic.[35]

In Galveston, the *Christian Advocate* and the *Apologete,* both religious weeklies, enjoyed a circulation of nearly seven thousand. *Port Folio* of Galveston and the *Rambler* of Austin flourished briefly as literary journals. Foreign language papers gained prominence during the fifties. *El Bejareño* first rolled off the press in San Antonio in 1855, and *Die Woechentliche Union,* successor to the *Zeitung* at Galveston, enjoyed a city circulation larger than its two English language rivals. Frederick Law Olmsted found the San Antonio *Staatz Zeitung* to contain "more news of matters of general interest than all the American Texan papers."[36] Olmsted showed a sharp preference for all things German, however, and one suspects his attitude might have been biased by the antislavery sentiments that he shared with the Germans.

Germans composed a near majority among the European immigrants in prewar Texas. In 1848 Viktor Bracht reported that fifteen thousand had come directly from Germany and another ten to fifteen thousand by way of the older states. An indication of the large influx of the Teutons is indicated in letters from Bracht to friends in 1846 and 1847: "Five thousand two hundred and forty-seven persons landed in Galveston from the middle of October of last year [1845] til the end of last April, transported on thirty ships (twenty-four from Bremen and twelve from Antwerp) . . . Of . . . [these] only two thousand five hundred have arrived . . . [at New Braunfels] and at Fredericksburg." At Galveston and "at Houston there are more Germans than Americans, and the use of any other language than German is almost an offense. That is the way it should be!"[37]

The first influx of Germans arrived in the late thirties, some from the older states, fleeing the effects of the Panic of 1837, and others from Germany itself. Large-scale immigration began with the work of the *Adelsverein,* or Association for the Protection of German Immigrants in Texas, organized by a group of German noblemen in June 1843.[38] Carl, Prince of Solms-Braunfels, headed the group which brought large numbers of Germans to Texas to found Fredericksburg, New Braunfels, and other German settlements in the interior. Their organization collapsed by 1847, but its effect on the settlements continued. By 1860 Germans were in the majority in three counties between Austin and San Antonio and composed a large part of the population in six other counties in the area. Some came through the port of Indianola, but the overwhelming majority came by way of Galveston and Houston, and many others remained behind in these communities.[39]

The urban Germans were in large part from the lower-middle and lower classes. Some were skilled laborers, others had experience as small tradesmen and craftsmen, and a few were professionals. The several noble immigrants, including two barons and a count, preferred the settlements to the cities. The Germans were almost uniformly, it seems, industrious, thrifty, clean, and ambitious. A few rose to positions of wealth or power prior to the

Civil War. They were not as readily assimilated as many other nationalities, for they had security in numbers. They tended to organize their own churches and social organizations and support their own newspapers.[40] The native American elements conceded the Germans' virtues throughout the forties and into the early fifties. As a case in point, in 1850 the mayor of San Antonio, urging that the city laws be printed in English, Spanish, and German, argued that, "In regard the German population, constituting as it does, the only really industrious and working people among us, sober and temperate in their habits, amenable to the laws when they understand them—in general intelligence comparing most favorably with any class of our Citizens, is the necessity most apparent."[41]

A few years later, however, Olmsted observed "the manners and ideals of the Texans and the Germans are hopelessly divergent, and the two races have made little acquaintance, observing one another apart with unfeigned curiosity, often tempered with mutual contempt."[42] The hostility toward the Germans arose in part because native American labor resented the large influx of German laborers and craftsmen who tended to lower the wage scale and were generally recognized as better workers.[43] Too, though most were unobtrusive, they all suffered from the outspoken prejudice of some of their leaders. Prince Carl was among the worst. The Prince announced in print that "no action is too vile for an American to perform, provided he thinks he will profit thereby . . . [They] are self-opinionated and boastful, unpleasing in their social dealings, and very dirty in their manners and habits."[44]

But none of these causes of friction quite equaled that created by the antislavery attitude of the Germans in a dominantly slave-oriented society. This explosive issue temporarily formed a wedge between the native Texans and the Germans. Dr. Adolph Douai, editor of the *San Antonio Zeitung*, took such an extreme abolitionist position in the columns of his newspaper that he drove the New Braunfels Germans, in mass meeting in mid-1855, to declare that they were not responsible for the sentiments and opinions of his paper. At the same time, however, they did not disclaim their antislavery attitudes. *Die Woechentliche Union,* published by Ferdinand Flake at Galveston, vigorously opposed the reopening of the slave trade.[45]

In May of 1854 about two hundred Germans from throughout the state held a mass meeting in San Antonio for the purpose of expressing their political principles, which included the gradual abolition of slavery. The meeting was a boon for the Know-Nothing or American Party, which was then beginning to organize in the state. The Texas platform of this nationally nativist, anti-Catholic party excluded the usual anti-Catholic resolutions, pointing out that they constituted religious intolerance. Their more obvious motive was not to offend the many potential members and sympathizers who would adhere to the other planks in the platform. Although sympathetic to slavery, the party was strongly pro-Union and thus attracted the support of many who disapproved of the racial premises but supported the unionist and slavery stands. Many of the urban newspapers, particularly the *State Times* of Austin, attacked the Germans, charging them with abolitionist tendencies. Edward Burleson, Jr., one of Austin's nativist leaders, began a vicious and unsuccessful campaign to attach the stigma of cruelty to Indians onto the Germans. Various other speakers questioned their loyalty to "southern institutions." Know-Nothings succeeded in electing their slates to municipal offices in Austin, Galveston, and San Antonio, and narrowly missed electing the governor in 1856.[46]

The Know-Nothings soon faded out of existence, leaving as their only positive contribution the formal organization of the Democratic Party, which was the true beginning of party systems in Texas. They also left in their aftermath a residue of hostile sentiments. A mob destroyed the offices of *Die Woechentliche Union* of Galveston early in 1861 because Ferdinand Flake, the paper's editor, dared to oppose secession. Not until after the Civil War would harmonious relations prevail among the native-born Americans and their German neighbors.[47]

Throughout the fifties relations between native Galvestonians and the Germans were better than on the mainland. Galveston was a cosmopolitan community and often attracted a more urbane immigrant. Germans, on the whole, shared more in the political activities of the city than they did elsewhere. The major entente, in fact, was between the native leaders and the Germans. More dependable than the native artisans, the latter were law abiding, paid their taxes, and were more likely to render the flattering homage to class and social distinctions than the rowdy native artisan. Thus, despite the prevalent unionist and antislavery attitudes among the Germans, the relationship between the island leaders and the German community was often good. The island workers, like their mainland counterparts, resented the Germans, and this attitude, no doubt, was part of the reason for the Germans maintaining their own social and cultural organizations.[48]

The German Reading Room occupied two floors of a large building in downtown Galveston and was only one of several in the state. The German Library of San Antonio held fourteen hundred volumes. The Turner Associations thrived during the fifties; Galveston's Association erected its own club house on the public square in 1859, at an estimated cost of over eight thousand dollars. The Houston Turnverein obtained its first property two years later. State Saengerfests were held annually after 1853, with the singing clubs of San Antonio, Houston, Galveston, Austin, Fredericksburg, and New Braunfels dominating the festivities. German rifle companies paraded in their colorful uniforms to the music of the German band. Houston German tradesmen organized their own volunteer fire brigade, which more than once dramatically rescued women and saved property. And in every community were several well-patronized family beer gardens.[49]

Although the Germans were the largest immigrant group, almost all other nationalities were represented in the Texas population. The Irish ranked a poor second among the Europeans, having only a fourth the number of their Teutonic neighbors. The French and English tied for third place. Irish immigrants arrived in Texas while it was a Mexican province, establishing San Patricio and other colonies and settling in several of the established towns. Others continued to come intermittently until the outbreak of the Civil War. Rapidly assimilated into the frontier communities, by secession they were indistinguishable from the native Americans. Often laborers, small tradesmen, and mechanics, some, like San Antonio's merchant elite, rose to positions of wealth and prominence. The English engaged in trade, practiced medicine, law, and, occasionally, opened small private schools. Frenchmen operated hotels, confectioneries, bakeries, liquor stores, and merchandising houses. Austin received a large influx of Swedish artisans and laborers brought by the immigration company, organized under the direction of Sir Svante Palm and S. M. Swenson.[50]

Next to the Germans in numbers were the Mexicans, who generally presented a dismal picture. Illiterate, unambitious, they lived a life apart from the mainstream of most communities, the objects of harsh discrimination because of their social condition and attitudes and their previous nationality. Occupationally, they were restricted to subsistence farming and carting. Since they were traditionally hostile to slavery, their lot grew no better as the Great Conflict approached. No more than a handful of Mexican families lived in the coastal cities, although the streets of

Houston were frequently crowded with transient cartmen. Relations between Austinites and Mexicans became so hostile that the latter were twice forcefully driven from the town during the fifties.[51]

San Antonio's population was at least one third, and possibly one half, of Mexican origin. A minute fraction of these, descended from the original Canary Island hidalgos, held their fellow Mexicans in contempt and mingled professionally and, occasionally, socially with the Americans. Except for these few, San Antonio's Mexicans virtually represented a caste. The city's population was the largest in the state, yet its property was valued at less than that of Austin, half its size, largely because of the impoverishment of its Mexican element. Their assimilation was negligible and their social life remained colorful. Despite an occasional puritanical outburst the city fathers usually left them to their traditional amusements of the fandango, card gambling, and cockfighting. Other than in their rather significant role as cartmen, the Mexicans exerted little influence in the economic or political life of the city or the state.[52]

Although at the bottom of the social and ethnic scale, the Negroes were as a whole materially better off than many others. Being a Negro in a Texas town meant being a slave, for less than two dozen free persons of color lived in all the major cities.[53] Yet even though Negroes lacked the dignity of human freedom and wretched as their condition might often have been, their material welfare was more assured and comfortable than that of the overwhelming majority of San Antonio Mexicans and many of the newly arrived immigrants.

Urban slaves represented a substantial investment; a good cook occasionally sold for as much as two thousand dollars. Few whites were going to harm seriously their personal property, and the blacks were assured of adequate food, shelter, medical care, and clothing. Families not only took care of their Negroes, but also often allowed them special privileges such as giving them last year's cast-off finery and allowing them to take the family carriage for a drive. A British visitor was amazed to find in Galveston "innumerable Negroes and Negresses parading about the streets in the most outrageously grand costumes—silks, satins, crinolines, hats with feathers, lace mantles, etc., forming an absurd contrast to the simple dresses of their mistresses. Many were driving about in their master's carriages, or riding on horses which are often lent to them on Sunday afternoons. All seemed intensely happy and satisfied with themselves."[54]

Few of the urban slaves would willingly permit themselves to be sold to rural owners, and when an exchange of this nature was initiated, the proposed rural master demanded a period of trial, which was more often than not unsuccessful. Without question the condition of the urban slaves was superior to that of their rural counterparts.

Whether black slave or Caucasian elite, the residents of the young Texas cities all seemed to sense that their communities were in a period of important transition. New attitudes and behavioral patterns developed, indicating an urban rather than a village orientation. Galveston solidified its cultural superiority over the state and posed with aristocratic pretensions, but it was gradually and subtly losing the economic battle for primacy with its mainland neighbor. Houston pursued the goal of control of transportation and trade along the Gulf coast with singular zeal, yet, internally, maintained a remarkable degree of egalitarianism and community harmony. San Antonio, plagued with its isolation, nonetheless developed a small hinterland trade, maneuvered for army contracts, and, strengthened by its cosmopolitan nature, continued to seek solutions to its "Mexican problem." Austin wished only to preserve its identity as political capital, and its growth and character could be measured in terms of the growth and character of the state. None of the four could be considered great cities, but by 1860 they had essentially formed the basic pattern of their characters. The Civil War was to complete the process.

VII
THE RESPONSE TO
CIVIL WAR

Texas enjoyed a unique role among the southern states during the Civil War. It suffered almost no military action or property damage, and at least during the first two or three years of the contest, it prospered economically. Although most able-bodied men were away with the armies, thousands of slaves poured in from Louisiana, Arkansas, and other Confederate states for safekeeping. They harvested the unusually high-yield crops produced between 1861 and 1864. Construction continued well into 1862. Several score miles of railroad track, laid largely by slaves, were added to the state's infant system and some of Texas' finest residences were built between 1861 and 1863.

Few abrupt alterations in the urban pattern occurred during this half-decade. Of the four major cities, the coastal ones suffered the greatest privations and setbacks, which, from the Unionist viewpoint, seemed divine retribution, for Galveston and Houston adamantly supported secession. Inflation plagued most of the communities, and even though the blockade of Galveston was not all Union authorities might have wished, most business at the island city came to a virtual standstill after 1861. Many aspects of Houston's economy were severely depressed after 1863. San Antonio benefited most by the war. The most populous Texas town, it now became for a time the state's commercial metropolis as well because of the shift in trade routes. The Confederate demand for meat boosted the cattle industry in San Antonio, and the town council continued to make concessions of land to army officials to assure the perpetuation of the city's role as a military center. Austin continued to thrive as the heart of the state's political system.

Municipal affairs centered largely on providing some type of stable currency, supporting military organizations, and encouraging wartime home industry. The city fathers had done little to broaden the scope of their authority after annexation, and urban services remained modest until Reconstruction. As a case in point, Houston had one fire engine in 1846 and added only one more by 1861. No city paved its streets, installed covered sewers, had transit systems, owned or granted franchises to water supply concerns, employed paid firemen, or operated successful permanent health departments until after the war. None except Galveston had street lighting, and that began on the eve of the war and extended for only one city block.[1] Ferdinand Flake bitterly denounced the aldermen of Galveston in 1866, and in so doing expressed views many Texas urbanites had held for years: "The rain stands in our streets forming pools of impassable water. Garbage and carrion destroy our health and invite pestilence.

Dogs, hogs, and goats are our only scavengers. Our wharves are rickety and dangerous, our streets are dark by night and muddy by day . . . The money that our citizens have spent in pistols for personal defense would make our houses safe from burglars, and our streets from assassins. The money spent in mending broken shins would keep our street crossings in good repair, and gas light would triple the business of the storekeepers, while promoting the comfort of everybody."[2] Before the war the merchant mayors and aldermen were primarily concerned with keeping taxes low; during the war providing improvements was impossible. Reconstruction was to bring with it many modern, municipally operated services, so desperately lacking in the prewar towns.

During the war each city contributed matériel to the military effort. The large foundries at Galveston and Houston cast shot, shell, and cannon, and the shops of the Galveston, Houston, and Henderson Railroad forged cannon. In San Antonio, a factory on Powderhouse Hill made cartridges from 1861 onward, and a tannery, capable of producing sufficient leather for 30,000 pairs of shoes every two months, opened in 1863.[3] In Austin, the Military Board established two ordnance factories. A cap and cartridge works which employed slaves put out between four and five thousand cartridges a day. A cannon foundry, Governor Lubbock reported, "was speedily put in successful operation and turned out a few first-class brass cannon that afterwards performed effective service for the Confederacy."[4] Texas' total industrial production for the war effort was not major, yet what there was came from its cities.

More impressive than the production of military matériel was the furnishing of military personnel. Although Texas was more removed from the areas of battle and less open to invasion than any other Confederate state, it put proportionately more men into uniform than any other southern state. Recruitment began in the cities. Terry's Texas Rangers formed in Houston, Tom Green's

Rifles joined up in Austin, and everywhere the local militia companies reorganized themselves into combat units. San Antonio was the military headquarters of the state, and its streets were filled with the noises of marching soldiers, particularly during the early days of the war. Cavalry units were enlistees' favorites, but many men volunteered for the less glamorous but equally essential infantry. A conservative estimate of the number of Texans in uniform during the war runs between fifty and sixty thousand. Not all, however, served the Confederate cause. Two regiments and several companies left the state to join federal forces. It is surprising that there were not more in view of the strong unionist sentiment in Texas.[5]

A quarter of the voters in the secession plebiscite favored continued ties with the northern states.[6] Many others voted for separation from the federal system but were opposed to joining a southern confederacy, preferring rather to return to the status of an independent republic. A decided minority of Texans were prepared to fight a war to establish a new southern nation of slave states. Texans were bitterly split on these issues, and nowhere was their diversity more obvious than in the cities.

The coastal towns, strongly rooted in southern traditions and the cotton-slave complex, reflected their regional attitude. In Galveston County, an overwhelming ninety-six percent of the voters chose secession, and in Harris County, where Houston is located, eighty-eight percent of those exercising their suffrage favored abandoning the union.[7] Apparently by the time of the election most of the unionists had resigned themselves to the overwhelming sentiment in their communities for separation. Some, however, fled to Mexico or to the federal lines.

Austin voted to remain with the North, and San Antonio's secessionist majority was only three percent.[8] Even stronger sentiment than is represented by the vote probably existed at San Antonio, where many unfranchised, illiterate Mexicans were against slavery. Even after secession militant voices of protest continued in the interior towns. On March 6, 1861 the *Alamo Express* reprinted the following editorial from the *Louisville Journal:* "The ingratitude of Texas seems likely to prove a very costly luxury to her. Her secession arrests passage of a bill in Congress for a mounted regiment to protect her frontier; it deprives her of the postal service which has been performed for her at the yearly expense of half a million dollars above receipts; and it cuts her off from the thirty-six millions of dollars which Congress has been determined to appropriate for the construction of a railroad throughout her whole length of seven or eight hundred miles to connect her with the Pacific states and the Pacific ocean. She has acted under the influence of atrocious misrepresentations and insane counsels and her long day of bitter regret is not far off."[9]

About a month later on the day before the firing on Fort Sumter, the *Express* editorialized that the Confederacy was "conceived in sin, shapen in iniquity, and born out of due time, because it was rushed into the world with indecent haste expressly to prevent the people from beholding its deformities." Jefferson Davis, it further held, was "vain, proud, weak, imprudent, ambitious, unprincipled, a vile traitor, a trained rebel, and an inflated bigot."[10] Union sentiment abated somewhat after the first year of the conflict.

Although nearly half of San Antonio's voters opposed separation from the northern states, the city profited by secession, for wartime economic realignments placed San Antonio in the heart of Texas trade routes. With the Union in control of the Mississippi and blockading the Gulf of Mexico, the southwestern states of Texas, Louisiana, and Arkansas were severed from the main body of the Confederacy. Blockade-running remained one method of maintaining foreign trade, but by far the most significant avenue for commerce during the war was through Mexico. The neighboring land across the Rio Grande was in the throes of its own civil war. Union sympathy with and support of the Juarez forces, which were concentrated in the north, complicated attempts to stop the transfer of contraband materials. In addition, the Confederacy carefully cultivated good relations with the governors of Nueva Leon, Tamaulipas, and Coahuila, a task which was not difficult since wartime trade with Texas brought in huge revenues. Getting cotton into Mexico, and guns, ammunition, and other matériel out was generally a simple matter.

San Antonio served as the hub of the Mexican trade, as it had since the beginning of European settlement, but the war brought the city, heretofore beyond the line of settlement, into focus as a major entrepôt for the cotton trade of not only Texas, but also of Arkansas and Louisiana. San Antonio merchants maintained agents in Monterrey, Tampico, and Matamoras throughout the war, and they and teamsters enriched themselves with war profits, much to the disgruntlement of the merchants of the coastal cities.[11]

Monterrey was the most significant center for the internal trade of Mexico. As early as 1862 cotton moved into its markets from Texas at the rate of two thousand bales per month. Cartmen brought back to San Antonio tons of powder destined for the cartridge factories there. That same year, the American vice-consul at Monterrey reported to the State Department that within the preceding three to four months trade with Texas had grown to such magnitude that enough goods were passing through to supply the whole rebel army! Monterrey was the major point of trade with Mexico itself, but even more important to Texans was the rapidly developed town of Matamoros, which was, in effect, Texas' major Civil War port.[12]

The sleepy little border town of Matamoros, Tamaulipas, Mexico, lies near the bank of the Rio Grande, forty miles from the Gulf of Mexico and directly opposite the Texas town of Brownsville. It was used as a port town before the Civil War, but no more than a dozen boats per year landed in its vicinity. With the beginning of the Union blockade, the village sprang to life. Mexican "citizens" flocked to the community from Texas, goods flooded in from San Antonio and other parts of the state, and the town grew astoundingly. Major factors, for example William Marsh Rice, left their home communities for the duration of the war in order to participate in this trade. River boats carried the cotton down to the Gulf and transferred it to ocean craft. A United States naval officer reported at one point early in the war that there were twenty vessels lying off the Rio Grande in the Gulf of Mexico loading cotton. These included one Prussian, eight English, one Bremen, two Danish, one American, and six Spanish ships. In 1863 regular steamer service ran between London and Matamoros, and trade was often brisk between the latter and the Union-held ports of New York, Philadelphia, and New Orleans.[13] As a wartime port for San Antonio, Matamoros flourished, but at the end of hostilities Corpus Christi became the logical water outlet for the city, and Matamoros reverted to its quiet obscurity.

Important as cotton was for San Antonio during the war, livestock formed the primary permanent basis for the city's export trade. The first postbellum years saw the beginning of a spectacular northward movement of animals from Texas, which, within a quarter of a century, amounted to ten million head of cattle and a million stock horses.[14] Dramatic as these postwar drives were, they should not obscure the fact that the establishment of the cattle trade and its concentration about San Antonio, the Texas center of that huge industry, lay during the war and, to an extent, in the antebellum period.

When the early Europeans came to Texas, they brought with them their native breeds of cattle. Many of these eventually ran wild, interbred, and some developed into a strange amalgamation, with Spanish strains dominating. By the 1850's they had become a potentially valuable natural resource. Conditions were too insecure to permit much trading activity during the period of the Republic, although some beefs left Texas regularly for New Orleans. After annexation business increased. As early as 1846, one rancher drove a thousand cattle as far north as Ohio, and by 1853 considerable numbers reached Missouri, Kansas, Iowa, and Illinois yearly for fattening, before midwestern farmers shipped them on to the St. Louis and Chicago markets. By 1859, however, northern sales virtually stopped.[15] Longhorns, though immune to the mortal Texas fever, carried infected ticks which transferred the germs to northern stock. Apprehensive Kansas, Missouri, and Illinois stock farmers secured protection from their legislatures barring the invading hordes and most Texas cattlemen believed the northern outlets were permanently closed.[16]

Throughout this same period stockmen were turning to California. The main trail west, the Whiting-Smith route, began at San Antonio. In 1854 beefs bringing between five and fifteen dollars per head in the region of the Alamo City sold to Sacramento and San Francisco buyers at between sixty and one hundred and fifty dollars apiece. Between 1850 and the outbreak of the war, thousands of animals covered the long trek between San Antonio and California.[17]

The Civil War ended the cattle drives to California and the northern states. Between 1861 and 1863, Texas ranchers provided the northern Confederate armies with their beef, but when Union forces blockaded the Mississippi and the Gulf of Mexico, this trade, too, stopped. Some of the producers continued to supply the Confederate forces stationed in Texas and Louisiana throughout the rest of the war, and some cattle were smuggled into Kansas and Indian Territory.[18]

Contrary to popular opinion, the cattle industry of Texas was not entirely based on open-range practices. Much of San Antonio's importance to the cattle trade lay in its proximity to established ranches. Many of the older ranchers near the Alamo City owned and enclosed all, or at least major parts, of their land. For example, the O'Conner Ranch owners fenced their holdings along the San Antonio River, from which they gleaned $80,000 in cattle sales in 1862. Colonel Richard King held title to nearly 85,000 acres, on which he ran 65,000 beefs. Rolideaux Ranch, of 142,840 acres, jutted into the Gulf of Mexico on a peninsula enclosed by thirty miles of plank fence.[19] These producers and others like them were ready for the huge northern market for Texas animals when the end of the war came.

Yankee farmers had badly depleted their stocks during the Civil War in satisfying the military and civilian demands for meat. At the same time Texas herds were multiplying so rapidly that the state was known as the cattle-hive of the nation. In 1866 alone, cowboys drove 200,000 head to the northern markets. The great trade centered on Chicago, whose Union Stock Yards opened on Christmas Day, 1865. San Antonio, the starting point for several trails, remained the metropolis of the Texas cattle empire, the focus of its commerce, finance, culture, and social life.[20]

It is ironic than San Antonio, with ambivalent feelings about secession, profited handsomely from the upheaval which followed, and that Galveston, which fervently supported separation, should suffer severely for its decision. Galveston was the site of one of the few invasions into the Texas Gulf coast. Business activity came to a halt in late 1861, and, at the same time, half the population left town, not to return until 1865. Although the island was militarily retaken early in 1863, Texans in truth abandoned the city for the duration of the war. The military events which caused this unhappy state began within two months after the fall of Fort Sumter.

Union forces began blockading Galveston early in July of 1861.

Soon after the arrival of the federal ships, the island militia fired upon them from the batteries which the rebels had earlier constructed along the shore. Half the town's population flocked to the beach; the ships returned the fire, killing one onlooker and injuring three others. The six or eight foreign consuls in residence at the port city unavailingly protested against this "uncivilized firing upon non-combatants," while frightened citizens fled the island in droves.[21] Some people returned, but only temporarily, for in May 1862 the blockaders demanded the surrender of the island; although the defenders refused, another hasty exodus of townspeople occurred. When the actual occupation by Union forces came on October 1, 1862, there were few civilians still on the island, except for those busily producing cannon at the foundry.

During the evacuation families and households moved to the mainland, particularly to Houston; businessmen closed their doors, boarded their windows, and, when possible, removed their stocks. Cartage anywhere in the city to the railhead near the bridge rose to the unprecedented amount of five dollars per load. After the final train left the island and the last steamers were plying toward Buffalo Bayou, the bridge was planked over and five thousand head of cattle were driven across to coastal pastures.[22]

On December 23, 1862, federal military units from New Orleans arrived to relieve the naval patrols. The troops landing at Kuhn's Wharf found the mayor waiting to greet them and to give them the keys to the deserted city. Meanwhile, Galveston exiles on the mainland were in an uproar, for Governor Lubbock had issued an order to burn the city. Such a sacrifice, they felt, was unnecessary. They easily persuaded General John Magruder, head of the Confederate forces, that the island should be retaken at all costs. Magruder, still smarting from criticism of his performance at Richmond, was eager to counteract these charges by an able performance. He converted two river steamers into cotton clads, armed them with cannon, faced one with railroad iron, and sent them into Galveston Bay on December 31, 1862, with over a hundred sharpshooters aboard each. Three hundred militia crossed the railroad bridge under cover of night and attacked the federal forces guarding the city. After a brief encounter with the superior federal ships, the Confederates won the battle; the ships not sunk or scuttled fled, and between three and four hundred federal soldiers were captured. Confederate casualties numbered twenty-six killed and one hundred and seventeen wounded.[23] One incident typified the particular tragedy of civil war above other wars. Confederate Major A. M. Lea, commander of the Texas riflemen, boarded the federal gunboat "Harriett Lane" to find his son, Union Lieutenant Tom Lea, second in command on the ship, dying of a bullet wound.[24] The incident brought home again to islanders the peculiar horrors of this war of father against son, brother against brother, and to the more perceptive, the stupidity and the wastefulness of the entire conflict.

Galveston was technically free. It would have the distinction of being the last southern port to surrender to federal forces at the end of the war. The blockade remained, but with New Orleans lost to the Union, Mobile and Galveston became the principal blockade-running ports of the Confederacy on the Gulf of Mexico.[25] Yet this brought little prosperity to Galveston, for the state, rather than private enterprise, handled most of the cotton sent through the port. Galveston's reverses during the conflict permanently harmed the city's future, for now added to its reputation of being vulnerable to storms and epidemics was the stigma of its being indefensible in time of war.

VIII

THE URBAN PATTERN

MATURES

The pattern for early urban development in Texas was formed by the end of the Civil War. Cities would rise on the upper Texas plains, but in the older section of the state none would seriously rival those already established. Galveston, Houston, San Antonio, and Austin had each developed its own particular characteristics and had shaped the design of its future growth. Moreover, by 1865 the permanent relationship between the four was cemented.

By 1865 Galveston's potentialities and shortcomings were clear. The community would continue to grow in population and economic strength for several decades, but the seeds of its eventual stagnation had already been planted. Its citizens were the most urbane, literate, and cultivated of the Texas peoples. They were ambitious and able, but they lacked foresight. The Galveston leadership looked to Europe for its guidelines and too often attempted to adapt to frontier situations the social patterns of class separation inherent in the older society. The elite isolated itself from the rest of the community. They emphasized their exclusiveness by using their fortunes for display and competitive consumption. They abdicated their political opportunities and responsibilities by withdrawing physically from the body politic into an island within the city. Moreover, the economic motivation of this group tended to define itself in terms of sharp individualism and immediate personal gain. These men of the upper class concerned themselves little with building a great city, but rather became preoccupied with amassing personal fortunes rapidly and exploiting the resources for their own use.

Nowhere was this attitude more pronounced or more fatal than in the area of transportation. Galveston existed because it was blessed by a natural harbor. For a time the city appeared to be at the point of an essential break in transportation for the Texas Gulf coast. Had the city's leadership seized the opportunity to build upon its advantage, the community might have become the metropolis of the Southwest. Instead, the merchant-elite created a despised monopoly through their wharf ownership and did little to improve either port or harbor. To have a first-class harbor capable of accommodating the largest of ocean vessels, Galveston needed only to cut a twelve-foot deep channel through a sand bar. With this melioration, substantial wharf extensions, and reasonable charges, the port situation would have been ideal and permanently attractive. Yet the plutocracy was uninterested.

The same attitude prevailed in railroad building. Farsighted men in America realized the future significance of the railroad to transportation. Many such men lived in Galveston, but those in power were either entirely contemptuous of promoters' ideas, were unwilling to risk the necessary capital, or were too dogmatic to alter their philosophies to meet the realities of the advantages of a state-owned system of railroads which would converge on Galveston and utilize its port facilities for worldwide trade. Thus, Galveston threw away its one great asset—its geographical advantage as a transportation center.

By 1865 other problems had begun to appear. The climate invited regular epidemics, which not infrequently decimated the population and deterred prospective immigrants. An informed and concerned municipal government, enforcing sanitation regulations, could have done much to reduce this problem. The violent storms of the Gulf left the flat island vulnerable to huge destruction of life and property. A wall such as that built after the storm of 1900 would have minimized this hazard, but such a venture required a far greater spirit of community cooperation than could be found in Galveston at this time. The Civil War proved that the island was highly vulnerable and that Texans could survive without Galveston. Indeed, when the governor ordered it burned, Texans appeared willing to discard it entirely. Galveston was militarily defensible only at great cost, a cost too high when compared with the advantages it offered.

Houston's more astute, farsighted, and cooperative leadership repeatedly benefited from Galveston's errors and disadvantages. Houston looked to earlier American frontiers for its patterns and guides, which proved more advantageous than Galveston's effort to emulate Europe. Early Houston serves as an excellent example for the thesis that an economic stake for all elements of the society makes for a more progressive community. Not only was wealth widely distributed, but the economic differences that did exist were not barriers to social and business intercourse. Wealthy merchants built their unimposing homes alongside those of the poor. There was little ostentation, for Houstonians believed that money should be invested in economic promotion. Even religious affiliation in Houston tended more to support the egalitarian churches than the traditional, ceremonial sects which predominated in Galveston. Money which Galvestonians spent for display, Houstonians put into economic improvements. While Galveston did little to improve its harbor, Houston worked constantly to clear and deepen the Bayou to accommodate larger vessels. While Galveston squabbled over the benefits and advantages of various railroad systems, Houston built railroads and became the hub of the Texas Gulf coast transportation system.

By 1865, San Antonio, the oldest and most populous of the four communities, had built up the cosmopolitan composition of Mexican, German, American, Irish, English, and French peoples which has given it twentieth-century fame as a picturesque tourist center. From its inception San Antonio controlled the Texas trade with Mexico, and, except for minor interruptions during the period from 1836 to 1865, emphasized this important role in the economy of Texas and the Southwest. From its beginning, too, San Antonio had been a military depot and the city fathers made repeated concessions to military authorities in order to preserve this basis of the city's economy. The cattle trade, a major foundation stone in San Antonio's nineteenth-century prosperity, flourished briefly in the fifties and early sixties and revived again with great vigor at the end of the Civil War.

San Antonio also had its problems. It was poor. Most people of Mexican ancestry posed a perpetual dilemma, for their culture rarely encouraged enterprise, and they depressed the general economic level of the community. San Antonio's leaders patiently worked with this problem, fought discrimination, and sought to elevate educational levels by operating the best public school system in the state. In one particular the Mexican-Americans played a major role in the economy. As teamsters, they constituted the backbone of the transportation system which tied San Antonio to its hinterland and to Mexico until the arrival of the railroad after the Civil War. Austin had no railroad until the Reconstruction period. Occasionally, the city's leadership would bestir itself to recommend the idea of a railroad to its fellow citizens, but little interest was aroused. Austin merchants seemed content to serve their own community. They sought no regional trade, nor appeared disturbed that San Antonio captured the commerce of the thriving German communities between the two cities. By the end of the Civil War, most Texans considered Austin the permanent capital. General Lamar's choice of sites proved to be a farsighted one, for although Austin was far beyond the frontier in 1836, by 1865 it was nearer the population center of a rapidly filling state. Its function was to house the core of the state's political system, and even though its planners envisioned a great commercial and industrial metropolis, this phase of their dreams would not materialize.

The four cities were markedly different in their characters. Galveston's European orientation and its emphasis on culture were unmistakable. Houston's aggressive competition for cotton and sugar trade from the rich river valleys and its constant quest to extend its merchandising frontiers followed the American southern urban pattern. San Antonio, ancient, lethargic, and democratic, gradually adopted American economic techniques, while preserving its varied ethnic patterns. Austin's population represented a melange of the various elements which composed Texas, and its motivation was political, not economic.

The founding of all four centers accompanied or preceded the opening of the rural frontiers. San Antonio, planted in the wilderness a century before the agricultural settlement of Texas, provided a pattern of urban importance for the region. Austin, established a hundred miles beyond the frontier, drew the frontier to it. Upon all these cities focused the major cultural, social, economic, and political activities of the state. Texans looked to them for guidance in art, architecture, music, the theater, and literature. They read urban newspapers, sought out urban society, borrowed money, traded raw materials, and purchased finished goods from urban merchants. They used urban industrial production. All roads converged upon the four cities for good reason: Galveston, Houston, San Antonio, and Austin were the focal points around which Texas flourished.

BIBLIOGRAPHY, NOTES, INDEX

BIBLIOGRAPHICAL NOTE

Early urban Texans, although not an illiterate people, were not notable record-keepers. The searcher does not often find unpublished
diaries or letter files that are helpful, for the best have been printed.
Several extensive collections, including the Ballinger, Gray, and
Maverick papers, occasionally did prove useful in casting light on
aspects of urban life rarely found in more publicized sources.

When extant, municipal records are major reservoirs of material
on urban growth. Unfortunately, many records of Texas cities have
been destroyed, damaged, or misplaced. Austin's archives from its
origin to 1862 have disappeared, as have Houston's for the years
between 1847 and 1865. Those of Houston's early history are often
badly watermarked, or burnt, or faded into illegibility. The same is
true of many pages in the Galveston city books. In contrast, San
Antonio's fathers have carefully kept their papers intact as far back
as the early Spanish period, and much of the material has been
indexed.

Census tracts contain an invaluable mine of information on economic, social, and cultural life. Those of the federal government for
1850 and 1860 are especially significant. However, care must be taken
in their use, for statistical errors occur, and standards of analysis vary
from city to city.

No newspaper's life extends throughout the entire period of this
study, but the *News* of Galveston and the *Telegraph and Texas
Register* of Houston do cover broad periods. Newspapers provide a

host of materials, often filled with distortions and outright error. Yet quality improved and coverage broadened with time. Many of the more militant editors helped me follow political and social currents. Rivaling newspapers in importance are travelers' accounts, early guides, and histories. Romantic tales of the Alamo and the Republic whetted the appetites of many curious spectators who flocked to Texas. Their impressions enlightened their contemporaries and benefited posterity with often unique insights into the young communities. Since these cities were small in the pre-Civil War era, the visitor faced no complex problem of analysis, and, unless he suffered a particular prejudice, inclination, or motivation, his recordings proved accurate. Many, however, did so suffer. Frederick Law Olmsted, the great urban landscape planner, wrote honestly and accurately on social and cultural matters, but his eye for accuracy in economic questions was sometimes blurred by his dislike of slavery. Prince Carl of Solms-Braunfels perceived many unusual urban characteristics, but his antipathy for Americans strongly slanted his view of many facets of the Texas urban culture. Emanuel Domenech saw things tainted by Protestantism, and Melinda Rankin found Romanism spreading insidiously. Jacob De Cordova's financial interest in Texas towns seemed to impel him to exaggerate their virtues. Viktor Bracht's Teutonic mind could see no beauty where there was disorder. One of the best early accounts is that of Mrs. Matilda C. Houstoun, a wealthy and literate Scotswoman, who visited Texas in a private yacht and intelligently and objectively analyzed what she found. Her work is far from comprehensive, though, for her hosts apparently showed her only the more pleasant features of life in these rude towns.

A number of unpublished histories lie in local archives, and some are equal if not superior to most printed works. Ben C. Stuart and Will Hayes, of Galveston, and Frank Brown, of Austin, lived during much of the period of which they wrote and used sources no longer extant. Jack Butterfield, of San Antonio, has written the most comprehensive nineteenth-century history of San Antonio, and it is as yet unpublished.

Printed historical studies of Texas towns are irregular in quality. Too many urban accounts have been written with motives which clash with the search for truth. No one has attempted a comparative history of any period, nor has anyone written a comprehensive study of any single city. The best urban histories are those recently written by trained historians who have concentrated on particular phases and eras of city life. Andrew Forest Muir's articles on economic features of antebellum Houston cannot be surpassed for meticulous detail and accuracy in research. Earl W. Fornell's study of Galveston during the 1850's appears in print after much of the research for this book had been completed, but his work proved to be helpful in confirming or challenging facts and interpretations previously found.

General references in this bibliography are only those used in the text. Unless specifically cited, collateral sources are not included. Many volumes on political, economic, social, and cultural history of the United States helped prepare the background for this study, and such pathfinding volumes as those of Adna Ferrin Weber, Carl Bridenbaugh, Blake McKelvey, Besse Louise Pierce, Arthur M. Schlesinger, Sr., and Richard C. Wade were invaluable. The author examined a plethora of pamphlets, letters, leaflets, brochures, sketches, clippings, photographs, and articles, which are too numerous to mention, but which all contribute to this book. Omitted also are works outside the chronological and geographical boundaries of this project. Extensive research, covering broad areas of time and space, preceded the organizational limiting of the book and played a vital role in its formation.

MANUSCRIPT COLLECTIONS

Austin, Texas History Center, University of Texas
 John Hunter Herndon Diary.
 Mary Maverick Papers.
 Samuel Maverick Papers and Diary.
 Thomas F. McKinney Papers.
 Robert Q. Mills Papers.
 Juan Augustin Morfi. "Memorias de la Provincia de Texas."
  Photostatic copy from the original in Library of Congress, Washington, D.C.
Galveston, Rosenberg Library
 William Pitt Ballinger Diary.
 Millie R. Gray Diary. ✓
 Charles W. Hayes. "Island and City of Galveston, 1527–1875."
 Ben C. Stuart. "Brief Chronology," "History of Galveston," and "Scrapbook."

PUBLIC RECORDS

Austin. Texas State Library. Archives Section. Executive Record Book, no. 40.

Austin. Office of the City Secretary. Record of the Mayor's Office and Board of Aldermen, November 16, 1862 to October 4, 1869.

Galveston. Office of the City Secretary. Ordinance Book, 1857–1865. Proceedings of the Mayor and Board of Aldermen of the City of Galveston, 1849–1865.

Galveston. Steward Title Company. Galveston City Company Records, 1838–1854.

Houston. Office of the City Secretary. Minutes and Ordinance Book, A: 1840–1847; B: 1865–1869.

Houston. Office of the County Clerk, Harris County. Probate Records, 1840–1847.

San Antonio. Office of the City Secretary. Journal of the City Council, A: June 1837–January 1849; B: January 1849–August 1856; C: August 1856–January 1865.

Washington, D.C. National Archives. Record Group 29. Schedules 1, 2, 3, 8. Free Inhabitants, Slave Inhabitants, Productions of Agriculture and Productions of Industry of the United States Census, 1850 and 1860.

NEWSPAPERS

Austin
Daily Bulletin, 1841–1842.
Austin City Gazette, 1839–1842.
Rambler, 1858–1859.
Southern Intelligencer, 1856–1860.
State Gazette, 1849–1858.
State Times, 1853–1855.
Texas Democrat, 1846–1847.
Texas Sentinel (or Centinel), 1840–1841, 1857.
Western Advocate, 1843.
Galveston
Civilian, 1838–1860.
Galvestonian, 1839.

News, 1844–1860.
Texas Portfolio, 1857.
Houston
  Citizen, 1843.
  Houstonian, 1841.
  Morning Star, 1839–1846.
  National Banner, 1838.
  National Intelligencer, 1839.
  Telegraph, 1856–1862.
  Telegraph and Texas Register, 1835–1856.
  Texian Democrat, 1844.
  Times, 1840.
San Antonio
  Alamo Express, 1860–1861.
  El Bejareño, 1855–1856.
  Herald, 1863.
  San Antonio Ledger, 1849–1855.

GENERAL SOURCES

Adams, Ephraim Douglass. *British Interests and Activities in Texas, 1838–1846.* Baltimore: Johns Hopkins Press, 1910.
———, ed. "Correspondence from the British Archives Concerning Texas, 1837–1846," *Quarterly of the Texas State Historical Association*, 15 (January 1912), 201–265.
Allen, William Youel. "Allen's Reminiscences of Texas, 1838–1842," ed. William S. Red, *Southwestern Historical Quarterly*, 17 (January 1914), 283–305; 18 (January 1915), 287–304.
Almonte, Juan N. *Noticia Estadística sobre Texas.* Mexico City: Ignacio Cumplido, 1835.
Audubon, John J. *The Life of John James Audubon, the Naturalist.* Ed. Lucy Audubon. New York: G. P. Putnam's Sons, 1901.
Ballou, Ellen Bartlett. "Scudder's Journey to Texas, 1859," *Southwestern Historical Quarterly*, 63 (July 1959), 1–14.
Bancroft, Hubert Howe. *History of the North Mexican States and Texas.* 2 vols. San Francisco: History Company, 1886–1889.
Barbey, Théodore. *Le Texas.* Paris: By the author, 1841.
Barker, Eugene C. "The African Slave Trade in Texas," *Quarterly of*

the *Texas State Historical Association*, 6 (October 1902), 145–158.

———— *The Life of Stephen F. Austin, Founder of Texas, 1793–1836: A Chapter in the Westward Movement of the Anglo-American People*. Dallas: Cokesbury Press, 1925.

———— *Mexico and Texas, 1821–1835*. University of Texas Research Lectures on the Causes of the Texas Revolution. Dallas: P. L. Turner Company, 1928.

————, ed. *Readings in Texas History for High Schools and Colleges*. Dallas: Southwest Press, 1929.

Barr, Alwyn. "Texas Coastal Defense, 1861–1865," *Southwestern Historical Quarterly*, 65 (July 1961), 1–31.

Barr, Amelia E. *All the Days of My Life: An Autobiography, the Red Leaves of a Human Heart*. New York: D. Appleton and Company, 1923.

Bartlett, John R. *Personal Narrative of Explorations and Incidents in Texas, New Mexico, California, Sonora, and Chihuahua, Connected with the United States and Mexican Boundary Commission during the Years 1850, '51, '52, and '53*. 2 vols. New York: D. Appleton and Company, 1854.

Benedict, J. W. "Diary of a Campaign Against the Comanches," *Southwestern Historical Quarterly*, 32 (April 1929), 304–305.

Biesele, Rudolph L. *The History of the German Settlements in Texas, 1831–1861*. Austin: Von Boeckmann-Jones Company, 1930.

———— "Prince Solm's Trip to Texas, 1844–1845," *Southwestern Historical Quarterly*, 40 (July 1936), 1–25.

———— "The Texas State Convention of Germans in 1854," *Southwestern Historical Quarterly*, 33 (April 1930), 247–261.

Bollaert, William. *Observations on the Geography of Texas*. London: William Clowes and Sons, 1850.

———— *William Bollaert's Texas*. Ed. W. Eugene Hollon and Ruth Lapham Butler. Norman: University of Oklahoma Press, 1956.

Bolton, Herbert Eugene, ed. *Spanish Exploration in the Southwest, 1542–1706*. New York: Barnes and Noble, 1963.

Bonnell, George W. *Topographical Description of Texas: To Which Is Added an Account of the Indian Tribes*. Austin: Clark, Wing, and Brown, 1840.

Bracht, Viktor, *Texas in 1848*. Trans. C. F. Schmidt. San Antonio: Naylor Printing Company, 1931.

Bracken, Dorothy K., and Maurine Whorton Redway, *Early Texas Homes*. Dallas: Southern Methodist University Press, 1956.

Braman, Don E. E. *Braman's Information about Texas*. Philadelphia: J. P. Lippincott and Company, 1857.

Briscoe, P. "The First Texas Railroad," *Quarterly of the Texas State Historical Association*, 7 (April 1904), 279–285.

Brown, Frank. "Annals of Travis County and the City of Austin from the Earliest Times to the Close of 1875." 12 vols. Typescript. Austin Public Library.

Brown, John Henry. *History of Texas from 1685 to 1892*. 2 vols. St. Louis: L. E. Daniell, Publisher, 1892–1893.

Bugbee, Lester G. "The Texas Frontier, 1820–1825," *Publications of the Southern History Association*, 4 (1900), 118–119.

Butterfield, Jack C. "The Free State of Bejar." MS, Daughters of the Republic of Texas Library, San Antonio.

Cabet, Etienne. *Almanach Icarien; Supplément à l'Almanach Icarien pour 1848*. Paris: Bureau du Populaire, 1848.

Carlson, Avery L. *A Monetary and Banking History of Texas from the Mexican Regime to the Present Day, 1821–1929*. Fort Worth: Fort Worth National Bank, 1930.

Carroll, Benjamin H., ed. *Standard History of Houston, Texas, from a Study of the Original Sources*. Knoxville, Tennessee: H. W. Crew, 1912.

Carroll, James M. *A History of Texas Baptists: Comprising a Detailed Account of Their Activities, Their Progress and Their Achievements*. Dallas: Baptist Standard Printing Company, 1923.

Castañeda, Carlos E. *Our Catholic Heritage in Texas, 1519–1936*. Vol. III: *The Mission Era: The Missions at Work, 1731–1761*. Vol. VI: *Transition Period: The Fight for Freedom, 1810–1836*. Vol. VII: *The Church in Texas Since Independence, 1836–1950*. Austin: Von Boeckmann-Jones, 1938–1958.

Chabot, Frederick C. *San Antonio and Its Beginnings, 1691–1731; Comprising the Four Numbers of the San Antonio Series with Appendix*. San Antonio: Naylor Printing Company, 1931.

"The City of Galveston, Texas," *De Bow's Review*, 3 (April 1847), 348–349.

Clark, Ira G. *Then Came the Railroads: The Century from Steam to Diesel in the Southwest*. Norman: University of Oklahoma Press, 1958.

Cohen, Henry, *et al. One Hundred Years of Jewry in Texas.* Dallas: Jewish Advisory Committee for the Texas Centennial Religious Program, 1936.

Connally, Ernest A. "Architecture at the End of the South: Central Texas," *Journal of the Society of Architectural Historians: Southern Issue,* 11 (December 1952), 9–10.

Corner, William, ed. *San Antonio de Bexar: A Guide and History.* San Antonio: Bainbridge and Corner, 1890.

Cotterhill, R. S. "The Beginnings of Railroads in the Southwest," *Mississippi Valley Historical Review,* 8 (March 1922), 318–326.

Crook, Carland Elaine. "San Antonio, Texas, 1846–1861." Unpub. Master's thesis, Rice University, Houston, 1964.

Cumberland, Charles C. "The Confederate Loss and Recapture of Galveston, 1862–1863," *Southwestern Historical Quarterly,* 51 (October 1947), 109–130.

Dale, Edward Everett. *The Range Cattle Industry: Ranching on the Great Plains from 1865 to 1925.* Norman: University of Oklahoma Press, 1960.

De Bow, James D. B. *Statistical View of the United States: Being a Compendium of the Seventh Census.* Washington, D.C.: Beverly Tucker, Senate Printer, 1854.

————, ed. "Commerce of Galveston," *De Bow's Review: Industrial Resources, Statistics . . .* 29 (December 1860), 783.

————, ed. "Commerce of Houston, Texas, September 1st, 1860," *De Bow's Review: Industrial Resources, Statistics . . .* 29 (December 1860), 529–530.

————, ed. "Education in Texas," *De Bow's Review: Industrial Resources, Statistics . . .* 19 (December 1855), 695–696.

————, ed. "Growth of Galveston, Texas," *De Bow's Review: Industrial Resources, Statistics . . .* 23 (December 1857), 554–555.

De Cordova, Jacob. *Texas: Her Resources and Her Public Men.* Philadelphia: E. Crozet, 1858.

Delaney, Robert W. "Matamoros, Port for Texas during the Civil War," *Southwestern Historical Quarterly,* 58 (April 1955), 473–487.

De Lono, A. *Galveston Directory for 1856–1857.* Galveston: Printed at the News Book and Job Office, 1856.

Dewees, William B. *Letters from an Early Settler of Texas.* Compiled by Cara Cardelle (pseud.) Louisville: Morton and Griswold, 1852.

Dictionary of American Biography. 20 vols. Ed. Dumas Malone and Allen Johnson. New York: Charles Scribner's Sons, 1928–1936.

Dillon, Charles H. "The Arrival of the Telegraph in Texas," *Southwestern Historical Quarterly,* 69 (October 1960), 200–211.

Domenech, Emanuel H. D. *Journal d'un Missionnaire au Texas et au Mexique, 1846–1852.* Paris: Librarie de Gaume Frères, 1857.

Dresel, Gustav. *Gustav Dresel's Houston Journal: Adventures in North America and Texas, 1837–1841.* Trans. and ed. Max Freund. Austin: University of Texas Press, 1954.

Dugas, Vera Lea. "Texas Industry, 1860–1880," *Southwestern Historical Quarterly,* 59 (October 1955), 151–183.

Dyer, Joseph O. *The Early History of Galveston.* Galveston: Oscar Springer, 1916.

——— *Galveston in Early Days.* Galveston: By the author, 1889.

Eby, Frederick. *Education in Texas: Source Materials.* University of Texas Bulletin, no. 1824. Austin: University of Texas, 1921.

Farrar, R. M. *The Story of Buffalo Bayou and the Houston Ship Channel.* Houston: Chamber of Commerce of Houston, 1926.

Fisher, Orceneth. *Sketches of Texas in 1840; Designed to Answer, in a Brief Way, the Numerous Enquiries Respecting the New Republic . . .* Springfield, Ill.: Walters and Weber, Printers, 1841.

Fletcher, Edward G. *The Beginnings of the Professional Theatre in Texas.* University of Texas Bulletin, no. 3621. Austin: University of Texas, 1936.

Fornell, Earl W. "The Abduction of Free Negroes and Slaves in Texas," *Southwestern Historical Quarterly,* 60 (January 1957), 369–380.

——— *The Galveston Era: The Texas Crescent on the Eve of Secession.* Austin: University of Texas Press, 1961.

Frantz, Joe B. *Gail Borden: Dairyman to a Nation.* Norman: University of Oklahoma Press, 1951.

Fremantle, Sir James Arthur Lyon. *The Fremantle Diary: Being the Journal of Lieutenant Colonel James Arthur Lyon Fremantle, Coldstream Guards, on His Three Months in the Southern States.* Ed. Walter Lord. Boston: Little, Brown and Company, 1954.

Friend, Llerena. "Additional Items for the Winkler Check List of

Texas Imprints, 1846–1860," *Southwestern Historical Quarterly*, 65 (July 1961), 101–107.

—— *Sam Houston: The Great Designer*. Austin: University of Texas Press, 1954.

—— "The Texan of 1860," *Southwestern Historical Quarterly*, 62 (July 1958), 1–17.

Gage, Larry Jay. "The City of Austin on the Eve of the Civil War," *Southwestern Historical Quarterly*, 63 (January 1960), 428–438.

Gallegly, Joseph. *Footlights on the Border: The Galveston and Houston Stage Before 1900*. The Hague: Mouton and Company, 1962.

Galveston Historical Society. *Historic Galveston Homes*. Galveston: By the Society, 1951.

Gambrell, Herbert P. *Anson Jones: The Last President of Texas*. Garden City, New York: Doubleday, 1948.

—— *Mirabeau Buonaparte Lamar: Troubadour and Crusader*. Dallas: Southwest Press, 1934.

Gammel, H. P. N., ed. *The Laws of Texas, 1822–1897*. 10 vols. Austin: Gammel Book Company, 1898.

Garrison, George P., ed. *Diplomatic Correspondence of the Republic of Texas*. 3 vols. Washington: Government Printing Office, 1908–1911.

Graham, Samuel B., ed. *Galveston Community Book: A Historical and Biographical Record of Galveston and Galveston County*. Galveston: Arthur H. Cawston, 1945.

Gregg, Josiah. *Commerce of the Prairies*. Ed. Max L. Moorhead. Norman: University of Oklahoma Press, 1954.

—— *Diary and Letters of Josiah Gregg: Southwestern Enterprises, 1840–1847*. Ed. Maurice Garland Fulton. Norman: University of Oklahoma Press, 1941.

Griffin, S. C. *History of Galveston, Texas. Narrative and Biographical*. Galveston: Arthur H. Cawston, 1931.

Haines, Francis. "The Northward Spread of Horses Among the Plains Indians," *American Anthropologist*, 40 (July-September 1938), 429–437.

Handy, Mary Olivia. *History of Fort Sam Houston*. San Antonio: Naylor Company, 1951.

Harris, August W. *Minor and Major Mansions in Early Austin*. Austin: By the author, 1955.

—— *Minor and Major Mansions & Their Companions in Early Austin: A Sequel.* Austin: By the author, 1958.

Harwood, Frances. "Colonel Amasa Turner's Reminiscences of Galveston," *Quarterly of the Texas State Historical Association,* 3 (July 1899), 44–48.

Hatcher, Mattie A. *The Opening of Texas to Foreign Settlement, 1801–1821.* Bulletin of the University of Texas, no. 2714. Austin: University of Texas, 1927.

Havins, T. R. "Texas Fever," *Southwestern Historical Quarterly,* 52 (July 1948), 147–162.

L'Héritier, Louis F. *Le Champ-d'Asile; Tableau topographique et historique du Texas, contenant des détails sur le sol, le climat et les productions de cette contrée; des documens authentiques sur l'organization de la colonie des réfugiés français; des notices sur ses principaux fondateurs; des extraits de leurs proclamations et autres actes publics: suivi de lettres éscrites par des colons à quelques-uns de leurs compatriotes.* Paris: L'advocat, 1819.

Heusinger, Edward W. *A Chronology of Events in San Antonio; Being a Concise History of the City, Year by Year, from the Beginning of Its Establishment to the End of the First Half of the Twentieth Century.* San Antonio: Standard Printing Company, 1951.

Historical Sketch of the First Baptist Church, of Galveston, Texas. Organized January 30, 1840. Galveston: News Steam Job Press, 1871.

Hogan, William R. "Pamela Mann: Texas Frontierswoman," *Southwest Review,* 20 (Summer 1935), 360–370.

——*The Texas Republic: A Social and Economic History.* Norman: University of Oklahoma Press, 1946.

Holden, William C. *Alkali Trails: Or, Social and Economic Movements of the Texas Frontier, 1846–1900.* Dallas: Southwest Press, 1930.

Holley, Mary Austin. *Letters of an Early American Traveller: Mary Austin Holley, Her Life and Her Works, 1784–1846.* Ed. Mattie Austin Hatcher. Dallas: Southwest Press, 1933.

Hooton, Charles. *St. Louis' Isle or Texiana: With Additional Observations Made in the United States and in Canada.* London: Simmonds and Ward, 1847.

Hoovestol, Paeder Joel. "Galveston in the Civil War." Unpub. Master's thesis, University of Houston, 1950.

Houston, Sam. *The Writings of Sam Houston, 1813–1863.* 8 vols. Ed. Amelia W. Williams and Eugene C. Barker. Austin: University of Texas Press, 1938–1943.

Houstoun, Matilda C. *Texas and the Gulf of Mexico: Or Yachting in the New World.* 2 vols. London: John Murray, 1844.

Hunt, Richard S., and Jesse F. Randel. *Guide to the Republic of Texas; Consisting of a Brief Outline of the History of its Settlement.* New York: J. H. Colton, 1839.

Irby, James A. "Confederate Austin." Unpub. Master's thesis, University of Texas, 1953.

Jacks, L. V. *Claude Debois: Bishop of Galveston.* St. Louis: B. Harder Book Company, 1946.

James, Marquis. *The Raven: A Biography of Sam Houston.* Indianapolis: Bobbs-Merrill, 1929.

James, Vinton Lee. *Frontier and Pioneer Recollections of Early Days in San Antonio and West Texas.* San Antonio: Artes Graficas, 1938.

Jefferson, Joseph. *The Autobiography of Joseph Jefferson.* New York: Century Company, 1890.

Johnson, Elmer H. *The Basis of the Commercial and Industrial Development of Texas: A Study of the Regional Development of Texas Resources.* Bulletin of the University of Texas, no. 3309. Austin: University of Texas, 1933.

✓ Johnson, Frank W. *A History of Texas and Texans,* 5 vols. Ed. Eugene C. Barker and E. W. Winkler. Chicago: American Historical Society, 1914.

Jones, Anson. *Memoranda and Official Correspondence Relating to the Republic of Texas, Its History and Annexation.* New York: D. Appleton and Company, 1859.

Kendall, George W. *Narrative of the Texan Santa Fé Expedition; Comprising a Description of a Tour Through Texas . . .* New York: Harper & Brothers, 1844.

Kennedy, Joseph C. G. *Agriculture of the United States in 1860; Compiled from the Original Returns of the Eighth Census under the Direction of the Secretary of the Interior.* Washington: Government Printing Office, 1864.

—— *Population of the United States in 1860; Compiled from the Original Returns of the Eighth Census under the Direction of the Secretary of the Interior.* Washington: Government Printing Office, 1864.

Kennedy, William. *Texas: Its Geography, Natural History, and Topography.* New York: Benjamin and Young, 1844.

———— *Texas: The Rise, Progress, and Prospects of the Republic of Texas.* 2 vols. London: R. Hastings, 1841.

Ker, Henry. *Travels Through the Western Interior of the United States from the Year 1808 up to the Year 1816, with a Particular Description of a Great Part of Mexico or New-Spain.* Elizabethtown, N.J.: By the author, 1816.

King, Dick. *Ghost Towns of Texas.* San Antonio: Naylor Company, 1953.

Konwiser, Harry M. *Texas Republic Postal System.* New York: Harry L. Lindquist, 1933.

Lamar, Mirabeau B. *The Papers of Mirabeau Buonaparte Lamar.* 6 vols. Ed. Charles A. Gulick, Jr. *et al.* Austin: A. C. Baldwin and Sons, 1920–1928.

Laws Passed by the Second Legislature of the State of Texas. Vol. II. Houston: Telegraph, State Printers, 1848.

Le Clerc, Frédéric. *Le Texas et sa révolution.* Paris: Imprimerie de H. Feurnier et Cᵉ, 1840.

Looscan, Adele B. "Harris County, 1822–1845," *Southwestern Historical Quarterly,* 18 (October 1914), 195–207; 18 (January 1915), 261–286; 19 (July 1915), 37–64.

Lozano, Rubén Rendón. *Viva Tejas: The Story of the Mexican-born Patriots of the Republic of Texas.* San Antonio: Southern Literary Institute, 1936.

Lubbock, Francis R. *Six Decades in Texas: Or Memoirs of Francis Richard Lubbock, Governor of Texas in Wartime, 1861–63. A Personal Experience in Business, War, and Politics.* Ed. C. W. Raines. Austin: Ben C. Jones and Company, 1900.

Lundy, Benjamin. *The Life, Travels, and Opinions of Benjamin Lundy, Including his Journeys to Texas and Mexico; With a Sketch of Contemporary Events, and a Notice of the Revolution in Hayti.* Philadelphia: William D. Parish, 1847.

Mahan, Alfred T. *The Gulf and Inland Waters.* Vol. III of *The Navy in the Civil War.* New York: Charles Scribner's Sons, 1883.

Maverick, Mary A. *Memoirs of Mary A. Maverick.* Ed. Rena Maverick Green. San Antonio: Standard Printing Company, 1921

Maverick, Samuel. *Samuel Maverick, Texan: 1803–1870; A Collection of Letters, Journals, and Memoirs.* Ed. Rena Maverick Green. San Antonio: Privately printed, 1952.

McCalla, William L. *Adventures in Texas, Chiefly in the Spring and Summer of 1840* . . . Philadelphia: By the author, 1841.

McClintock, William A., ed. "Journal of a Trip through Texas and Northern Mexico in 1846–1847," *Southwestern Historical Quarterly,* 34 (October 1930), 141–158.

McCoy, Joseph G. *Historic Sketches of the Cattle Trade of the West and Southwest.* Southwest Historical Series, vol. VIII. Ed. Ralph P. Bieber. Glendale, California: Arthur H. Clark Company, 1940.

McKay, S. S. "Texas and the Southern Pacific Railroad, 1848–1860," *Southwestern Historical Quarterly,* 35 (July 1931), 1–27.

Mease, James. "Notice sur le Texas," *Bulletin de la Société de Géographie,* 8 (1827), 2–13.

Merrill, James M. *The Rebel Shore: The Story of Union Sea Power in the Civil War.* Boston: Little, Brown and Company, 1957.

Miller, Edmund Thornton. *A Financial History of Texas.* Bulletin of the University of Texas, no. 37. Austin: The University of Texas, 1916.

Moore, Francis, Jr. *Map and Description of Texas Containing Sketches of Its History, Geology, Geography and Statistics* . . . Philadelphia: H. Tanner Jr., 1840.

Morgan, William M. *Trinity Protestant Episcopal Church of Galveston, 1841–1953: A Memorial History.* Houston: Anson Jones Press, 1954.

Muir, Andrew Forest. "The Destiny of Buffalo Bayou," *Southwestern Historical Quarterly,* 47 (October 1943), 91–106.

———— "The Free Negro in Harris County, Texas," *Southwestern Historical Quarterly,* 46 (January 1943), 214–238.

———— "Railroads Come to Houston, 1857–1861," *Southwestern Historical Quarterly,* 64 (July 1960), 42–63.

———— "Railroad Enterprise in Texas, 1836–1841," *Southwestern Historical Quarterly,* 47 (April 1944), 339–370.

———— "William Marsh Rice, Houstonian," *East Texas Historical Journal,* 2 (February 1964), 32–35.

Newel, Chester. *History of the Revolution in Texas, Particularly of the War of 1835 & '36* . . . New York: Wiley and Putnam, 1838.

Newton, Lewis W., and Herbert P. Gambrell. *A Social and Political History of Texas.* Dallas: Southwest Press, 1932.

Nichols, Ruth G. "Samuel May Williams," *Southwestern Historical Quarterly,* 56 (October 1952), 189–210.

Nixon, Patrick Ireland. *A Century of Medicine in San Antonio: The Story of Medicine in Bejar County, Texas.* San Antonio: By the author, 1936.

———— *A History of the Texas Medical Association, 1853–1953.* Austin: University of Texas Press, 1953.

North, Alfred Thomas. *Five Years in Texas; Or What You Did Not Hear during the War from January 1861 to January 1866. A Narrative of His Travels, Experiences, and Observations, in Texas and Mexico.* Cincinnati: Elm Street Printing Co., 1871.

Nunn, William C. *Texas Under the Carpetbaggers.* Austin: University of Texas Press, 1962.

Oates, Stephen B. "Recruiting Confederate Cavalry in Texas," *Southwestern Historical Quarterly,* 64 (April 1961), 463–477.

Oberste, William H. *Texas Irish Empresarios and Their Colonies: Power & Hewetson, McMullen & McGloin. Refugio-San Patricio.* Austin: Von Boeckmann-Jones, 1953.

Odell, Arabella Gertrude. "Reopening the African Slave Trade in Texas." Unpub. Master's thesis, University of Texas, 1946.

Olmsted, Frederick Law. *A Journey Through Texas; or, A Saddle-Trip on the Southwestern Frontier.* New York: Dix, Edwards & Company, 1857.

Page, Frederick B. *Prairiedom: Rambles and Scrambles in Texas or New Estrémadura.* New York: Paine and Burgess, 1846.

Pagés, Pierre M. F. *Travels Round the World in the Years 1767, 1768, 1769, 1770, 1771.* 3 vols. London: J. Murray, 1791–1792.

Parker, Amos A. *Trip to the West and Texas. Comprising a Journey of Eight Thousand Miles, Through New-York, Michigan, Illinois, Missouri, Louisiana and Texas, in the Autumn and Winter of 1834–5.* Boston: Benjamin B. Mussey, 1836.

Paxton, Philip [pseud. for Samuel A. Hammett]. *A Stray Yankee in Texas.* New York: Redfield and Company, 1853.

Peareson, P. E. "Reminiscences of Judge Edwin Waller," *Quarterly of the Texas State Historical Association,* 4 (July 1900) 33–53.

Peyton, Green [pseud. for Green Pevton Wertenbaker]. *San Antonio, City in the Sun.* New York: McGraw-Hill, 1946.

Phelan, Macum. *A History of Early Methodism in Texas, 1817–1866.* Nashville: Cokesbury Press, 1924.

Pike, Zebulon M. *An Account of Expeditions to the Sources of the Mississippi and Through the Western Parts of Louisiana . . .* Philadelphia: C. and A. Conrad, 1810.

Potts, Charles S. *Railroad Transportation in Texas.* Bulletin of the University of Texas, no. 119. Humanistic Series, no. 7. Austin: University of Texas, 1909.

Ramsdell, Charles William. *Reconstruction in Texas.* Studies in History, Economics and Public Law, vol. XXXVI, no. 1. Edited by the Faculty of Political Science of Columbia University. New York: Columbia University, 1910.

Rankin, Melinda. *Texas in 1850.* Boston: Damrell and Moore, 1850.

Ransom, Harry. "A Renaissance Gentleman in Texas: Notes on the Life and Library of Svante Palm," *Southwestern Historical Quarterly,* 53 (January 1950), 225–238.

Red, William S. *A History of the Presbyterian Church in Texas.* Austin: Steck Company, 1936.

Reed, St. Clair Griffin. *A History of the Texas Railroads and of Transportation Conditions under Spain and Mexico, and the Republic and the State.* Houston: St. Clair Publishing Company, 1941.

Reid, John C. *Reid's Tramp; or, A Journal of the Incidents of Ten Months Travel Through Texas, New Mexico, Arizona, Sonora, and California . . .* Selma, Alabama: John Hardy, 1858.

Report of the Commissioner of Patents, Agriculture, 1850 to 1860. Washington: Government Printing Office, 1851–1861.

Rice, Bernardine. "San Antonio: Its Early Beginnings and Its Development Under the Republic." Unpub. Master's thesis, University of Texas, 1941.

Richardson, Rupert N. *The Comanche Barrier to South Plains Settlement: A Century and a Half of Savage Resistance to the Advancing White Frontier.* Glendale, Calif.: Arthur H. Clark Company, 1933.

——— *Texas: The Lone Star State.* Englewood Cliffs, N.J.: Prentice Hall, 1958.

Richardson, Willard, *et al.,* eds. *Galveston Directory, 1859–60; With a Brief History of the Island, Prior to the Foundation of the City.* Galveston: Galveston News Book and Job Office, 1859.

——— *The Texas Almanac for 1858* . . . Galveston: Richardson and Company, 1857.

——— *The Texas Almanac for 1860* . . . Galveston: Richardson and Company, 1859–1860.

Riegel, Robert E. "Trans-Mississippi Railroads during the Fifties," *Mississippi Valley Historical Review,* 10 (September 1923), 153–172.

Roemer, Ferdinand. *Texas; With Particular Reference to German Immigration and the Physical Appearance of the Country.* Trans. Oswald Mueller. San Antonio: Standard Printing Company, 1935.

Rosenquist, Carl M., and Harry E. Moore. "The Bases of Urbanism in Texas," *Southwestern Social Science Quarterly,* 14 (September 1933), 109–119.

Sánchez, José María. *Viaje á Texas en 1828–1829; Diario del teniente D. José María Sánchez, Miembro de la Comisíon de Límites.* Mexico City: Papeles Históricos Mexicanos, 1939.

Santleben, August. *A Texas Pioneer: Early Staging and Overland Freighting Days on the Frontiers of Texas and Mexico.* Ed. I. D. Affleck. New York: Neale Publishing Company, 1910.

Savardan, Augustin. *Un Naufrage au Texas; Observations et impressions rescueillies pendant deux ans et demi au Texas à travers les États-Unis d'Amérique.* Paris: Garnier Frères, 1858.

Sayles, John, and Henry Sayles, compilers. *Early Laws of Texas; General Laws from 1836 to 1879* . . . St. Louis: Gilbert Book Company, 1891.

Schmidt, C. F. "Viktor Frederick Bracht: A Texas Pioneer," *Southwestern Historical Quarterly,* 35 (April 1932), 279–289.

Schmitz, Joseph W. *Thus They Lived: Social Life in the Republic of Texas.* San Antonio: Naylor Company, 1935.

Schoen, Harold. "The Free Negro in the Republic of Texas," *Southwestern Historical Quarterly,* 39 (April 1936), 292–308; 40 (October 1936), 85–113; 40 (January 1937), 169–199; 40 (April 1937), 267–289; 41 (July 1937), 83–108.

Sheridan, Francis C. *Galveston Island, or A Few Months Off the Coast of Texas: The Journal of Francis C. Sheridan, 1839–1840.* Ed. Willis W. Pratt. Austin: University of Texas Press, 1954.

Siegel, Stanley. *A Political History of the Texas Republic, 1836–1845.* Austin: University of Texas Press, 1956.

Simonds, Frederic William. *The Geography of Texas, Physical and Political*. New York: Ginn and Company, 1905.

Sitterson, Joseph Carlyle. *Sugar Country: The Cane Sugar Industry in the South, 1753–1950*. Lexington: University of Kentucky Press, 1953.

Smith, Ashbel. *An Account of the Yellow Fever Which Appeared in the City of Galveston, Republic of Texas, in the Autumn of 1839, with Cases and Dissections*. Galveston: Hamilton Stuart, 1839.

Smith, Edward. *Account of a Journey Through North-Eastern Texas, Undertaken in 1849, for the Purposes of Emigration* . . . London: Hamilton, Adams, and Company, 1849.

Smyrl, Frank H. "Unionism in Texas, 1856–1861," *Southwestern Historical Quarterly*, 68 (October 1964), 172–295.

Solms-Braunfels, Carl. *Texas, 1844–1845*. Trans. unknown. Houston: Anson Jones Press, 1936.

Speiser, Adel. "The Story of the Theater in San Antonio." Unpub. Master's thesis, St. Mary's University, San Antonio, 1948.

Spell, Lota M., ed. and trans. "The Grant and First Survey of the City of San Antonio," *Southwestern Historical Quarterly*, 66 (July 1962), 73–89.

——— "Music in Texas," *Quarterly Journal of Studies in Civil War History*, 4 (September 1958), 301–306.

Spratt, John S. *The Road to Spindletop: Economic Change in Texas, 1875–1901*. Dallas: Southern Methodist University Press, 1955.

A Statement Respecting the Necessity and Advantages to the Commercial and Agricultural Interests of Texas of a Ship Channel from the Outer Galveston Bar to the City of Houston, the Head of Tide Water in Buffalo Bayou. Houston: A. C. Gray and Company, 1870.

Stephens, A. Ray, ed. "Letter from the Texas Secession Convention, 1861: Willard Richardson to George Ware Fulton," *Southwestern Historical Quarterly*, 65 (January 1962), 394–396.

Stiff, Edward. *A New History of Texas* . . . Cincinnati: George Conclin, 1847.

Streeter, Thomas W. *Bibliography of Texas, 1795–1845*. Vol. I: *Texas Imprints*. Cambridge: Harvard University Press, 1955.

Stuart, Ben C. "Hamilton Stuart: Pioneer Editor," *Southwestern Historical Quarterly*, 21 (April 1918), 384.

Suhler, Samuel A. "Significant Questions Relating to the History of Austin, Texas, to 1900." Unpub. diss., University of Texas, 1966.

Terrell, Alexander W. "The City of Austin from 1839 to 1865," *Quarterly of the Texas State Historical Association*, 14 (October 1910), 113-128.

Texas in 1840; Or the Emigrants' Guide to the New Republic . . . New York: William W. Allen, 1840.

Texas in 1837: An Anonymous, Contemporary Narrative. Ed. Andrew Forest Muir. Austin: University of Texas Press, 1958.

Texas Library and Historical Commission. *Journal of the Secession Convention of Texas, 1861.* Ed. Ernest W. Winkler. Austin: Austin Printing Company, 1912.

Texas Newspapers, 1813-1939: A Union List of Newspaper Files Available in Offices of Publishers, Libraries, and a Number of Private Collections. Prepared by Historical Records Survey Program, Division of Professional and Service Projects, Works Projects Administration of Texas. Works Projects Administration. Houston: San Jacinto Museum of History Association, 1941.

Tiling, Moritz P. G. *History of the German Element in Texas from 1820 to 1850 and Historical Sketches of the German Texas Singers' League and Houston Turnverein from 1853 to 1913.* Houston: By the author, 1913.

To the Voters of the State of Texas: Bid for the Location of the Seat of Government at Austin by the Citizens of Austin. Austin: William H. Cushney, 1850.

Vielé, Teresa G. *Following the Drum: A Glimpse of Frontier Life.* New York: Rudd and Carleton, 1858.

A Visit to Texas; Being the Journal of a Traveller Through Those Parts Most Interesting to American Settlers. With descriptions of scenery, habits . . . Mobile: Woodruff, Fiske, and McGuin, 1836.

Walker, Francis A. *The Statistics of the Population of the United States: Ninth Census.* Vol. I. Washington: Government Printing Office, 1872.

—————— *The Statistics of the Wealth and Industry of the United States: Ninth Census.* Vol. III. Washington: Government Printing Office, 1872.

Wall, E. L., ed. *The Port Situation at Galveston.* Galveston News Company, 1928.

Waugh, Julia Nott. *Castro-Ville and Henry Castro, Empresario*. San Antonio: Standard Printing Co., 1934.

Webb, Walter P., *et al.*, eds. *The Handbook of Texas*. 2 vols. Austin: Texas State Historical Association, 1952.

Western Texas, the Australia of America; or, The place to live. Cincinnati: E. Mendenhall, 1860.

Wharton, Clarence R. *Texas Under Many Flags*. 5 vols. Chicago: American Historical Society, 1930.

Winkler, Ernest W., ed. *Check List of Texas Imprints, 1846–1860*. Austin: Texas State Historical Association, 1949.

——, ed. *Platforms of Political Parties of Texas*. Bulletin of the University of Texas, no. 53. Austin: University of Texas, 1916.

—— and Llerena Friend, eds. *Check List of Texas Imprints, 1861–1876*. Austin: Texas State Historical Association, 1949.

Woodman, David, Jr. *Guide to Texas Emigrants*. Boston: M. Hawes, 1835.

Wooster, Ralph A. "Foreigners in the Principal Towns of Ante-Bellum Texas," *Southwestern Historical Quarterly*, 66 (October 1962), 208–220.

——, compiler. "Notes on Texas' Largest Slaveholders, 1860," *Southwestern Historical Quarterly*, 65 (July 1961), 72–79.

Wooten, Dudley G., ed. *A Comprehensive History of Texas 1685 to 1897*. 2 vols. Dallas: William G. Scarff, 1898.

Works Projects Administration. *Houston: A History and Guide*. Compiled by workers of the Writers' Program of the Works Projects Administration. Sponsored by the Harris County Historical Society. American Guide Series. Houston: Anson Jones Press, 1942.

—— *San Antonio: An Authoritative Guide to the City and Its Environs*. Compiled and written by the Federal Writers' Project of the Works Projects Administration in the State of Texas; San Antonio Conservation Society, cooperating sponsor. American Guide Series. San Antonio: Clegg Company, 1938.

—— *Texas: A Guide to the Lone Star State*. Compiled by workers of the Writers' Program of the Works Projects Administration in the State of Texas. American Guide Series. New York: Hastings House, 1940.

Yoakum, Henderson K. *History of Texas from Its First Settlement in 1685 to Its Annexation to the United States in 1846.* 2 vols. New York: Redfield, 1855.

Young, Samuel O. *A Thumb-Nail History of the City of Houston, from Its founding in 1836 to the Year 1912.* Houston: Rein and Sons, 1912.

NOTES

CHAPTER I   THE YOUNG TOWNS OF A NEW REPUBLIC

1. Ephriam D. Adams, ed., "Correspondence from the British Archives Concerning Texas, 1837–1846," *Quarterly of the Texas State
Historical Association,* 15 (January 1912), 233.

2. John J. Audubon, *The Life of John James Audubon, the Naturalist,* ed. Lucy Audubon (New York: G. P. Putnam's Sons, 1901),
pp. 408–409.

3. Adams, ed., "Correspondence from the British Archives," p. 233.

4. Alexander W. Terrell, "The City of Austin from 1839 to 1865,"
Quarterly of the Texas State Historical Association, 14 (October 1910),
114. Even if Lamar did not use these exact words, they are an accurate
reflection of his grandiose vision of a future Republic of Texas extending to the Pacific.

5. *Ibid.,* pp. 124–125, 127.

6. San Antonio, Office of the City Secretary, Journal of the City
Council, A: June 1837–January 1849, September 4, 1837 (no pagination); December 27, 1847, p. 130.

7. Unless specifically cited, information in this section may be found
in Eugene C. Barker, ed., *Readings in Texas History for High Schools
and Colleges* (Dallas: Southwest Press, 1929); Herbert Eugene
Bolton, ed., *Spanish Exploration in the Southwest, 1542–1706* (New
York: Barnes & Noble, 1963); John Henry Brown, *History of Texas
from 1685 to 1892,* 2 vols. (St. Louis: L. E. Daniell, Publisher, 1892);
Rupert N. Richardson, *Texas: The Lone Star State* (Englewood Cliffs,

N. J.: Prentice-Hall, 1958); Clarence R. Wharton, *Texas under Many Flags*, 5 vols. (New York: American Historical Society, 1930).

8. Francis Haines, "The Northward Spread of Horses Among the Plains Indians," *American Anthropologist*, 40 (July–September 1938), 420–438; Rupert N. Richardson, *The Comanche Barrier to South Plains Settlement* (Glendale, Calif.: Arthur H. Clark Company, 1933).

9. Frederick C. Chabot, *San Antonio and Its Beginnings, 1691–1731* (San Antonio: Naylor Printing Company, 1931), p. 7.

10. Carlos E. Castañeda, *Our Catholic Heritage in Texas, 1519–1936*, vol. III: *The Mission Era: The Missions at Work, 1731–1761* (Austin: Von Boeckmann-Jones Co., 1938), p. 90.

11. Pierre P. F. Pagés, *Travels Round the World in the Years 1767, 1768, 1769, 1770, 1771*, translator unknown (London: J. Murray, 1791), I, 91–92, 96–97; Juan Agustín de Morfi, "Memorias de la Provincia de Texas," Libro IV, photostat at the University of Texas Archives, from original in Library of Congress, no pagination; Chabot, *San Antonio*, p. 9.

12. Chabot, *San Antonio*, p. 8.

13. *Ibid.*, p. 7 Castañeda, *Catholic Heritage*, III, 93; William Corner, ed., *San Antonio de Bexar: A Guide and History* (San Antonio: Bainbridge and Corner, 1890), pp. 43–44.

14. Zebulon M. Pike, *An Account of Expeditions to the Sources of the Mississippi, and Through the Western Parts of Louisiana, . . .* (Philadelphia: C. & A. Conrad, 1810), pp. 265–269.

15. Walter P. Webb et al., eds., *The Handbook of Texas* (Austin: Texas State Historical Association, 1952), I, 328.

16. Castañeda, *Catholic Heritage*, vol. VI: *Transition Period: The Fight for Freedom, 1810–1836*, pp. 186–187.

17. H. P. N. Gammel, ed., *The Laws of Texas, 1822–1897* (Austin: Gammel Book Company, 1898), I, 32.

18. José María Sánchez, *Viaje á Texas en 1828–29* (Mexico: Papeles Historicos Mexicanos, 1939), p. 27; Lester G. Bugbee, "The Texas Frontier, 1820–1825," *Publications of the Southern History Association*, 4 (1900) 118–119; William B. Dewees, *Letters from an Early Settler of Texas* (Louisville: Morton & Griswold, 1852), pp. 35–36.

19. Dewees, *Letters*, pp. 34–35; Sánchez, *Viaje á Texas*, p. 29.

20. Benjamin Lundy, *The Life, Travels, and Opinions of Benjamin Lundy, Including His Journals to Texas and Mexico; with a Sketch of Contemporary Events, and a Notice of the Revolution in Hayti*

(Philadelphia: William D. Parrish, 1847), pp. 48, 124; Juan N. Almonte, *Noticia Estadística sobre Texas* (Mexico City: Ignacio Cumplido, 1835), pp. 25, 40. Almonte was an important Mexican official, who later became Supreme Chief of Mexico. His report on Texas is considered to be the most reliable of the period.

21. Eugene C. Barker, *The Life of Stephen F. Austin, Founder of Texas, 1793–1836: A Chapter in the Westward Movement of the Anglo-American People* (Dallas: Cokesbury Press, 1925), pp. 37–38.

CHAPTER II THE INLAND SETTLEMENTS: AUSTIN AND SAN ANTONIO

1. Francis C. Sheridan, *Galveston Island or A Few Months Off the Coast of Texas. The Journal of Francis C. Sheridan, 1839–1840,* ed. Willis W. Pratt (Austin: University of Texas Press, 1954), p. 90.

2. Matilda C. Houstoun, *Texas and the Gulf of Mexico* (London: John Murray, 1844), I, 262, 307; II, 109.

3. Sheridan, *Galveston Island,* p. 95.

4. *Ibid.*

5. *Ibid.,* pp. 37, 47–48. See also Houstoun, *Texas and the Gulf of Mexico,* II, 107; Charles Hooton, *St. Louis' Isle or Texiana; With Additional Observations Made in the United States and in Canada* (London: Simmons and Ward, 1847), pp. 20–22.

6. Sheridan, *Galveston Island,* pp. 39–40.

7. Hooton, *St. Louis' Isle,* p. 10.

8. *Ibid.;* Houstoun, *Texas and the Gulf of Mexico,* I, 271.

9. William R. Hogan, *The Texas Republic* (Norman: The University of Oklahoma Press, 1946), pp. 11–12, 164, 191–217, 219–220.

10. *Ibid.,* p. 103; Ferdinand Roemer, *Texas; With Particular Reference to German Immigration and the Physical Appearance of the Country,* trans. Oswald Mueller (San Antonio: Standard Printing Company, 1935), p. 45; Webb, *Handbook.*

11. Henri Castro, founder of the colony, lost his fortune in the venture, which failed to achieve great success. The town of Castroville continues to exist with a population of about 1,800.

12. Sheridan, *Galveston Island,* p. 89.

13. Gammel, *Laws,* II, 325–327.

14. *Telegraph and Texas Register* (Houston), October 14, 1837; January 5, 1839; January 23, 1839; May 1, 1839.

15. *Telegraph and Texas Register*, January 23, 1839.

16. *City Gazette* (Austin), August 17, 1842.

17. Frank Brown, "Annals of Travis County and of the City of Austin from the Earliest Time to the Close of 1875," 12 vols., typescript, Austin Public Library, IX, 5–8.

18. William Bollaert, *William Bollaert's Texas*, ed. W. Eugene Hollon and Ruth Lapham Butler (Norman: University of Oklahoma Press, 1956), pp. 195–196, 198.

19. *City Gazette* (Austin), August 17, 1842; Brown, "Annals," XI, 5–8.

20. Executive Record Book, No. 40, pp. 169–170. Texas State Library, Archives Section.

21. Webb, *Handbook*, I, 64–65; Alexander W. Terrell, "City of Austin"; Brown, "Annals," IX, 42–44; Samuel A. Suhler, "Significant Questions Relating to the History of Austin, Texas, to 1900," unpub. diss., University of Texas, 1966, pp. 167–272.

22. P. E. Peareson, "Reminiscences of Judge Edwin Waller," *Quarterly of the Texas State Historical Association*, 4 (July 1900), 45–48; Mirabeau Buonaparte Lamar, *The Papers of Mirabeau Buonaparte Lamar*, Charles A. Gulick, Jr. *et al.*, eds., 6 vols. (Austin: A. C. Baldwin & Sons, 1920–1927), II, 587–588; Brown, "Annals," VI, 15.

23. Terrell, "City of Austin," p. 117; Brown, "Annals," VI. 15–17; *Telegraph and Texas Register* (Houston), October 9, 1839; Herbert P. Gambrell, *Mirabeau Buonaparte Lamar: Troubadour and Crusader* (Dallas: Southwest Press, 1934), p. 250; Peareson, "Reminiscences of Edwin Waller," p. 47.

24. William Kennedy, *Texas: The Rise, Progress and Prospects of the Republic of Texas*, 2 vols. (London: R. Hastings, 1841), II, 410–411.

25. Brown, "Annals," VII, 45; IX, 14–38; *City Gazette* (Austin), August 17, 1842.

26. *Texas in 1840; or the Emigrant's Guide to the New Republic* (New York: William W. Allen, 1840), p. 63.

27. *Texas Sentinel* (Austin), April 15, 1841; Kennedy, *Texas*, II, 411.

28. Brown, "Annals," V, 70; VII, 4; see also *Texas in 1840*.

29. Brown, "Annals," VI, 13–19, 21; VII, 38.

30. *Daily Bulletin* (Austin), November 27, 1841; December 27, 1841; *Texas Sentinel* (Austin), July 5, 1841.

31. *Texas Sentinel* (Austin), May 20, 1841.

32. Brown, "Annals," VII, 49, 63.

33. *Texas Sentinel* (Austin), February 18, 1841; *City Gazette* Austin," pp. 120–121.

34. Brown, "Annals," VII, 22–23; microfilmed selections of unpublished correspondence between Saligny and the French Ministry of Foreign Affairs were presented to the City of Austin in 1965 by the French ambassador to the United States.

35. Brown, "Annals," VIII, 7, 11; XII, 8; Terrell, "The City of Austin," pp. 120–121.

36. Brown, "Annals," VI, 28; VII, 5, 41, 59; VIII, 11, 30.

37. *Ibid.*, VII, 4, 66; XII, 9; Kennedy, *Texas*, II, 411.

38. *Texas Sentinel* (Austin), February 11, 1841.

39. Mary A. Maverick, *Memoirs: San Antonio's First American Woman*, ed. Rena Maverick Green (San Antonio: Standard Printing Company, 1921), p. 27.

40. Bollaert, *Texas*, p. 166; Richardson, *Comanche Barrier*, pp. 109–111.

41. Diary of Samuel A. Maverick, University of Texas Archives, Austin.

42. Frederic B. Page, *Prairiedom: Rambles and Scrambles in Texas or New Estrémadura* (New York: Paine and Burgess, 1846), 126–132.

43. Solms-Braunfels Papers, Library of Congress, Washington, D.C., XLIX, 153–156, cited in Rudolph L. Biesele, "Prince Solm's Trip to Texas, 1844–1845," *Southwestern Historical Quarterly*, 40 (July 1936), 10; J. W. Benedict, "Diary of a Campaign Against the Comanches," *ibid.*, 32 (April 1929), 304–305; Edward Stiff, *A New History of Texas* (Cincinnati: George Conclin, 1847), p. 29.

44. Roemer, *Texas*, pp. 119–120.

45. Solms-Braunfels Papers, XL, 10; see also Auguste Frételliére, "Adventures of a Castrovillian," included in Julia Nott Waugh, *Castro-Ville and Henry Castro, Empresario* (San Antonio: Standard Printing Co., 1934), pp. 91–92.

46. Kennedy, *Texas*, I, 74–75.

47. Roemer, *Texas*, p. 133.

48. Page, *Prairiedom*, p. 132.

49. Orceneth Fisher, *Sketches of Texas in 1840* (Springfield, Ill.:

Walters and Weber, Printers, 1841), p. 36; Frétellière, "Adventures," p. 91; Roemer, *Texas*, p. 120.

50. Solms-Braunfels Papers, XL, 10; Bollaert, *Texas*, p. 349.

51. "City of San Antonio, Journal of the City Council" (hereafter referred to as SA Journal City Council), A, 32.

52. *Ibid.*, A, 8, 43, 45, 47, 52, 80.

53. Frétellière, "Adventures," p. 93; see also Roemer, *Texas*, p. 121–123.

54. SA Journal City Council, A, 109; Roemer, *Texas*, p. 124; Scrapbook of Valentine Bennet, photostat in University of Texas Archives, Austin, and quoted in Bernadine Rice, "San Antonio: Its Early Beginnings and Its Development Under the Republic," unpub. Master's thesis, University of Texas, 1941, p. 99.

55. George W. Kendall, *Narrative of the Texan Santa Fé Expedition*, 2 vols. (New York: Harper & Brothers, 1844), I, 46–47.

56. Mary A. Maverick to Mrs. A. Adams, August 25, 1838, and February 21, 1841, Maverick Papers, University of Texas Archives, Austin; Mary A. Maverick, *Memoirs*, pp. 55–56; Frederick C. Chabot, *With the Makers of San Antonio* (San Antonio: Artes Graficas Press, 1937), pp. 304–316.

57. Roemer, *Texas*, pp. 124–125.

58. *Telegraph and Texas Register* (Houston), June 14, 1843.

59. Jack C. Butterfield, "The Free State of Bejar," Daughters of the Republic of Texas Library, San Antonio, p. 51c.

60. Bollaert, *Texas*, p. 231.

61. Roemer, *Texas*, pp. 130–131.

62. SA Journal City Council, A, 2–92, has been the source of information for the remainder of this chapter.

63. Solms-Braunfels Papers, XL, 10.

CHAPTER III   "THE GREAT EMPORIUMS": HOUSTON AND GALVESTON

1. *Telegraph and Texas Register* (Columbia, Texas), November 16, 1836.

2. Francis R. Lubbock, *Six Decades in Texas: or Memoirs of Francis Richard Lubbock*, ed. C. W. Raines (Austin: Ben C. Jones & Co., 1900), p. 46; *Texas in 1837: An Anonymous, Contemporary Narrative*, ed. Andrew Forest Muir (Austin: University of Texas Press, 1958),

p. 28; Gustav Dresel, *Gustav Dresel's Houston Journal: Adventures in North America and Texas, 1837–1841*, ed. Max Freund (Austin: University of Texas Press, 1954), p. 32.

3. Lubbock, *Six Decades*, p. 51.

4. Gammel, *Laws*, I, 1298–1299.

5. *Telegraph and Texas Register*, June 9, 1838; December 1, 1838; December 15, 1838; December 30, 1840; *Morning Star*, October 3, 1839; October 5, 1839; January 21, 1840; December 16, 1841; June 12, 1841. All newspapers cited in this chapter were published in Houston unless otherwise noted.

6. *Telegraph and Texas Register*, December 30, 1840; Gammel, *Laws*, I, pp. 1298–1299.

7. *Telegraph and Texas Register*, December 1, 1838; December 15, 1838; *Morning Star*, September 7, 1839; February 19, 1840; Minutes of the Houston City Council, A, 16, 42, 69.

8. *Telegraph and Texas Register*, January 26, 1843; February 1, 1843; *Weekly Times*, April 30, 1840; *Morning Star*, October 30, 1841; January 31, 1843.

9. Dresel, *Journal*, pp. 77–78; Lamar, *Papers*, III, 57; Diary of Milly R. Gray, Galveston Public Library.

10. *Telegraph and Texas Register*, August 11, 1841; March 27, 1839; December 1, 1838.

11. *Morning Star*, October 7, 1839; September 19, 1840; *Telegraph and Texas Register*, February 5, 1840.

12. *Telegraph and Texas Register*, October 30, 1839; January 25, 1843.

13. *Ibid.*, May 16, 1838; August 4, 1838.

14. *Ibid.*, February 5, 1840; Minutes, Houston City Council, A, 40, 45; Lamar, *Papers*, II, 339.

15. *Telegraph and Texas Register*, January 30, 1839; January 23, 1839; and Samuel Maverick, *Samuel Maverick, Texan: 1803–1870*, ed. Rena Maverick Green (San Antonio: Privately printed, 1952), pp. 81–82.

16. *Morning Star*, April 9, 1839; August 16, 1839; February 17, 1842.

17. *Ibid.*, December 24, 1839; May 15, 1841; April 27, 1841.

18. *Telegraph and Texas Register*, October 13, 1838; November 14, 1838; December 27, 1843.

19. *Ibid.*, July 14, 1841; June 22, 1842; *Morning Star*, October 12, 1843.

20. *Telegraph and Texas Register*, October 21, 1837; January 27, 1838; December 29, 1841.

21. *Ibid.*, November 30, 1843; May 1, 1844; *Morning Star*, January 23, 1841.

22. *Telegraph and Texas Register*, November 10, 1838; June 5, 1839; Minutes, Houston City Council, A, 17, 96; *Morning Star*, February 27, 1840; March 2, 1845; March 8, 1845.

23. *Telegraph and Texas Register*, February 3, 1838; June 10, 1840; *Morning Star*, April 22, 1840.

24. *Telegraph and Texas Register*, October 27, 1838; *Morning Star*, March 4, 1840; April 27, 1841.

25. *Telegraph and Texas Register*, January 12, 1838; May 5, 1838; November 14, 1838; December 1, 1838.

26. *Ibid.*, October 7, 1837; October 11, 1837; October 14, 1837; October 21, 1837; *Morning Star*, June 8, 1838; July 10, 1839; July 15, 1839; July 24, 1839; July 30, 1839.

27. *Morning Star*, June 18, 1839; December 26, 1840; November 16, 1841; December 14, 1841; *Telegraph and Texas Register*, June 19, 1839; November 6, 1844.

28. *Morning Star*, December 20, 1839.

29. Probate Records, Harris County, F, 14, 15, 21, 22; C, 26, 27; E, 221–222; Ashbel Smith, *An Account of the Yellow Fever which Appeared in the City of Galveston* (Galveston: Hamilton Stuart, 1839); Ashbel Smith, Papers, Journals, University of Texas Archives, Austin.

30. *Telegraph and Texas Register*, March 5, 1845; see also issue of December 2, 1837.

31. *Ibid.*, May 2, 1837; April 6, 1839; January 5, 1842; *Morning Star*, April 8, 1839; June 18, 1839; June 24, 1839.

32. *Telegraph and Texas Register*, May 9, 1837; May 30, 1837; October 21, 1837; February 13, 1839; *Morning Star*, June 15, 1840.

33. *Telegraph and Texas Register*, January 27, 1838; December 8, 1838; October 21, 1840; *Morning Star*, April 22, 1840; January 23, 1841; March 26, 1842; October 14, 1843; June 28, 1845; June 28, 1845.

34. Edward G. Fletcher, *The Beginnings of the Professional Theater in Texas*, University of Texas Bulletin, no. 3621 (Austin: University

of Texas, 1936), pp. 10–18; *Telegraph and Texas Register,* June 16, 1838; July 28, 1838; February 13, 1839; March 6, 1839; Probate Records Harris County, E, 517–518.

35. *Morning Star,* May 6, 1839.

36. *Ibid.,* June 9, 1838; June 23, 1838; Fletcher, *Professional Theater in Texas,* pp. 10–18.

37. Stiff, *A New History of Texas,* pp. 71–72.

38. *Ibid.,* pp. 80–81.

39. *Telegraph and Texas Register,* April 27, 1842; June 25, 1838; January 20, 1838; June 30, 1838; *Morning Star,* May 11, 1839.

40. *Telegraph and Texas Register,* February 20, 1839; June 24, 1840; March 2, 1842.

41. *Ibid.,* June 24, 1840; April 13, 1842; January 25, 1843; Herndon, "Diary of a Trip from Kentucky to Texas, 1837–1838," typescript, University of Texas Archives, Austin, p. 294.

42. *Telegraph and Texas Register,* July 8, 1837; *Morning Star,* October 5, 1839.

43. *Morning Star,* December 25, 1841.

44. Dresel, *Journal,* pp. 36, 39; *Telegraph and Texas Register,* February 20, 1839; December 18, 1839; April 13, 1842; January 10, 1844; May 1, 1839.

45. *Morning Star,* June 20, 1839; October 8, 1839; January 26, 1841; *National Intelligencer,* June 20, 1839.

46. Lamar, *Papers,* I, 562.

47. Eugene C. Barker and Amelia W. Williams, eds., *The Writings of Sam Houston, 1813–1863,* 8 vols. (Austin: University of Texas Press, 1938–1943), II, 190.

48. *Morning Star,* January 6, 1842.

49. Dresel, *Journal,* p. 37.

50. Philip Paxton [pseud. for Samuel A. Hammett], *A Stray Yankee in Texas* (New York: Redfield and Company, 1853), p. xiv.

51. *Telegraph and Texas Register,* October 27, 1837; Dresel, *Journal,* p. 99.

52. Dresel, *Journal,* pp. 37–38.

53. *Morning Star,* April 20, 1839; September 8, 1839; February 20, 1840; March 9, 1840; April 30, 1840; July 23, 1840; July 15, 1843.

54. *Telegraph and Texas Register,* December 22, 1838; November 11, 1837; December 8, 1838; *Morning Star,* October 15, 1839.

55. Barker and Williams, eds., *The Writings of Sam Houston; Tele-*

graph and Texas Register, May 5, 1838; September 29, 1838; *Morning Star*, June 15, 1840; *Texian Democrat* (Houston), January 20, 1844.

56. *Morning Star*, June 18, 1839.

57. J. M. Carroll, *A History of Texas Baptists* (Dallas: Baptist Standard Printing Company, 1923), pp. 150–151; *Telegraph and Texas Register*, December 16, 1837; *Morning Star*, July 6, 1839.

58. *Telegraph and Texas Register*, May 16, 1838; July 7, 1838; December 1, 1838.

59. Casteñeda, *Catholic Heritage*, vol. VII: *The Church in Texas since Independence, 1835–1950*, pp. 19–20; *Morning Star*, August 17, 1841.

60. *Morning Star*, July 21, 1842; July 9, 1844; *Telegraph and Texas Register*, March 8, 1843; October 15, 1845.

61. William Y. Allen, "Allen's Reminiscences of Texas, 1838–1842," ed. William S. Red, *Southwestern Historical Quarterly*, 18 (January 1915), 298: see also 17 (January 1914), 283–305.

62. Andrew Forest Muir, "Railroad Enterprise in Texas, 1836–1841," *Southwestern Historical Quarterly*, 47 (April 1944), 339–345.

63. See *Telegraph and Texas Register* issues between January 1, 1837 and January 1, 1842; also *Texas in 1837*, p. 34.

64. *Telegraph and Texas Register*, September 23, 1837; March 26, 1845; *Morning Star*, April 26, 1839; February 6, 1840.

65. Herndon, "Diary of a Trip," p. 283.

66. *Morning Star*, June 12, 1841; *Telegraph and Texas Register*, October 6, 1841; Adele B. Looscan, "Harris County, 1822-1845," *Southwestern Historical Quarterly*, 19 (July 1915), 43.

67. *Morning Star*, May 12, 1842; November 17, 1842; *Telegraph and Texas Register*, March 26, 1845.

68. G. W. Hayes, "Island and City of Galveston," typescript, Rosenberg Library, Galveston, p. 177.

69. Gammel, *Laws*, I, 1130–1131.

70. Joe B. Frantz, *Gail Borden: Dairyman to a Nation* (Norman: University of Oklahoma Press, 1951), p. 130.

71. *Ibid.*, pp. 136–137; *Texas in 1837*, pp. 8–10; Hayes, "Galveston," pp. 279–280.

72. S. C. Griffin, *History of Galveston, Texas* (Galveston: A. H. Cawston, 1931), p. 42; Smith, *An Account of the Yellow Fever*, p. 34.

73. William Kennedy, *Texas*, II, 407–408; *Texas in 1840*, pp. 17–18.

74. Hayes, "Galveston," p. 375.

75. Griffin, *History of Galveston, Texas*, p. 36.

76. Hayes, "Galveston," p. 369.

77. *Ibid.*, pp. 338–340; Ben C. Stuart, "Hamilton Stuart: Pioneer Editor," *Southwestern Historical Quarterly*, 21 (April 1918), 384; Griffin, *History of Galveston, Texas*, p. 35; Hayes, "Galveston," pp. 379–381; Gammel, *Laws*, II, 598–600.

78. Richard S. Hunt and Jesse F. Randel, *Guide to the Republic of Texas; Consisting of a Brief Outline of the History of Its Settlement* (New York: J. H. Colton, 1839), pp. 51–55; Matilda C. Houstoun, *Texas and the Gulf of Mexico*, I, 257–258; Emanuel H. D. Domenech, *Journal d'un missionnaire au Texas et au Mexique, 1846–1852* (Paris: Librarie de Gaume Frères, 1857), p. 25.

79. Griffin, *History of Galveston, Texas*, pp. 35–36; Frantz, *Borden*, p. 139.

80. Ben C. Stuart, "The City's Story," Rosenberg Library, Galveston, copied from an article in the *Galveston Daily News*, June 4, 1889; Griffin, *History of Galveston, Texas*, p. 26; Hayes, "Galveston," pp. 334–336.

81. Gammel, *Laws*, II, 411–412, 440–447; Hayes, "Galveston," pp. 401–411; Griffin, *History of Galveston, Texas*, p. 27.

82. Hayes, "Galveston," pp. 336–342, 357, 426–427.

83. Roemer, *Texas*, p. 43; Hooton, *St. Louis' Isle*, p. 11; Houstoun, *Texas*, II, 249.

84. Sheridan, *Galveston Island*, p. 49.

85. Hooton, *St. Louis' Isle*, pp. 38–39.

86. *Ibid.*, pp. 13–14; Hayes, "Galveston," p. 362.

87. Gammel, *Laws*, II, 1336; Griffin, *History of Galveston, Texas*, pp. 31–32; Hayes, "Galveston," pp. 476–477.

88. Hooton, *St. Louis' Isle*, p. 72.

89. Stuart, "History of Galveston"; Griffin, *History of Galveston, Texas*, p. 38.

90. Houstoun, *Texas*, I, 264–265.

91. Stuart, "History of Galveston."

92. Griffin, *History of Galveston, Texas*, pp. 38–39.

93. Houstoun, *Texas*, II, 110; Stuart, "History of Galveston"; C. F. Schmidt, "Viktor Frederick Bracht: A Texas Pioneer," *Southwestern Historical Quarterly*, 35 (April 1932), 281.

94. Sheridan, *Galveston Island,* pp. 34, 36, 49–50; Roemer, *Texas,* p. 48.

95. Ruth G. Nichols, "Samuel May Williams," *Southwestern Historical Quarterly,* 56 (October 1952), 204–206; Hayes, "Galveston," p. 398; Griffin, *History of Galveston, Texas,* p. 39.

96. Sheridan, *Galveston Island,* p. 46; Roemer, *Texas,* pp. 45–48; Hayes, "Galveston," pp. 470–471.

CHAPTER IV   OX-CARTS AND STEAM ENGINES

1. Frederick Law Olmsted, *A Journey Through Texas; or a Saddle-Trip on the Southwestern Frontier* (New York: Dix, Edwards & Co., 1857), p. 246.

2. St. Clair G. Reed, *A History of the Texas Railroads and of Transportation Conditions under Spain and Mexico and the Republic and the State* (Houston: St. Clair Publishing Co., 1941), pp. 41, 65–69.

3. *Ibid.,* pp. 43–45; Richardson, *Texas: The Lone Star State,* pp. 158–159.

4. *Telegraph and Texas Register* (Houston), May 2, 1855.

5. Willard Richardson *et al.,* eds., *Texas Almanac, 1860,* p. 145; Reed, *Railroads,* p. 47.

6. Reed, *Railroads,* p. 47.

7. *Ibid.,* pp. 47–48; Ira G. Clark, *Then Came the Railroads: The Century from Steam to Diesel in the Southwest* (Norman: University of Oklahoma Press, 1958), p. 9.

8. Webb, *Handbook,* II, 545; Olmsted, *A Journey Through Texas,* pp. 150–151.

9. Reed, *Railroads,* p. 676; *Telegraph and Texas Register,* December 3, 1852; July 22, December 9, 1853; May 19, 1858; Willard Richardson *et al.,* eds., *Galveston Directory for 1859–60* (Galveston: News Book and Job Office, 1859), p. 85.

10. *Texas Democrat* (Austin), March 11, 1846.

11. Reed, *Railroads,* p. 40.

12. *Ibid.,* p. 41; Charles S. Potts, *Railroad Transportation in Texas,* Bulletin of the University of Texas no. 119, Humanistic Series no. 7 (Austin: University of Texas, 1909), p. 10.

13. Jacob De Cordova, *Texas: Her Resources and Her Public Men* (Philadelphia: E. Crozet, 1858), p. 336; Viktor Bracht, *Texas in 1848*, trans. C. F. Schmidt (San Antonio: Naylor Printing Company, 1931), p. 58; *Galveston News, passim*.

14. Andrew Forest Muir, "The Destiny of Buffalo Bayou," *Southwestern Historical Quarterly*, 47 (October 1943), 96–97.

15. Roemer, *Texas*, pp. 44–45; Melinda Rankin, *Texas in 1850* (Boston: Damrell and Moore, 1850), pp. 155–157.

16. *Telegraph and Texas Register*, December 15, 1858.

17. *Galveston News*, October 14, 1906.

18. *Ibid.*, June 4, 1889; Earl W. Fornell, *The Galveston Era* (Austin: University of Texas Press, 1961), pp. 15–16.

19. Richardson, *Galveston Directory, 1859–60*, p. 45; Fornell, *Galveston*, p. 16; Reed, *Railroads*, pp. 490–491.

20. E. L. Wall, ed., *The Port Situation at Galveston* (Galveston: Galveston News Company, 1928), pp. 3–5; Reed, *Railroads*, p. 491; *Telegraph and Texas Register*, 1855–1858, *passim*.

21. R. M. Farrar, *The Story of Buffalo Bayou and the Houston Ship Channel* (Houston: Chamber of Commerce of Houston, 1926).

22. *Ibid.; A Statement Respecting the Necessity and Advantages to the Commercial and Agricultural Interests of Texas of a Ship Channel from the Outer Galveston Bar to the City of Houston, the Head of Tide Water in Buffalo Bayou* (Houston: A. C. Gray, 1870), pp. 4–5; Wall, *Port Situation*, pp. 3–5; Reed, *Railroads*, pp. 490–492; *Telegraph*, January 17, 1859.

23. *Telegraph*, September 23, 1876.

24. *New Orleans Times*, September 21, 1876, quoted in Farrar, *Buffalo Bayou*, unpaginated.

25. Hayes, "Galveston," p. 470; *Galveston News, passim;* De Cordova, *Texas*, p. 242; Roemer, *Texas*, p. 44.

26. H. Stuart, "Commerce of Galveston," *De Bow's Review and Industrial Resources, Statistics, etc.*, 25 (1858), 710.

27. Webb, *Handbook*, II, 603.

28. Reed, *Railroads*, pp. 1–2, 6–7; *Telegraph and Texas Register* (Columbia, Texas), November 19, 1836; Benjamin H. Carroll, ed., *Standard History of Houston, Texas, from a Study of the Original Sources* (Knoxville, Tenn.: H. W. Crew, 1912), p. 27.

29. Clark, *Then Came Railroads*, pp. 14–15; Reed, *Railroads*, pp. 18–22; Gammel, *Laws*, I, 1188–1192.

30. Clark, *Then Came Railroads*, p. 15; Reed, *Railroads*, pp. 30–38; Muir, "Railroad Enterprise in Texas," pp. 345–370; Gammel, *Laws*, I, 1507–1512; II, 130–134, 488–491.

31. *Telegraph and Texas Register*, May 2, 1855.

32. *Telegraph and Texas Register*, July 20, September 11, 1857; Richardson, *Texas Almanac, 1868*, pp. 118–123.

33. *Galveston News*, April 22, 1856.

34. Fornell, *Galveston*, pp. 160–163; *Telegraph and Texas Register*, April 16, 1856.

35. Fornell, *Galveston*, pp. 167–168; Reed, *Railroads*, pp. 50–51.

36. *Galveston News*, April 22, 1856.

37. Reed, *Railroads*, pp. 49–52.

38. Fornell, *Galveston*, pp. 159–165.

39. William Pitt Ballinger, Diary, June 17, 1859, Rosenberg Library, Galveston.

40. Fornell, *Galveston*, pp. 159–179; *Telegraph and Texas Register*, March 17, April 16, 22, May 7, 19, June 23, 25, August 4, 1856; Olmsted, *A Journey Through Texas*, pp. 505–506.

41. Reed, *Railroads*, pp. 53–56.

42. *Ibid.*, pp. 53–57; Carroll, *Houston*, p. 227; Gammel, *Laws*, III, 632–636.

43. Letters between Jonathan Fay Barrett and John Grant Tod, 1853, John Grant Tod Papers, private collection of Mrs. Rosa Tod Hamer and John Tod Hamer, Houston, cited in Fornell, *Galveston*, p. 181. An excellent account of this period of railroad building is to be found in Andrew Forest Muir, "Railroads Come to Houston, 1857–1861," *Southwestern Historical Quarterly*, 64 (July 1960), 42–63.

44. Clark, *Then Came Railroads*, p. 15; Reed, *Railroads*, pp. 56–59; *Telegraph and Texas Register*, October 15, 1852.

45. *Telegraph and Texas Register*, February 27, 1856; P. Briscoe, "The First Texas Railroad," *Southwestern Historical Quarterly*, 7 (April 1904), 279–285.

46. Reed, *Railroads*, pp. 61–62.

47. Gammel, *Laws*, IV, 329–331; Carroll, *Houston*, p. 229.

48. Reed, *Railroads*, pp. 79–84; *Telegraph and Texas Register*, February 3, 25, 27, October 25, December 24, 1856; Clark, *Then Came Railroads*, p. 28.

49. Richardson, *Texas Almanac, 1860*, pp. 130, 202; Reed, *Railroads*, pp. 79–84; Gammel, *Laws*, IV, 808–816.

50. Reed, *Railroads,* pp. 65–66; Clark, *Then Came Railroads,* p. 28; Carroll, *Houston,* p. 228.

51. Reed, *Railroads,* pp. 65–69; *Telegraph and Texas Register,* June 27, July 5, 1852; Clark, *Then Came Railroads,* p. 28.

52. Reed, *Railroads,* pp. 65–69; *Telegraph and Texas Register,* December 24, 1856; June 30, 1858; Carroll, *Houston,* p. 228.

53. *Telegraph and Texas Register,* May 30, 1855; *Galveston News,* January 11, 1859; Reed, *Railroads,* pp. 75–79; Clark, *Then Came Railroads,* p. 29; Carroll, *Houston,* pp. 228–230.

54. Ordinance Book, 1857–1865, Office of the Galveston City Secretary, pp. 10, 17, 41; Fornell, *Galveston,* p. 189; Richardson, *Texas Almanac, 1860,* pp. 134–135; *Telegraph and Texas Register,* May 11, 1857; De Cordova, *Texas,* p. 236.

55. Reed, *Railroads,* pp. 84–87; *Telegraph and Texas Register,* September 2, 1857; January 3, May 31, 1861; Gammel, *Laws,* IV, 744–749; Carroll, *Houston,* pp. 229–230; "Commerce of Houston, Texas, September 1st, 1860," *De Bow's Review and Industrial Resources, Statistics, etc.,* 29 (1860), 529.

56. Reed, *Railroads,* pp. 84–87.

57. *Ibid.,* pp. 89–92; Clark, *Then Came Railroads,* pp. 29–31.

58. Webb, *Handbook,* II, 544; Richardson, *Texas Almanac, 1858,* pp. 118, 120; SA Journal City Council, B, 126, 131; Reed, *Railroads,* pp. 89–92.

CHAPTER V   QUEEN COMMERCE

1. U.S. Congress, House, *House Executive Document No. 78, Report of the Commissioner of Agriculture for the Year 1862,* 37th Cong., 3d sess. (Washington, D.C.: Government Printing Office, 1863), p. 105; Reed, *Railroads,* p. 79; Joseph C. G. Kennedy, *Agriculture of the United States in 1860; Compiled from the Original Returns of the Eighth Census* (Washington, D.C.: Government Printing Office, 1864), p. 149 (hereafter cited as Kennedy, *Agriculture, Eighth Census*).

2. Kennedy, *Agriculture, Eighth Census,* pp. 140–149; Muir, "Destiny of Buffalo Bayou," p. 91; Reed, *Railroads,* p. 79; James L. Watkins, *King Cotton: A Historical and Statistical Review, 1790 to 1908* (New York: By the author, 1908), p. 219.

3. "Growth of Galveston, Texas," *De Bow's Review*, 23 (1857); ✓ *su*
555.

4. *Telegraph and Texas Register* (Houston), October 16, 1860; Muir, "Railroads Come to Texas, 1857–1861," pp. 53–54.

5. De Cordova, *Texas*, p. 237; Kennedy, *Agriculture, Eighth Census*, p. 49; "Commerce of Galveston, Texas, 1860," *De Bow's Review*, 29 (1860), 529. By 1858, most cotton was shipped directly to Europe or the North: Europe, 49,576 bales; New York, 39,078 bales; Boston, 22,885 bales; New Orleans, 5,822 bales ("Commerce of Galveston," *De Bow's Review*, 25 [1858], 710).

6. Joseph Carlyle Sitterson, *Sugar Country: The Cane Sugar Industry in the South, 1753–1950* (Louisville: University of Kentucky Press, 1953), p. 187.

7. *Ibid.*, pp. 42–44, 49–51; "Growth of Galveston, Texas," *De Bow's Review*, 23 (1857), 555.

8. Kennedy, *Agriculture, Eighth Census*, p. 149; De Cordova, *Texas*, p. 298.

9. Olmsted, *Journey Through Texas*, p. 363; Kennedy, *Agriculture, Eighth Census*, pp. 140–149.

10. Kennedy, *Agriculture, Eighth Census*, pp. 140–149.

11. Joseph C. G. Kennedy, *Population of the United States in 1860; Compiled from the Original Returns of the Eighth Census* (Washington: Government Printing Office, 1864), pp. 486–487 (hereafter cited as Kennedy, *Population, Eighth Census*).

12. Olmstead, *Journey Through Texas*, p. 363; Fornell, *Galveston*, p. 115.

13. Fornell, *Galveston*, pp. 115–119, 241–264; *Telegraph and Texas Register*, May 25, 1857.

14. *Galveston Civilian*, June 20, 1857; *Galveston News*, June 20, 1857; *Telegraph and Texas Register*, July 1, 1857.

15. Olmstead, *Journey Through Texas*, p. 424.

16. Hayes, "Galveston," p. 488; Fornell, *Galveston*, pp. 226–227; Webb, *Handbook*, I, 608; Rudolph L. Biesele, *The History of the German Settlements in Texas, 1831–1861* (Austin: Von Boeckmann-Jones Company, 1930), pp. 201, 225.

17. Schedule No. 2, R.G. 29, Slave Inhabitants of the United States Census, 1850, and Schedule No. 2, R.G. 29, Slave Inhabitants of the United States Census, 1860, National Archives, Washington, D.C.; *s.v.* "Galveston," "Houston," "San Antonio," and "Austin."

18. Kennedy, *Population, Eighth Census,* p. 491.

19. Schedule No. 1, R.G. 29, Free Inhabitants of the United States Census, 1860 (hereafter cited as Schedule No. 1, Census, 1860), *s.v.* "Galveston," "Houston," "San Antonio," and "Austin."

20. *Ibid., s.v.* "San Antonio"; Olmstead, *Journey Through Texas,* pp. 152–153.

21. Olmstead, *Journey Through Texas,* p. 152. See also John C. Reid, *Reid's Tramp, or a Journal of the Incidents of Ten Months Travel Through Texas, New Mexico, Arizona, Sonora and California* (Selma, Ala.: John Hardy, 1858), p. 58.

22. Schedule No. 1, Census, 1860, *s.v.* "San Antonio."

23. Kennedy, *Population, Eighth Census,* p. 486; Schedule No. 1, Census, 1860, *s.v.* "Austin."

24. *Austin Democrat,* March 18, 1848.

25. Brown, "Annals," XVIII, 24; Schedule No. 1, Census, 1860, *s.v.* "Austin."

26. Webb, *Handbook,* II, 326–327, 697–698.

27. Schedule No. 1, Census, 1860, *s.v.* "Austin" and "San Antonio."

28. De Cordova, *Texas,* p. 229.

29. Commerce of Houston, Texas, Sept. 1st, 1860," *De Bow's Review,* 29 (December 1860), 530.

30. De Cordova, *Texas,* p. 230.

31. *Dictionary of American Biography,* XV, 546–547; Schedule No. 1, Census, 1860, *s.v.* "Houston."

32. Schedule No. 1, Census, 1860, *s.v.* "Houston."

33. "Growth of Galveston, Texas," *De Bow's Review,* 23 (1857), 554–555; Fornell, *Galveston,* p. 24; John R. Bartlett, *Personal Narrative,* 2 vols. (New York: D. Appleton, 1854), II, 537.

34. *Dictionary of American Biography,* XIII, 13–14; Schedule No. 1, Census, 1860, *s.v.* "Galveston."

35. Gammel, *Laws,* II, 130–134, 1031; Hayes, "Galveston," p. 472; *Telegraph and Texas Register,* April 29, 1837; Muir, "Railroad Enterprise in Texas," pp. 339–370.

36. Samuel B. Graham, ed., *Galveston Community Book: A Historical and Biographical Record of Galveston and Galveston County* (Galveston: A. H. Cawston, 1945), p. 137–138; Hayes, "Galveston," p. 476.

37. Richardson, *Texas,* p. 166; Hayes, "Galveston," p. 472; Gammel, *Laws,* II, 406–407.

38. Graham, *Galveston Community Book,* pp. 136–138; *Galveston News,* January 8, 1847.

39. *Telegraph and Texas Register,* October 18, 21, 1857; *Galveston News,* October 20, 1857; Hayes, "Galveston," p. 473.

40. Samuel May Williams Papers, 1855–58, Rosenberg Library, Galveston, cited in Fornell, *Galveston,* p. 42; Hayes, "Galveston," p. 475.

41. Hayes, "Galveston," pp. 473–474; Fornell, *Galveston,* pp. 50–52; *Telegraph and Texas Register,* January 16, 1857; *Galveston News,* February 3, 4, 1857; A. L. Carlson, "Samuel May Williams," *Dictionary of American Biography,* XX, 289–290.

42. Abigail Curlee, "Robert Mills," *Dictionary of American Biography,* XIII, 13–14.

43. *Ibid.;* Hayes, "Galveston," p. 473; *Telegraph and Texas Register,* September 9, 1857.

44. Fornell, *Galveston,* p. 57.

45. Webb, *Handbook,* II, 697.

46. Olmsted, *Journey Through Texas,* pp. 152–153.

47. Schedule No. 8, Products of Industry, of the United States Census, 1860, Record Group 29, National Archives, Washington, D.C. (hereafter cited as Schedule No. 8, Census, 1860), *s.v.* "Houston" and "Galveston."

48. Schedule No. 8, Census, 1850, *s.v.* "San Antonio" and "Bejar County."

49. Schedule No. 8, Census, 1850, *s.v.* "Austin" and "Travis County"; see also Brown, "Annals," XX, 25.

50. Schedule No. 8, Census, 1850, *s.v.* "Houston" and "Harris County."

51. Schedule No. 8, Census, 1860, *s.v.* "Galveston"; Graham, *Galveston Community Book,* pp. 123–125; Hayes, "Galveston," pp. 480–481.

52. According to the 1850 Census, Borden owned more real estate than anyone else in Galveston except Samuel May Williams; Schedule No. 1, Census, 1860, *s.v.* "Galveston."

53. Frantz, *Borden,* pp. 197–200.

54. *Ibid.,* pp. 203–204; Carl W. Witman, "Gail Borden," *Dictionary of American Biography,* II, 459–460.

55. Schedule No. 8, Census, 1850, *s.v.* "Galveston"; Schedule No.

1, Census, 1850, *s.v.* "Galveston"; Frantz, *Borden*, pp. 203–204, 206–207.

56. *Ibid.*, pp. 204–205, 209, 212–214, and reproduced handbill facing p. 194.

57. *Ibid.*, pp. 211, 213.

58. *Ibid.*, pp. 211–212, 220; Olmsted, *Journey Through Texas*, pp. 81, 87.

59. Frantz, *Borden*, pp. 216–219, 260.

CHAPTER VI   SOCIAL PATTERNS AND CULTURAL ASPIRATIONS

1. Kennedy, *Population, Eighth Census*, p. 487.

2. Olmsted, *Journey Through Texas*, pp. 150–151.

3. William A. McClintock, ed., "Journal of a Trip Through Texas and Northern Mexico in 1846–1847," *Southwestern Historical Quarterly*, 34 (October 1930), 144–148; August Santleben, *A Texas Pioneer: Early Staging and Overland Freighting Days on the Frontier of Texas and Mexico*, ed. I. D. Affleck (New York: Neal Publishing Company, 1910), p. 272

4. Olmsted, *Journey Through Texas*, p. 149; Reid, *Reid's Tramp*, p. 58; Ernest A. Connally, "Architecture at the End of the South: Central Texas," *Journal of the Society of Architectural Historians; Southern Issue*, 11 (December 1952), 9–10; Claude B. Aniol, *San Antonio: City of Missions* (New York: Hastings House, 1942), p. 38.

5. Dorothy K. Bracken and Maurine Whorton Redway, *Early Texas Homes* (Dallas: Southern Methodist University Press, 1956), pp. 16–19; Connally, "Architecture," pp. 10–11.

6. Olmsted, *Journey Through Texas*, p. 112; Rankin, *Texas in 1850*, p. 155; Brown, "Annals," XV, 20, 33; XVII, 51; De Cordova, *Texas*, pp. 260–261; *Texas State Gazette* (Austin), October 26, 1850.

7. Connally, "Architecture," pp. 8–12; Bracken and Redway, *Early Texas Homes*, pp. 54–57, 60–61. At this writing, several examples of Cook's architecture have been preserved and are similar to their original design.

8. Bracken and Redway, *Early Texas Homes*, pp. 56, 59.

9. De Cordova, *Texas*, pp. 239–240; *Galveston News*, January 21, 1857; December 17, October 27, 1858.

10. Galveston Historical Society, *Historic Galveston Homes* (Galveston: By the society, 1951), Bracken and Redway, *Early Texas Homes,* pp. 174–186. For a delightful pictorial study of nineteenth-century Galveston, see Howard Barnstone, *The Galveston That Was* (New York: Macmillan Company, 1966).

11. Schedule No. 1, Census, 1860, *s.v.* "Galveston."

12. Schedule No. 1, Census, 1860, *s.v.* "Houston"; Bracken and Redway, *Early Texas Homes,* pp. 164–165.

13. William Manning Morgan, *Trinity Protestant Episcopal Church of Galveston, Texas, 1841–1953* (Houston: Anson Jones Press, 1954), pp. 50–57, 314–316, 327, 346–350, 370–371; Richardson, *Galveston Directory, 1859–60,* p. 64; Census, Social Statistics Tracts, 1860, R.G. 29, National Archives, Washington, D.C., *s.v.* "Galveston"; *Telegraph and Texas Register,* December 28, 1857, and May 1, 1860; Domenech, *Journal d'un Missionnaire,* p. 26; De Cordova, *Texas,* p. 239; Henry Cohen *et al., One Hundred Years of Jewry in Texas* (Dallas: Jewish Advisory Committee for the Texas Centennial Religious Program, 1936), p. 23; Rankin, *Texas in 1850,* pp. 156–157.

14. Census, Social Statistics Tracts, 1860, *s.v.* "Houston"; Domenech, *Journal d'un Missionnaire,* p. 28.

15. Brown, "Annals," XII, 9–12; XIV, 20; XVI, 6; XVIII, 23; XIX, 27; Census, Social Statistics Tracts, 1860, *s.v.* "Austin."

16. De Cordova, *Texas,* p. 268; Census, Social Statistics Tracts, 1860, *s.v.* "San Antonio."

17. Rankin, *Texas in 1850,* p. 157.

18. Joseph Gallegly, *Footlights on the Border: The Galveston and Houston Stage Before 1900* (The Hague: Mouton & Co., 1962), pp. 49, 53, 74, 87, 176.

19. *Galveston Civilian,* March 30, 1858.

20. *Ibid.,* April 17, 1857; *Telegraph and Texas Register* (Houston), January 30, March 16, July 20, 24, 1857, May 1, 1860; Fornell, *Galveston,* pp. 108–115; Brown, "Annals," XII, 25.

21. Joseph Jefferson, *The Autobiography of Joseph Jefferson* (New York: Century Company, 1890), pp. 62–63.

22. Frederick Eby, *Education in Texas: Source Materials,* University of Texas Bulletin, no. 1824 (Austin: University of Texas, 1921), pp. 264–270; *Early Laws of Texas,* comp. John Sayles and Henry Sayles (St. Louis: Gilbert Book Co., 1891), II, 329.

23. S.A. Journal, City Council, A, 105; B, 204–205, 261, 271, 334.

24. Census, Social Statistics Tracts, 1860, *s.v.* "San Antonio," "Houston"; Griffin, *History of Galveston, Texas,* p. 31. Parents who could pay tuition were required to do so in the Houston public schools.

25. Census, Social Statistics Tracts, 1860, *s.v.* "San Antonio" and "Galveston"; Butterfield, "The Free State of Bejar," p. 59; Fornell, *Galveston,* p. 71; *Galveston News,* November 10, 1857.

26. Butterfield, "Free State of Bejar," p. 59; De Cordova, *Texas,* p. 268; Census, Social Statistics Tracts, 1860, *s.v.* "San Antonio."

27. Carroll, *Houston,* p. 293; *Telegraph and Texas Register,* December 21 and 28, 1857; Census, Social Statistics Tracts, 1860, *s.v.* "Galveston" and "San Antonio."

28. *Telegraph and Texas Register,* May 4, 1857.

29. Census, Social Statistics Tracts, 1860, *s.v.* "San Antonio," "Austin," "Galveston," and "Houston."

30. *Ibid.;* Fornell, *Galveston,* p. 76; Brown, "Annals," XVIII, 22.

31. *Galveston News,* April 28, 1857.

32. Brown, "Annals," XVIII, 11; Census, Social Statistics Tracts, 1860, *s.v.* "Galveston" and "Houston"; *Telegraph and Texas Register,* April 17, 1860; *Galveston News,* December 8, 1857.

33. Brown, "Annals," XI, 55; Fornell, *Galveston,* p. 102; Census, Social Statistics Tracts, 1860, *s.v.* "Galveston," "Houston," "San Antonio," and "Austin."

34. Census, Social Statistics Tracts, 1860, *s.v.* "Texas."

35. *Ibid.;* De Cordova, *Texas,* pp. 263, 272; Fornell, *Galveston,* pp. 140–154; Brown, "Annals," XL, 42–45; Ernest W. Winkler, ed., *Check List of Texas Imprints, 1846–1860* (Austin: Texas State Historical Association, 1949), pp. xvii–xx. Copies of newspapers listed in the text may be found at the Newspaper Collections, Main Library, University of Texas, Austin, or at other depositories throughout the state.

36. Richardson, *Galveston Directory, 1859–60,* pp. 8, 91; Fornell, *Galveston,* p. 150; Census, Social Statistics Tracts, 1860, *s.v.* "Galveston" and "San Antonio"; Hayes, "Galveston," pp. 488–489; Winkler, *Check List,* p. xviii; Olmsted, *Journey Through Texas,* p. 133.

37. Kennedy, *Eighth Census, Population,* p. 487; Bracht, *Texas in 1848,* pp. 65, 167, 192.

38. Olmsted, *Journey Through Texas,* p. 160; Fornell, *Galveston,* p. 129; Moritz Tiling, *History of the German Element in Texas from 1820–1850 and Historical Sketches of the German Texas Singers'*

League and Houston Turnverein from 1850–1913 (Houston: By the author, 1913), pp. 10–11.

39. Carl Solms-Braunfels, *Texas, 1844–45* (Houston: Anson Jones Press, 1936), pp. 2-3; Tiling, *German Element,* p. 122.

40. Tiling, *German Element,* pp. 10–11; Olmsted, *Journey Through Texas,* pp. 140–147, 427–440; Bracht, *Texas in 1848;* Biesele, *History of the German Settlements.*

41. S. A. Journal, City Council (Mayor's Report), A, 32.

42. Olmsted, *Journey Through Texas,* p. 431.

43. *Galveston News,* February 5, June 23, 1856; *Telegraph and Texas Register,* August 9, September 6, 1859.

44. Solms-Braunfels, *Texas, 1844–45,* pp. 47–49.

45. Olmsted, *Journey Through Texas,* pp. 133, 140, 431–440; Biesele, *History of the German Settlements,* p. 225; Fornell, *Galveston,* pp. 150–152.

46. Ernest W. Winkler, ed., *Platforms of Political Parties in Texas,* Bulletin of the University of Texas, no. 53 (Austin: University of Texas, 1916), pp. 29, 58–61, 68–71; Brown, "Annals," XVII, 17, 18, 28, 29; *Austin State Times* (1854–55), *passim.*

47. Richardson, *Texas: The Lone Star State,* pp. 129–132; Winkler, *Check List,* pp. 68–71; Hayes, "Galveston," p. 488; Fornell, *Galveston,* pp. 288–289.

48. *Telegraph and Texas Register,* September 30, 1857, September 14, 1859; *Galveston News,* December 17, 1856.

49. Richardson, *Galveston Directory, 1859–60,* pp. 47, 80; *Galveston News,* January 22, 1861; Census, Social Statistics Tracts, 1860, *s.v.* "San Antonio," "Galveston"; Lota M. Spell, "Music in Texas," *Civil War History,* 4 (1958), 301–305; Tiling, *German Element,* pp. 137–159, 160.

50. Kennedy, *Eighth Census, Population,* p. 490. For a breakdown of the numbers, wealth, and occupations of urban immigrants see Ralph A. Wooster, "Foreigners in the Principal Towns of Ante-Bellum Texas," *Southwestern Historical Quarterly,* 66 (October 1962), 208–220. See also Census, Social Statistics Tracts, 1860, *s.v.* "San Antonio," "Houston," "Galveston," "Austin"; Webb, *Handbook,* I, pp. 326–327, 697–698.

51. John R. Bartlett, *Personal Narrative,* I, 40; Brown, "Annals," XVI, 40; Olmsted, *Journey Through Texas,* pp. 160, 163–165.

52. Olmsted, *Journey Through Texas,* pp. 160, 162–163; Butter-

field, "Free State of Bejar," p. 12; Santleben, *A Texas Pioneer*, p. 272; Census, Social Statistics Tracts, 1860, *s.v.* "San Antonio" and "Austin"; S. A. Journal, City Council, B, 279, 326.

53. Kennedy, *Eighth Census, Population*, pp. 486–487.

54. James Arthur Lyon Fremantle, *The Fremantle Diary: Being the Journal of Lieutenant Colonel James Arthur Lyon Fremantle, Coldstream Guards, on His Three Months in the Southern States*, ed. Walter Lord (Boston: Little, Brown, 1954), pp. 58–59.

CHAPTER VII   THE RESPONSE TO CIVIL WAR

1. Griffin, *History of Galveston, Texas*, p. 47.

2. *Flake's Bulletin*, February 14, 1866, cited in Hayes, "Galveston," pp. 658–659.

3. Hayes, "Galveston," p. 502; *San Antonio Herald*, May 9, 1863.

4. Lubbock, *Six Decades in Texas*, pp. 368–369. See also Brown, "Annals," XXIII, 3–4, 65.

5. Hayes, "Galveston," pp. 483–486; Samuel S. O. Young, *A Thumb-Nail History of the City of Houston, from its founding in 1836 to the year 1912* (Houston: Rein and Sons, 1912), p. 42; Brown, "Annals," XXIII, 30; Stephen B. Oates, "Recruiting Confederate Cavalry in Texas," *Southwestern Historical Quarterly*, 64 (April 1961), 463–477; Webb, *Handbook*, I, 351, II, 728; Charles William Ramsdell, *Reconstruction in Texas*, Studies in History, Economics, and Public Law, vol. XXVI, no. 1, ed. Faculty of Political Science of Columbia University (New York: Columbia University, 1910), pp. 21–22; Willard Richardson, *Texas Almanac for 1860*, p. 254.

6. Texas Library and Historical Commission, *Journal of the Secession Convention of Texas, 1861*, ed. Ernest W. Winkler (Austin: Austin Printing Company, 1912), pp. 87–90.

7. *Ibid.*, pp. 88, 91.

8. *Ibid.*, pp. 88–90.

9. *Alamo Express*, March 6, 1861.

10. *Ibid.*, April 11, 1861.

11. Robert W. Delaney, "Matamoros, Port for Texas during the Civil War," *Southwestern Historical Quarterly*, 58 (April 1955), 478–480; *Telegraph and Texas Register*, June 18, 1862.

12. *New York Times,* September 6, 1862, and *Official Records, War of the Rebellion,* series 3, vol. II, 949, both cited in Delaney, "Matamoros," pp. 478, 498.

13. *Official Naval Records, War of the Rebellion,* series I, vol. XIX, 180, cited in Delaney, "Matamoros," p. 483; Andrew Forest Muir, "William Marsh Rice, Houstonian," *East Texas Historical Journal,* 2 (February 1964), 32–35.

14. Webb, *Handbook,* I, 316.

15. Edward Everett Dale, *The Range Cattle Industry: Ranching on the Great Plains from 1865 to 1925* (Norman: University of Oklahoma Press, 1960), pp. 6–8; Joseph G. McCoy, *Historic Sketches of the Cattle Trade of the West and Southwest,* Southwest Historical Series, vol. VIII, ed. Ralph P. Beiber (Glendale, California: Arthur H. Clark Company, 1940), pp. 21–32.

16. T. R. Havins, "Texas Fever," *Southwestern Historical Quarterly,* 52 (October 1948), 148–162; McCoy, *Cattle Trade,* pp. 32–39.

17. McCoy, *Cattle Trade,* pp. 25–26.

18. Dale, *Range Cattle Industry,* pp. 10–11; McCoy, *Cattle Trade,* pp. 41–46; William C. Holden, *Alkali Trails: Or Social and Economic Movements of the Texas Frontier, 1846–1900* (Dallas: Southwest Press, 1930), pp. 23–24.

19. *Report of the Commissioner of Agriculture for the Year 1870,* p. 347.

20. *Ibid.,* p. 346, 350–351; McCoy, *Cattle Trade,* pp. 46–50; Holden, *Alkali Trails,* pp. 24–25.

21. Lubbock, *Six Decades in Texas,* pp. 386–388; Hayes, "Galveston," p. 148.

22. Hayes, "Galveston," pp. 492–510; Alfred Thomas North, *Five Years in Texas . . .* (Cincinnati: Elm Street Printing Co., 1871), pp. 102–113; James M. Merrill, *The Rebel Shore: The Story of Union Sea Power in the Civil War* (Boston: Little, Brown, 1957), pp. 113, 173–175.

23. Alfred T. Mahan, *The Gulf and Inland Waters,* vol. III of *The Navy in the Civil War* (New York: Charles Scribner's Sons, 1883), pp, 108–109; Charles C. Cumberland, "The Confederate Loss and Recapture of Galveston, 1862–1863," *Southwestern Historical Quarterly,* 51 (October 1947), 109–130.

24. Hayes, "Galveston," pp. 495–500; North, *Five Years in Texas,* pp. 111–113. North incorrectly identified the participants in this

tragedy as General Sidney Sherman and his son, Lieutenant Sidney Sherman, both of Galveston, who also fought on opposite sides during the war.

25. Merrill, *The Rebel Shore*, pp. 175–176; Mahan, *The Gulf and Inland Waters*, p. 249.

INDEX